D1175073

The New CEOs

The New CEOs

Women, African American, Latino, and Asian American Leaders of *Fortune* 500 Companies

Richard L. Zweigenhaft and G. William Domhoff

ROWMAN & LITTLEFIELD PUBLISHERS, INC.
Lanham • Boulder • New York • Toronto • Plymouth, UK

Published by Rowman & Littlefield Publishers, Inc.
A wholly owned subsidiary of The Rowman & Littlefield Publishing Group, Inc.
4501 Forbes Boulevard, Suite 200, Lanham, Maryland 20706
http://www.rowmanlittlefield.com

Estover Road, Plymouth PL6 7PY, United Kingdom

British Library Cataloguing in Publication Information Available

Library of Congress Cataloging-in-Publication Data

Zweigenhaft, Richard L.
 The new CEOs : women, African American, Latino, and Asian American leaders of *Fortune* 500 companies / Richard L. Zweigenhaft and G. William Domhoff.
 p. cm.
 ISBN 978-1-4422-0765-3 (cloth : alk. paper) — ISBN 978-1-4422-0767-7 (electronic)
 1. Chief executive officers. 2. Women chief executive officers. 3. Minority executives.
4. Women executives. I. Domhoff, G. William. II. Title.
 HD38.2.Z94 2010
 658.4'2—dc22   2011002320

∞™ The paper used in this publication meets the minimum requirements of American National Standard for Information Sciences—Permanence of Paper for Printed Library Materials, ANSI/NISO Z39.48-1992.

Printed in the United States of America

Contents

Preface

It has been a little over three decades since we began our collaborative efforts on the changes that were taking place in what was once a homogenous white Christian male power structure. We first studied the gradual inclusion of Jews in the corporate elite in the 1960s and 1970s after decades of exclusion, then the successful careers of young low-income African Americans who had been accepted into a then-unique program leading to entrance into high-status preparatory schools and Ivy League colleges, and finally the growing presence of women and people of color in positions of power on corporate boards of directors, in the federal government, and at the top of the military.

In this book, we now take a further step in our attempt to understand diversity by studying the seventy-four women and people of color who have been in what are by all odds the most important positions of power in the United States, outside of the presidency, the chief corporate officers (CEOs) of the large corporations that have dominated the American economy since the beginning of the twentieth century. It is a study that could not have been undertaken fifteen years ago because there were only a few women or people of color running major corporations (and, therefore, the "sample size" would have been too small for any meaningful patterns to emerge). Although there was increasing corporate diversity in the 1980s and 1990s, it could only be found on boards of directors and in personnel and public relations offices, not in the corner offices on the highest floors of the skyscrapers.

As has been the case for each of our previous books, many people have helped us, and we wish to thank them for their assistance. Three current or recent undergraduates were crucial in helping us to gather data for some of the studies we report on in the text: Kyle Riplinger, a recent graduate of Guilford College, helped conduct the study described in appendix 2 (he is the coauthor of that appendix); Heather Jackson, a recent graduate of the University of North Dakota, did web research for us that allowed us to double-check and to update the information reported in appendix 1; and Isaac Studebaker and Elizabeth Hayton, both Early College students at Guilford College, helped us gather some of the data that went into various studies that we present in chapter 6.

Faculty members at schools around the country have helped us in a variety of ways. Some of them we thank in the text, or in notes, but we wish to thank them here as well in this list of those to whom we are greatly indebted. We thank both Dan Clawson, professor of sociology at the University of Massachusetts, Amherst, and Peter Dreier, professor of political science, Occidental College, for the extremely useful feedback they gave us on early versions of what was to become chapter 5; Roderick Harrison, a sociology professor at Howard University, for guiding us to invaluable data sets, and then going beyond the call to find what we needed in these data sets and sending us summary tables that we used to create the tables on education and income in chapter 6; Rory Kramer, a graduate student in sociology at the University of Pennsylvania, who shared his work on "diversifiers" with us and guided us to online data about the racial makeup of the Ivy League schools; Robert Livingston, assistant professor of management and organizations at Kellogg School of Management, Northwestern University, and Nicholas Pearce, a doctoral student at the Kellogg School, who generously provided us with the grayscale photographs of CEOs that they used to study "babyfaceness" in CEOs; Frederick R. Lynch, associate professor of government at Claremont McKenna College, who shared his ideas about the diversity movement with us; Tom Pettigrew, research professor of social psychology at the University of California, Santa Cruz, for helping us to understand the complex nature of the contact between dominant groups and excluded groups and how that contact affects the likelihood of social action; Earl Smith, professor of sociology and the Rubin Distinguished Professor of American Ethnic Studies at Wake Forest University, for an early reading of our prospectus and one chapter, and for the ongoing support he has given us over the years; Cliff Staples, professor of sociology at the University of North Dakota, for generously allowing us to use the extensive information he has gathered on board memberships and memberships in policy groups; and Nancy DiTomaso, professor and chair of the Department of Management and Global Business at Rutgers University, for the useful perspectives she provided to us about the diversity movement and for helping us to see the key role that Roosevelt Thomas played in that movement.

We also received invaluable help from a number of people who work for nonprofit organizations. These include Jan Combopiano, vice president and chief knowledge officer, and Emily Troiano, director of the Information Center, both of whom work for Catalyst, and both of whom were generous in providing reports on the progress of women in corporate America written over the years by that excellent organization; Ancella Livers, the executive director of the Institute for Leadership Development & Research at the Executive Leadership Council, who in a phone interview and in e-mails gave us information about the role of the Executive Leadership Council in the pipeline that sometimes leads African Americans to the CEO office; and Sandra Timmons, the president of the A Better Chance program, whose ongoing friendship and encouragement has meant a lot to us, and who, for this project, provided useful information from a 2005 survey of ABC alumni and also gave us a copy of the extensive 2005 *ABC Alumni Directory.*

We also thank Roosevelt Thomas for his generous willingness to let us interview him about his early academic career and about the transition he made from academe to diversity work, and Eric Conger (Conger Minor, Wesleyan, 1968) for using his social capital (or maybe for letting the first author use his social capital) to help us make contact with William Perez, former CEO of Nike and Wrigley (and we thank William Perez for responding to our e-mail).

We wish to thank those who work at the Guilford College Library (especially Susan McClanahan, the Access Services manager, who responded so diligently to the many interlibrary loan requests made by the first author); Virginia Ferguson (for scanning many documents for the first author); Guilford College for providing the first author with a sabbatical leave in the fall of 2009; and Adrienne Israel, vice president for academic affairs and academic dean at Guilford College, whose office provided funds to support some of the research done during the first author's sabbatical leave.

Finally, we are deeply grateful to Sarah Stanton, the acquisitions editor at Rowman & Littlefield, for her enthusiasm about this project, and her helpful editorial suggestions. We are also grateful to Jin Yu and Lynda Phung for shepherding this manuscript through the production process in such a conscientious and good-natured manner.

Our research relationship originated in a friendship that developed as teammates on intramural basketball and softball teams in the early 1970s when we were both at the University of California, Santa Cruz: Zweigenhaft (a nimble point guard and shortstop) as a graduate student in social psychology and Domhoff (a hard-driving shooting guard and power-hitting outfielder) as a professor who concentrated on the study of political power. After he completed his Ph.D. and accepted a position at Guilford College, Zweigenhaft studied the extent to which Jews were part of the local power structure in Greensboro, North Carolina, his new hometown. After writing an article about the Jews of Greensboro, and then another that compared Greensboro with nearby Winston-Salem, and then a third that included the entire South, he convinced Domhoff to join him in a larger project, a book about Jews in the American power structure. Doing the research and writing the book that resulted from it were so enjoyable that Domhoff subsequently persuaded Zweigenhaft to continue the collaboration on a study that looked at questions related to why and when the wealthy white establishment took in new members, in this case the integration of elite boarding schools. A few years after this second book was published, Zweigenhaft proposed a third project, a comparison of those in the power elite (that is, the top leaders in the corporations, the federal government, and the military) in the 1990s with those studied in the 1950s by C. Wright Mills in his now-classic book, *The Power Elite*. We wrote substantially updated second editions of the second and third books (on blacks who attended elite boarding schools and on diversity in the power elite), so this is either our fourth book or our sixth book.

We are pleased that our friendship not only survived this thirty-year collaboration but was strengthened by it. We hope we have contributed to the store of social science knowledge through this and our previous books. We have learned a great deal by working together, far more than we ever could have learned on these topics working individually. We hope that readers find as much pleasure in reading this book as we have derived from writing it.

To make this book readable for the general public and for undergraduates, but also useful to social scientists with an interest in original research, we have tried to strike a balance by using accessible and nontechnical language in the main text and placing more detailed findings (and most of the statistical analyses) in tables, notes, and three appendices. At the same time, we think that students might benefit from seeing, in appendix 2, the research strategies we and others have employed in showing that skin color and facial features, such as being "baby-faced," can make a very real difference in who reaches top corporate positions.

Setting the Stage

The Changing Role of the CEO
and the Recent Emergence of Women,
African American, Latino, and Asian American CEOs

Not that long ago virtually all of the chief executive officers of the largest corporations in the United States were white men. Most were Presbyterians and Episcopalians, educated at Ivy League schools, and two-thirds of them came from either the upper middle or upper classes. By December 31, 2010, twenty-four white women, fourteen African Americans, fifteen Latino men, and twenty Asian Americans had been CEOs of *Fortune* 500 corporations. Almost all of these seventy-three CEOs were appointed between 1999 and 2010. We call them "the new CEOs." In January 2011, another African American began his tenure as CEO of a *Fortune* 500 company, bringing the total to seventy-four.

As can be seen in figure 1.1, the increase for the four main underrepresented groups has been dramatic, although the actual numbers in any given

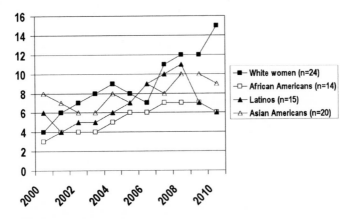

Figure 1.1.   The number of white women, African American, Latino, and Asian American CEOs, 2000–2009

year remain quite small. A few of the new CEOs have served in interim appointments, and others have not lasted long, but some have remained CEOs for more than a decade. As is apparent, the rise in the growth in the overall number of new CEOs has been fairly steady, from a total of 21 in 2000 to 37 in 2010, with a peak of 40 in 2008. The number of women has increased most dramatically (from 4 to 15), but the increases have been more modest for African Americans (from 3 to 6), and for Asian Americans (from 8 to 9). There were 6 Latino CEOs in 2000 and 6 in 2010. Even at the time of the peak number, when there were 40 in 2008, this represented only 2 percent of all *Fortune* 500 CEOs, and the other 460 CEOs were white males.

Still, the presence of seventy-four women, African Americans, Latinos, and Asian American *Fortune* 500 CEOs represents a major change from the makeup of those who held the same positions only ten to fifteen years ago. They provide a large enough sample to explore some questions about the past, the present, and the future. Who are they, where have they come from, and why did the companies that appointed them do so? Are we likely to see more of them, and, if so, which ones and why? And now that there are enough of them to look at them as a group, not just as individuals, is there any evidence that they differ meaningfully from the white male CEOs who came before them, or the white males who still predominate in chief executive positions?

When Katharine Graham's husband committed suicide in 1963, she became the CEO of the *Washington Post* (her father had owned the paper).[1] The *Washington Post* did not make the *Fortune* 500 until 1972 (and even then it barely made the list—it was #478). When she retired in 1991 (at which time it had moved up to #267), she was one of only three women CEOs of *Fortune* 500 companies.

When Coca-Cola named Roberto Goizueta its CEO in 1981, he became the first Latino to head a *Fortune*-level company (Coca-Cola was #56 in 1981). Five years later, when Gerald Tsai, born in Shanghai, became the CEO of the American Can Company, he became the first Asian American CEO of a *Fortune* 500 corporation (it was #140 on the 1986 list). In 1999, two companies on the *Fortune* 500 list named African American men as CEOs—Franklin Raines at Fannie Mae (#26) and Lloyd Ward at Maytag (#379).[2] These initial appointments—the first woman in 1963, the first Latino in 1981, the first Asian American in 1986, and the first African Americans in 1999—were signs of more to come. The appointments of another sixty-nine new CEOs did not occur in a vacuum. Not only had the culture changed in its treatment of, and views about, women, blacks, Latinos, and Asian Americans, but the corporate world had changed as well.

When William Miller of the Harvard University Research Center in Entrepreneurial History looked at the backgrounds of 190 men who were business leaders between 1901 and 1910, he found that 79 percent had fathers who were businessmen or professionals. American historians, he concluded, "stress this elite's typically lower-class foreign, or farm origins. . . . Yet poor immigrant boys and poor farm boys together actually make up no more than 3 percent of the business leaders who are the subject of this essay. . . . Poor immigrant and poor farm boys who become business leaders have always been more conspicuous in American history books than in American history" (Miller 1962, 328).

Mabel Newcomer, the chair of the economics department at Vassar, studied the highest ranking businessmen of 1900, 1925, and 1950. She, too, found that more than 70 percent were the sons of businessmen or professionals (Newcomer 1955, 55, 62–63). In his study of the top executives of 1950, C. Wright Mills also found that about 70 percent were the sons of businessmen or professionals. "For at least two generations now," Mills wrote, "the families of the top executives of the big American corporations have, as a group, been far removed from wage work and the lower white-collar ranks. In fact, their families are in a substantial proportion citizens of good report in the local societies of America" (Mills 1956, 128). This pattern has persisted. Writing in the late 1990s, Peter Temin, an economist at MIT, found that the business elite had remained remarkably stable in terms of class background (see Temin 1997 and 1998).

In his detailed study, Mills found that the top executives in the middle of the twentieth century came to their executive positions in one of four ways. About 6 percent of Mills's sample was what he called "entrepreneurs"—they had started a business with their own money, or the money of others they knew, and the business had grown. Another 11 percent were "inheritors"— they had secured their executive positions because their fathers or other relatives owned the company. About 13 percent had not started their careers as businessmen but were "professionals" with skills the corporations needed— most were lawyers, trained in the intricacies of corporate law. Finally, the remaining 68 percent of Mills's sample were "career men" who moved steadily upward through the corporate world, usually working for only one company but sometimes moving from one company to another. Mills notes that in 1870 more than six in ten executives came to the top positions in their companies from outside the corporation, but by 1950 the pattern had reversed—almost seven in ten came from within the company (139).

Moreover, Mills argues that in order to reach these top executive positions they had to fit into the corporate milieu created by the others who were already in the highest circles of the corporate hierarchy. This called for conformity, the kind of conformity that was popularized in best-selling midcentury books that appeared at the same time as *The Power Elite*, like William H. Whyte's *The Organization Man* (1956), and Sloan Wilson's novel *The Man in the Gray Flannel Suit* (it came out as a book in 1955 and as a movie in 1956). As Mills puts it: "To be compatible with the top men is to act like them, to look like them, to think like them: to be of and for them" (141). The CEOs in the mid-twentieth century, whether they came from inside or outside the corporation, were "company men."

A. A. Berle, writing in 1959, a few years after the publication of Mills's *The Power Elite* (a book that Berle much disliked), describes the top executives at the largest companies in the following way, contrasting them to the wealthy founders who had previously run America's largest companies:

> Few know, and most do not care, who are the current managers of General Electric or Aluminum Company of America, of United States Steel or American Telephone and Telegraph Company, of Allied Chemical or the Great Atlantic and Pacific Tea Company. In the publicly held corporations an American businessman ordinarily cannot honestly make a large fortune in the sense that Morgan, Vanderbilt, Belmont, Rockefeller, Mellon, and Davis made fortunes a generation ago. He can do quite nicely, make a comfortable stake, secure an excellent pension, and perhaps make a little on the side. With reasonable good fortune he can honestly become "little rich" and make comfortable provision for his family. But his son will have to go out and look for a job like anyone else. (Berle 1959, 4)

In the eyes of many commentators, this new era, which some call "managerial capitalism," was far superior to what had gone before ("owner-based capitalism"), and few foresaw the dramatic changes that were soon to come. As Rakesh Khurana, a professor at the Harvard Business School who has written extensively on corporate leadership, puts it, "The superiority of managerial capitalism over owner-based capitalism as an economic arrangement was almost a given in any treatment of the modern corporation" (Khurana 2002, 53). Ironically, although the new CEOs were said to be far more prone to conformity and far less individualistic or rebellious than the often temperamental founders and owners who had preceded them, the changed role of CEOs and other top executives during managerial capitalism came to be characterized as a "managerial revolution" (Baltzell 1964, 254; Domhoff and Ballard 1968, 270; Khurana 2002, 55).

Increasingly, CEOs chose the outside directors who served on their company's boards, and, as a result, these directors "although legally responsible to shareholders, in fact felt more beholden to the CEOs who invited them to serve on their companies boards" (Khurana 2002, 53). Moreover, when it came to choosing a successor, at times the incumbent CEO simply informed the board who he had chosen to replace him. By the early 1980s, according to Khurana, many CEOs went through elaborate "executive tournaments" in which they presented the contending internal candidates with corporate challenges to address. Reginald Jones, the CEO of General Electric who retired in 1981 and who recommended that the company hire Jack Welch, sat down, unannounced, with seven or eight candidates and posed the following dilemma: "Well, look now, Bill, you and I are flying in one of the company planes and this plane crashes. (Pause) Who should be the next chairman of the General Electric Company?" (Khurana 2002, 62).

With Reagan's election in 1980 and his administration's commitment to a laissez-faire approach to the market and to deregulation, CEOs of *Fortune*-level companies faced new challenges. Corporate raiders seeking to buy vulnerable companies "engulfed and devoured" many companies in the 1960s, leading to innumerable panic stories in the business press, but this practice became even more prevalent by the 1980s, which saw a series of unfriendly takeovers, leveraged buyouts, and mergers. Khurana (2002, 56) refers to "the greedy takeover artists epitomized by T. Boone Pickens or the 'barbarians' of Kohlberg Kravis Roberts" (Burrough and Helyar 1990). Joe Nocera, now a business writer for the *New York Times*, was a thirty-year-old reporter working for the *Texas Monthly* in 1982 when he wrote his first business profile, an inside story account of an attempted unfriendly takeover of Cities Services, then the 39th largest company in America, by T. Boone Pickens and his company, Mesa Petroleum (Cities was twenty times larger than Mesa, which had not yet made it into the *Fortune* 500). More than twenty-five years later, when he looked back to the night he met Pickens, Nocera remembers the scorn Pickens held for the CEOs who had been hired in previous decades: "They were decidedly *not* entrepreneurs, the men who ran America's large corporations; they were—and I can still hear the scorn in his voice—corporate bureaucrats. At that point in his career, Boone hadn't yet conducted his first 'corporate raid,' and was barely known in business circles outside of Texas. His ideas about the primacy of the shareholder, which were also being developed by a handful of others, including a financier named Carl Icahn, were only just beginning to enter the business culture" (Nocera 2008b, 4).

The new dynamics created by the confluence of deregulation, unfriendly corporate takeovers, and leveraged buyouts may have led to changes in the ways large corporations chose their CEOs and in what those companies looked for when they made such appointments. Most boards of directors now employ independent headhunting search firms (four such firms, not surprisingly called the Big Four, have captured most of this lucrative market) to assist in the search process. As Khurana emphasizes in the title and subtitle of his 2002 book (*Searching for a Corporate Savior: The Irrational Quest for Charismatic CEOs*), search committees no longer sought staid, predictable, company men but, rather, sought charismatic individuals who could, individually, save a company (both the goal and the process employed, he claims, were irrational).

By the late 1980s, then, about one-fourth of those who emerged as CEOs at *Fortune* 500 companies were hired from the outside or had not worked for those companies for very long, and their style and their values differed dramatically from those they replaced. In *Barbarians at the Gate: The Fall of RJR Nabisco*, Wall Street journalists Bryan Burrough and John Helyar contrast Ross Johnson, who became CEO first of Standard Brands and then (through a merger) of Nabisco and then (through another merger) of RJR Nabisco, with the CEOs of earlier decades:

> He was a new breed of chief executive for a new age of American business. The old-timers at Standard Brands had seen themselves as corporate stewards. "Your company is the ship," they would say, "the chief executive is only the captain." That steady-as-she-goes ethos was fine for men scarred by the 1930s and scared to make waves. But Johnson, like many of his peers, hadn't lived through a Depression, hadn't fought a world war, and wasn't about to acknowledge limits. He was no old-style team player but a Broadway Joe or Reggie Jax, an iconoclastic superstar, a cool, television-age man, loyal to little but his own whims. (Burrough and Helyar 1990, 38)

Although the new headhunting approach to finding and hiring CEOs was meant to broaden the candidate pool, and to find creative charismatic leaders who could—as the cliché goes—think outside the box, the very makeup of the search committees, the hired headhunting firms, and the candidate pools more often than not worked against successful hires. The search committees tended to consist of members of the boards who were less involved and less knowledgeable, the headhunter firms mostly employed former CEOs of *Fortune* 500 companies, and most of those in the candidate pools were current and former *Fortune* 500 CEOs. In their faddish and misguided search for leaders with charisma—an ill-defined quality that seemed to be a combination of personality attributes and the presentation of self—the committees often failed to look in depth at what was probably the best predictor of future effectiveness—past work experience (Khurana 2002, 178).

THE RISE IN CEO COMPENSATION—AND POWER

As many sociologists and economists have observed for many years, and as almost everyone else came to realize after the economic crash in the fall of 2008, compensation for CEOs has increased dramatically over the past thirty years. Analysts have compared compensation for CEOs then and now with pay for the average worker, with pay for minimum wage, with pay for the

CEOs of companies in Europe, with profits (or losses) that their companies had experienced, with pay for the president of the United States, or with any number of other economic indicators. All of these comparisons show that from around the time Ronald Reagan was elected in 1980 modern CEOs became immensely rich, even if they were failures as CEOs. Generally those citing the rise in compensation use words like "remarkable," "colossal," and "stupendous." Dennis Gilbert has been tracking these patterns in a textbook on the American class structure for years. In the eighth edition of that book, he writes the following:

> Earnings have soared . . . among the CEOs of major corporations. From 1980 to 2000, the real earnings of CEOs rose by over 600%—a remarkable increase in an era of stagnant wages. The gulf separating the typical CEO from the typical American worker has grown to colossal proportions. The average CEO of a major corporation earned a stupendous 475 times the wage of an average blue-collar worker in 1999, up from roughly 42 times in 1980. (Gilbert 2011, 62)

Such (remarkable, colossal, stupendous) compensation packages were unheard of prior to the 1980s. "Golden parachutes, golden handcuffs, and the whole panoply of mechanisms for lavishly rewarding CEOs," writes Khurana, "without regard to performance . . . were unheard of before" the new era that included many raids, takeovers, and buyouts by small groups of very rich investors (Khurana 2002, 193).

After the meltdown of the stock market in 2008, which was followed by closer scrutiny of CEO compensation packages, CEOs were, on average, paid less, and some companies dropped such perks as the use of corporate jets for personal travel. In 2008, according to an analysis by the Associated Press ("Stock Surge a Bonanza for Top CEOs," Associated Press, May 10, 2010, *News & Record*, A8), the median CEO pay package dropped 7 percent, and in 2009 it dropped another 11 percent—all the way down to $7.2 million. Because more packages included stock compensation, however, and because the stock market did well in 2009, many CEOs made more money than ever. As one management consultant put it, "The dirty secret of 2009 is that CEOs were sitting on more wealth by the end of the year than they had accumulated in a long time." One of the women discussed in chapter 2, Carol Bartz, the CEO of Yahoo since January 2009, was the highest paid CEO in 2009—her compensation package was $47.2 million (in her first year on the job).

A study by the Institute for Policy Studies showed not only that CEO salaries soared in 2009, but that the highest-paid CEOs worked at companies that had eliminated the most jobs. This study found that "in 2009, the CEOs who slashed their payrolls the deepest took home 42 percent more compensation than the year's chief executive pay average for S&P 500 companies" (Anderson, Collins, Pizzigati, and Shih 2010, 4). This includes some of the seventy-four new

CEOs we examine in this book. For example, Fred Hassan, the Pakistani-born CEO of Schering-Plough, about whom we write in chapter 4, was paid about $50 million in 2009, and his company laid off sixteen thousand employees between November 2008 and March 2010 (in the conclusion to chapter 5, we provide details about the five new CEOs who are among the biggest job slashers).

To show graphically the dramatic increase in CEO compensation before the peak of the boom in 2006 and 2007, figure 1.2 shows, simply, the average compensation for CEOs from 1990 through 2005 and production workers' average pay, the Standard & Poor Index, corporate profits, and federal minimum wage, with all figures adjusted for inflation. As we have said, the CEOs made off like bandits.

But how could such a large gap develop between the CEOs and the rest of the population? The most relevant factor involves the way in which CEOs now are able to rig things so that the board of directors, which they help select—and which includes some fellow CEOs on whose boards they sit—gives them the pay they want. The trick is in hiring outside experts, called "compensation consultants," who give the process a thin veneer of economic respectability.

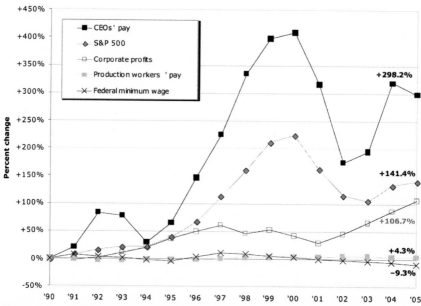

Figure 1.2.   CEOs' average pay, production workers' average pay, the S&P 500 index, corporate profits, and the federal minimum wage, 1990–2005 (all figures adjusted for inflation)

Source: Executive Excess 2006, the 13th Annual CEO Compensation Survey from the Institute for Policy Studies and United for a Fair Economy.

The process has been explained in detail by a former CEO of DuPont, Edgar S. Woolard, Jr., who became chair of the New York Stock Exchange's executive compensation committee after his retirement. His experience suggests that he knows whereof he speaks, and he speaks because he's concerned that corporate leaders are losing respect in the public mind. He says that the business page chatter about CEO salaries being set by the competition for their services in the executive labor market is "bull." As to the claim that CEOs deserve ever higher salaries because they "create wealth," he describes that rationale as a "joke" (Morgenson 2005, 1).

According to Woolard:

> The compensation committee talks to an outside consultant who has surveys that you could drive a truck through and pay anything you want to pay, to be perfectly honest. The outside consultant talks to the H.R. vice president, who talks to the C.E.O. The C.E.O. says what he'd like to receive. It gets to the H.R. person who tells the outside consultant. And it pretty well works out that the C.E.O. gets what he's implied he thinks he deserves, so he will be respected by his peers. (Morgenson 2005, 1)

The board of directors buys into what the CEO asks for because the outside consultant is an "expert" on such matters. Furthermore, handing out only modest salary increases might give the wrong impression about how highly the board values the CEO. And if someone on the board should object, there are the three or four CEOs from other companies who will make sure it happens. It is a process with a built-in escalator.

As for why the consultants go along with this charade, they know which side their bread is buttered on. They realize the CEO has a big hand in whether they are hired again. So they suggest a package of salaries, stock options and perks, and retirement benefits that they think will please the CEO, and they, too, grow rich in the process. And certainly the top executives just below the CEO don't mind hearing about the boss's raise. They know it will mean pay increases for them, too (see Morgenson 2006 for an excellent detailed article on the main consulting firm that helps CEOs and other corporate executives raise their pay).

There is a much deeper power story that underlies the self-dealing and mutual back-scratching by CEOs now carried out through interlocking directorates and seemingly independent outside consultants. It is not one we can fully discuss here, but it is likely that it involves several factors. First of all, it reflects the decrease in the bargaining power of lower-level employees following the all-out corporate attack on unions in the 1970s, which we show in the final chapter to be related to corporate acceptance of greater diversity in the workforce. That decline in union power made possible and was increased by both outsourcing to small nonunionized firms within the United States and the movement of production to developing countries, which were originally facilitated by the breakup of the New Deal coalition, Republican victories in presidential and congressional elections, and the rise of the New Right (Domhoff 1990, chap. 10; Domhoff 2007). We suspect that offshoring and the decline of unions signals the shift of the United States from a high-wage to a low-wage economy, with professionals protected by the fact that foreign-trained doctors and lawyers haven't been allowed to compete with their American counterparts in the direct way that low-wage foreign-born workers are, although that too may be changing as more and more corporations outsource their routine legal work to law factories in India (Timmons 2010, B1).

Second, the rise in CEO pay may reflect the increasing power of chief executives as compared to major owners and stockholders in general, not just their increasing power over workers. CEOs may now be the center of gravity in the corporate community, displacing the leaders in wealthy owning families (e.g., the second and third generations of the Walton family, the owners of Wal-Mart). True enough, the CEOs are sometimes ousted by their generally go-along boards of directors, but they are very powerful while they are in office.

Whatever the mix of factors that has increased CEO compensation to astronomical levels in recent decades, we also want to note that the growth in the pay differential may have made them more autocratic and out of touch with their employees and other ordinary Americans than in the past. As recent research shows, CEOs become "meaner" as the degree of difference between them and other employees increases (Desai, Brief, and George 2010a). This finding is in keeping with, and augments, a growing number of research studies by social psychologists revealing that even the slightest power differentials can distort the perceptions of those who have become more powerful. They soon fail to understand how less-powerful people perceive and feel about situations, are more likely to condemn cheating while cheating more themselves, and come to believe they have more control over events than they in fact do (Fast, Gruenfeld, Sivanathan, and Galinsky 2009; Galinsky, Magee, Inesi, and Gruenfeld 2006; Lammers, Stapel, and Galinsky 2010). They also tend to distance themselves from others and to think more abstractly, whereas those who lack power in experimental situations suffer from impairments in their thinking abilities even though they were as capable as other participants before the studies began (Smith 2006; Smith, Jostmann, Galinsky, and Dijk 2008).

Experimental studies of the effects of power and lack of power complement the numerous epidemiological investigations showing that people on the lower rungs of the social ladder die younger and suffer more physical and mental illnesses, even in the case of those who make a comfortable living and are not materially deprived in any way (e.g., Adler, Singh-Manoux, Schwartz, Stewart, Matthews, and Marmot 2008). Of the greatest relevance for our study of people at or near the highest levels of power, there is even a difference between those in charge and those just below them in an ongoing longitudinal study of British civil servants: "Most striking was the significant difference in mortality between high-level civil servants who were well-paid professionals and those one level above them at the very top" (Adler 2009, 664). The German saying that "life is like a chicken coop ladder," used as the title of a book on culture by anthropologist Alan Dundes (1984), probably goes too far as a general characterization of human society because of the many opportunities for cooperation, love, and autonomy. However, its graphic imagery alerts us to the fact that relations between CEOs and their employees may have adverse consequences, often deadly, which go far beyond the size of their respective paychecks because of the many negative effects of the chronic stress that is generated by a lack of power.

OUR FRAMEWORK

In our previous work, which was not based on CEOs but on members of corporate boards, members of presidential cabinets, and those who made it into the highest levels of the military, we concluded that four factors explained who did and who did not make it into what C. Wright Mills called the power elite (by which he meant those who occupied the highest positions in the corporate, political, and military elites, and for the purposes of our research meant corporate directors of *Fortune*-level boards, members of presidential cabinets, and those who held the status of general or the equivalent in the military). The first of these was socioeconomic class. Despite many claims to the contrary, we found that women, African Americans, Latinos, and Asian Americans who were born to privilege were more likely to make it into these leadership positions. It was not mandatory—there are some genuine rags to riches stories for people in each of those groups—but we found clear evidence that being born into the upper one-third of the class structure was one of a number of important predictors of who ultimately made it to the top. It was not, however, the only predictor.

Education was a second factor related to successful entry into the leadership elite. The members of underrepresented groups who made it to the top were consistently better educated than the white men who had long populated those higher circles of power. They were more likely to attend prestigious colleges and universities, and they were more likely to earn graduate and professional degrees.

Skin color was a third factor of importance that influenced who did and who did not make it. We performed controlled studies in which raters assessed the skin color of African Americans and Latinos in top leadership positions, and prominent African Americans and Latinos who were not in such positions, and the findings showed conclusively that those with lighter skin were more likely to rise in these institutional hierarchies.

Finally, we concluded that the newcomers were able to manage their identities in ways that communicated that they were not likely to disrupt or threaten those already in power. They had, or they had learned, a style that allowed them to fit in comfortably with those in power. They could show the white male power structure that they were "just like them" in more ways than the white men realized.

These four factors—class, education, skin color, and style—are not mutually exclusive. Many of those we studied, for example, had learned to manage their identities in ways that fit in with white men in power by having attended elite boarding schools and colleges where they were surrounded by privileged whites. Similarly, many of those African Americans and Latinos with light skin had been born into economic comfort. Still, these four categories proved quite useful when we tried to understand the pathways to power for those from previously excluded groups.

In this study of CEOs, we will apply the same four categories to see if they again are useful in explaining why the new CEOs made it to their positions when others did not.

Two Caveats

Before we turn, in the next three chapters, to a look at the women, the African Americans, and the Latinos and Asian Americans who have become CEOs, we need to address two issues. First we want to explain why we are including chapters on women, African American, Latino and Asian American CEOs but are not including chapters on Catholic and Jewish CEOs. In the middle of the twentieth century what many have called a WASP (white Anglo-Saxon Protestant) Establishment began to assimilate Catholics into its ranks (see Baltzell 1964; Alba and Abdel-Hady 2005; Alba 2009) and, a few decades later, it began to assimilate Jews. In our previous books (Zweigenhaft and Domhoff 1982, 1998, 2006) we have detailed the dramatic increase in the presence of Jews in elite positions, including the fact that (as he had hoped when we interviewed him in 1981) many Jews did follow Irving Shapiro of DuPont into the CEO offices of other *Fortune* 500 companies that were not founded or owned by Jews. We will not detail again the increased presence of Jews in the corporate elite, but we do wish to emphasize, as we have in our previous work, that much can be learned about what makes newcomers acceptable (and unacceptable) in the halls of power by studying how Jews, and which Jews, made it into the higher circles. In chapter 5 we will draw on a sample of Jewish CEOs of *Fortune* 500 companies in the analyses that we make (these Jewish CEOs are one of two "control" groups we will also draw on to compare with the women, African American, Latino, and Asian American CEOs—the other control group consists of a sample of non-Jewish white male CEOs).

Second, in our previous work we have stressed that many of the categories we have used (such as "Jews," "African Americans," "Latinos") can be difficult to define, can be ambiguous, can overlap, and can interact. In an interview study the first author did in the early 1980s of Harvard MBAs, one woman made this point quite clearly when she asserted that she thought being female was a more substantial barrier in the corporate world than was the fact that she was Jewish, but that both were factors in the challenges that she faced: "It's the whole package," she said. "I heard secondhand from someone as to how I would be perceived as a pushy Jewish broad who went and got an MBA. Both elements, being Jewish and being a woman, together with having the MBA, were combined to create a stereotype" (Zweigenhaft 1984, 17). In our books on diversity in the power elite (Zweigenhaft and Domhoff 1998, 2006), we argue that in order to understand who does and who does not make it to the highest leadership positions, it is important to take into account class background but that other factors, such as whether a person is female, Jewish, Latino, or African American, also matter. In keeping with this emphasis, the concept of "intersectionality" has gained prominence in sociology and in cultural studies since the early 1990s (Crenshaw 1991). This theoretical perspective emphasizes that categories like "women" or "Jews," as socially and culturally constructed categories, are not dichotomous and that they must be seen and used contextually. Therefore, as we are about to turn to chapters on women CEOs, African American CEOs, Latino and Asian American CEOs, we want to stress at the outset that these categories are often quite difficult to define, that there is overlap among the categories (for example, Andrea Jung, the CEO of Avon since November 1999, is both a woman and an Asian American), and there are important interactions that must be considered as one employs these at times arbitrary categories (although she and her publicists at times have been misleading about her parents' class background, Andrea Jung is not only female and Asian American but she is from a privileged background).

With that intersectional caveat in mind, let us turn in the next chapter to the women who have become CEOs of *Fortune* 500 companies.

2

The Women *Fortune* 500 CEOs

It was a classic story of a man who married the boss's daughter. In this case, the owner's well-educated and accomplished daughter married a bright young lawyer in 1940, and, although he knew nothing about the business when he married her, within a few years he was running the company. But then, in 1963, the story took an unexpected turn: he committed suicide. To the surprise of many, the owner's daughter, Katharine Graham, decided to take over the leadership of the company, the *Washington Post*.

Graham expected to be an interim caretaker for the paper, but instead she stayed on, and when she died in 2001 at the age of eighty-four, the *New York Times* wrote that she had "transformed the *Washington Post* from a mediocre newspaper into an American institution" (Berger 2001, A1). Two key moments in that transformation were the 1971 decision to publish the Pentagon Papers (standing with the *New York Times* in its challenge to the Nixon administration about the bogus justifications for the country's involvement in Vietnam) and, a year later, the decision to publish the series of articles on Watergate, a series that lead to Nixon's resignation. By the time she stepped down as CEO in 1991, the *Washington Post* was a multi-million dollar communications empire. When the company first made the *Fortune* 500 list, in 1972, Katharine Graham became the first woman CEO of a *Fortune* 500 company.

As Richard Vancil notes in his book *Passing the Baton: Managing the Process of CEO Succession*, the title of CEO was not used universally until fairly late in the twentieth century. He studied a sample of 227 companies from 1960 through 1984 and found that the use of the CEO title had increased dramatically. "As late as 1967," he wrote, "only half of the companies in the sample were using the title" (Vancil 1987, 291). Katharine Graham, assuming the leadership of her company as she did in 1963, did not use the term CEO to refer to herself until much later, but she was the de facto CEO well before she used the term. Almost all of the new CEOs we write about in this book became CEOs in the last decade, so this is not an issue for them.

Graham is a case study for intersectionality, for she demonstrates quite well the multiple and interacting influences within any individual. She was female, she was from a wealthy upper class family that interacted socially and professionally with the most prominent people in the country, her manic-depressive husband had at times treated her abusively, and, as she only belatedly discovered when she was a student at Vassar, she was partly Jewish. Her mother was Lutheran, and her parents were married in a Lutheran ceremony, even though her father was Jewish. Katharine and her four siblings were baptized in their home as Lutherans, but the family had a pew at the tiny St. John's Episcopal Church (where the rector was a friend of the family). Katharine explained in her autobiography: "For the most part religion was not part of our lives. . . . Remarkably, the fact that we were half Jewish was never mentioned any more than money was discussed. I was totally—incredibly—unaware of anti-Semitism, let alone of my father's being Jewish" (Graham 1997, 52). Like her parents, she was married in a Lutheran ceremony.

The second woman to become CEO of a *Fortune* 500 company, Linda Wachner, had a very different trajectory to the top. Born in New York City in 1946, Wachner was raised in Queens by Herman Wachner, a fur salesman, and his wife Shirley, a saleslady at Saks Fifth Avenue (like Katharine Graham, Wachner's father was Jewish—but so, too, was her mother). Linda had a sister who was eighteen years older, so she essentially was raised as an only child. After graduating from the State University of New York at Buffalo, where she majored in economics and business administration, she became a buyer for department stores. In 1970, while on a business trip in Florida, she met Seymour Applebaum, an executive at a dressmaking company, and they married in 1973 (she was twenty-seven and he was sixty). Applebaum, who had a heart condition, died ten years later (they had no children). Wachner's older sister had died two years earlier, her father had died many years earlier, and when her mother died in 1987, she had no immediate family.

She joined Warnaco in 1974 and within a year she became vice president of the lingerie division. It was apparent that she was smart, aggressive, and ambitious, and when the president of the company reminded her that it had taken a hundred years for a woman to become a vice president and that she should temper her expectations about when further promotions would occur, she left. Within two years she had become president and chief operating officer at Max Factor. When the Beatrice companies took over Max Factor in 1984, Wachner—well aware that she was living in an era of corporate takeovers, with buyouts and mergers seeming to take place everywhere she looked—raised $280 million with the help of a New York investment firm in the hopes of buying the company from Beatrice. The offer fell through; she left Max Factor and within a few months arranged a $905 million dollar deal to buy the cosmetics division of Revlon, but someone else offered more and that deal fell through also. Undeterred, in 1986 she went after Warnaco, her former company, and her hostile bid, a leveraged buyout for more than $500 million, was successful. With this purchase, Wachner became the second woman to head a *Fortune* 500 company—Warnaco had been on the *Fortune* 500 list every year since 1966, and in 1986 it was #405.

Wachner got rid of some managers and hired others, and she dropped slow-selling products and picked up others (including Calvin Klein underwear and Chaps by Ralph Lauren). In 1992 *Fortune* magazine named her America's most successful businesswoman, but she also developed a reputation among her employees, her colleagues, and in the press as both tough and tough to work with. *Fortune* labeled her "America's toughest woman boss," and "the Queen of Impatience." The *Daily Mail* of London called her "hell on high heels." She was known for autocratic behavior that included abusive and de-meaning treatment of her employees, for her use of obscene language, and for her use of racial and ethnic slurs (Kaufman 2001a, 6). Her behavior puts us on notice that perhaps we should not expect to find the new CEOs as a group behaving much differently from their white male counterparts.

Like more and more CEOs of the 1980s and 1990s, she was extremely well compensated. By 1996 she was the highest paid female executive in the country, with a compensation package at about $10 million. Although the company stock fell 27 percent from 1998 to 1999, and the company lost $32 million, her compensation increased. As *Fortune* put it in 2000, explaining why she was still on their list of the fifty most powerful women in American business even though her company was not doing well: "Her power is in her pay. She got a compensation package worth an estimated $73 million last year" (Sellers 2000, 106). Graef Crystal, a compensation expert, estimated that from 1993 to 1998 Wachner had been paid $158 million in salary and bonuses from Warnaco and Authentic Fitness (another company that she ran, subsequently purchased by Warnaco). "At the end of the day," he claims, "she is worth more than the company. . . . She proved there can be a negative correlation between pay and performance" (Kaufman 2001b, C14).

By 2000, however, things began to unravel for Warnaco and for Wachner. In May 2000 Calvin Klein, who had previously sung her praises, sued her (mainly, it seems, for selling his high-priced vanity jeans in low-rent out-lets like Costco and J. C. Penney), calling her "abusive," "unprofessional," and "vile" (Sellers 2000). Shareholders who claimed that she had withheld information on the actual financial condition of the company also sued her. In June 2001, $3.1 billion in debt, Warnaco declared bankruptcy (the value of the stock had dropped from $44 a share in July 1998 to $0.39) and a restructuring committee was formed (the day after declaring bankruptcy, the company cancelled its lease of a helicopter, at $33,800 a month, and its lease of a corporate jet at $234,800 per month; Schoolman 2001). In November 2001, the Warnaco board pulled the plug, firing Wachner without severance (Kaufman 2001b). (Wachner sued the bankrupt company for severance pay of $25 million, demanding that the company place her claim in front of those of other creditors—they subsequently settled for $3.5 million.)

Marion Sandler was the third woman to become the CEO of a *Fortune* 500 company—technically she was co-CEO, along with her husband. She was born in 1931 in Biddeford, Maine, where her parents owned a hardware and plumbing supply store and had become successful in real estate. After graduating from Wellesley, one of the first (if not the first) in what was to prove to be a long line of famous women business leaders who graduated from there (Dobrzynski 1995), and earning an MBA from NYU, she became one of the first women security analysts on Wall Street. She met her husband, a lawyer from a working class lower east side New York family, at a party in the Hamptons.

They married in 1961. Within two years they had created Golden West Financial Corporation and, for $3.8 million, purchased a bank called Golden West Savings and Loan Association, a transaction mostly financed by Marion's brother, a successful businessman, and moved to California (Fost 2006). The bank, which had a main office and one branch, was what was then called a "thrift" or a "savings and loan"—it took deposits and made mortgage loans. As *New York Times* business writer Joe Nocera (2008a) explains, "They were not afraid of trying things the industry had never tried before. . . . During their tenure, Golden West's stock rose at an annual rate of 19 percent, a remarkable long-term record."

By the late 1980s the Sandlers had become major supporters of a number of progressive causes and organizations (Nocera calls them "philanthrocapitalists"). Over the years they had made sizable donations to such well-known liberal organizations as Human Rights Watch and the American Civil Liberties Union; in addition, they started the Center for American Progress (by late 2008 they had donated more than $20 million to it), and they gave another $30 million for the first three years of ProPublica, a foundation dedicated to investigative journalism (Nocera 2008a). In their support for progressive causes, the Sandlers are unusual among extremely wealthy corporate leaders in that they have been part of a liberal-labor coalition. More typically, corporate leaders are either moderate conservatives or ultraconservatives, and the corporate foundations they set up support causes or institutions that further their moderately conservative or ultraconservative beliefs.[1]

The Sandlers and a company they owned, by then called World Savings Bank, had pioneered a lending practice that they called Pick-A-Pay. More commonly called "option adjustable rate mortgages" (or option ARMs), these adjustable mortgages, which became increasingly popular during the Reagan era of deregulation, allowed homeowners to vary the amounts they paid, and these loans allowed for small payments early on, with larger payments due over time. Some of the loans allowed homeowners to pay so little that the payments did not cover the interest and thus the principal on their loans increased rather than decreased. The loans initially were especially attractive to professionals whose incomes fluctuated a great deal—those, for example, who depended on end-of-the-year bonuses but never knew how large those bonuses might be. Over time, however, mortgage companies, including World Savings Bank, began to market to a larger clientele, including many low-paid blue collar workers, many of whom could barely afford, or could not afford, to make their mortgage payments. By late 2008, many analysts and regulators considered these loans "the Typhoid Mary of the mortgage industry" (Moss and Fabrikant 2008).

Golden West thrived during the housing boom that preceded the financial crash of fall 2008, and grew to have assets of approximately $125 billion and twelve thousand employees. Between 1998 and 2005, the number of Pick-A-Pay loans by World Bank had quadrupled but were starting to slow. The next year, in what the *New York Times* called "a hastily arranged deal," Wachovia bought Golden West for $24 billion. The Sandlers, who maintained that they sold their firm because they were growing older and wanted to devote themselves to philanthropy, owned 10 percent of the stock, and thus took in about $2.4 billion from the deal.

Wachovia's purchase of Golden West proved costly, as the bank subsequently endured many billions of dollars of losses on the World Bank portfolio. As Wachovia, along with other banks, desperately sought to stay afloat, it was purchased by Wells Fargo, which in turn took over what proved to be billions of dollars of losses. As analysts and the media watched things fall apart, many began to reevaluate the Sandlers, whose public image just months before had been exemplary ("To listen to the Sandlers," wrote Nocera [2008a] in March 2008, "is to be in the presence of the kind of proud, righteous liberals who went out of fashion a long time ago"). By December 2008, as the *New York Times* described in an article titled "Once Trusted Mortgage Pioneers, Now Pariahs,"[2] the most painful and widely publicized attack on the Sandlers came in a *Saturday Night Live* skit in which one of the actors claimed that the Sandlers "should be shot." *Time* magazine listed the Sandlers

#12 on their list of "the 25 people to blame for the financial crisis" (the list also included Phil Gramm, Alan Greenspan, Bill Clinton, George Bush, and "American consumers"—in *Time*'s online poll, the Sandlers moved up to #10 with 107,188 "votes," trailing Phil Gramm, #1, with 140,450).

These three women—Katharine Graham, Linda Wachner, and Marion Sandler—were the first wave of women CEOs of *Fortune* 500 companies. As we've shown, Graham was the daughter of a founder, Wachner became CEO through a hostile leveraged buyout, and Sandler cofounded the company that she and her husband ran for many years. Graham was born in 1917 (and died in 2001), Sandler was born in 1931, and Wachner in 1946—Graham and Sandler came of age well before, and Wachner slightly before, the effects of the women's movement of the late 1960s began to penetrate the corporate world. They grew up in a culture that for the most part expected women to play subservient roles in and outside the family. They opened the doors, however, for many other, younger, women, as can be seen in table 2.1, which lists the names of the twenty-eight women who now have been CEOs of *Fortune* 500 companies, the companies they worked for, and the years the company was first on the *Fortune* 500 list with them as CEO.

THE NEXT TWENTY-FIVE WOMEN CEOS
OF *FORTUNE* 500 COMPANIES

Although four of the twenty-five women CEOs of *Fortune* companies who came after Graham, Wachner, and Sandler were born in the late 1940s, nineteen of them were born in the 1950s, and two were born in the 1960s. When this wave of future *Fortune* 500 CEOs graduated from high school, in the late 1970s or early 1980s, expectations and opportunities for women were changing. The next three women appointed *Fortune* 500 CEOs were Jill Barad, who became CEO of Mattel in 1997, Carly Fiorina, who became CEO of Hewlett-Packard in 1999, and Andrea Jung, who became CEO of Avon in 1999. By the time these three women, all born in the 1950s, graduated from college, more and more women were going to law school, more were going to medical school, and more were getting MBAs (in 1965, about 1 percent of the MBA students at Harvard were women, but by 1983 more than 25 percent of the students were; see Rowan 1983, 64; and Blagg 1983, 77). Even those who did not go on to obtain higher degrees but who entered the working world directly out of college, joined a workforce with changing views of what roles women could play and what they could do.

In 1962, Felice Schwartz founded Catalyst, a nonprofit agency specializing in women's job issues. The organization sought to help women in business

Table 2.1. Women CEOs of *Fortune* 500 Companies, 1972–2010

Number	CEO	Born	First Year on List with Woman as CEO, Ranking, and Company	Tenure as CEO
1	Graham, Katharine	1917–2001	1972, #479: Washington Post	1977–1991
2	Wachner, Linda	1946–	1986, #405: Warnaco	1986–2001
3	Sandler, Marion	1931–	1989, #446: Golden West Financial	1973–2006
4	Barad, Jill	1951–	1997, #318: Mattel	1997–2000
5	Fiorina, Carly	1954–	1999, #13: Hewlett-Packard	1999–2005
6	Jung, Andrea	1959–	1999, #312: Avon	1999 –
7	Fuller, Marce	1960–	2001, #52: Mirant (prev. So. Energy Inc.)	2001–2005
8	Hallman, Cinda*	1945–2008	2001, #443: Spherion*	2001–2004
9	Mulcahy, Anne	1952–	2001, #120: Xerox	2001–2009
10	Russo, Patricia	1953–	2002, #141: Lucent (merged: Alcatel)	2002–2008
11	Scott, Eileen	1953–	2002, #406: Pathmark Stores	2002–2005
12	Sammons, Mary	1946–	2003, #128: Rite Aid	2003–2010
13	Ivey, Susan	1958–	2004, #280: Reynolds American	2004–2011
14	Barnes, Brenda	1953–	2006, #111: Sara Lee	2005–2010
15	Whitman, Meg	1956–	2006, #458: eBay	1998–2007
16	Woertz, Patricia	1953–	2007, #56: Archer Daniels	2006–
17	Rosenfeld, Irene	1953–	2007, #64: Kraft	2006–
18	Nooyi, Indra	1955–	2007, #63: PepsiCo	2006 –
19	Rosput Reynolds, Paula	1956–	2007, #363: Safeco	2006–2008
20	Babrowski, Claire	1958–	2007, #466: RadioShack (interim CEO, 2005–2006)	2007–2007
21	Meyrowitz, Carol	1954–	2007, #133: TJX	2007–
22	Braly, Angela	1961–	2008, #33: WellPoint	2007–
23	Gold, Christina	1947–	2008, #473: Western Union	2006–
24	Elsenhans, Lynn	1956–	2008, #56: Sunoco	2008–
25	Kullman, Ellen	1956–	2009, #75: DuPont	2009–
26	Bartz, Carol	1948–	2009, #345: Yahoo	2009–
27	Burns, Ursula	1958–	2009, #147: Xerox	2009–
28	Sen, Laura	1956–	2009, #269: BJ's Wholesale Club	2009–

*Spherion appeared on the *Fortune* list in 2001 as #443, and therefore we include her. Catalyst does not include Cinda Hallman on its list because its classification is based on the revenue year, not the publication year. On Catalyst's list she appears as the CEO of a company that in 2001 was ranked between 501 and 1000 (Jan Combopiano, e-mail message to first author, August 29, 2009).

and in the professions achieve their maximum potential, and it sought to help employers capitalize on the abilities of their female employees. In 1977, in response to requests from some corporations, Catalyst began its Corporate Board Resource, which was designed to draw on its database of high-achieving women "to help board chairmen carefully select and recruit female directors." In 1993, Catalyst began to publish an annual *Census of Women Board Directors*. Sheila Wellington, the president of Catalyst, explained how eager companies were to let Catalyst know they had added women to their boards: "Hardly had the ink dried on the 1993 Census before more corporations were calling to alert us to the fact that they'd added a woman to their boards. For months, we fielded calls relaying names of female additions to boards" (Wellington 1994).

The number of women on the boards of *Fortune* 500 companies has increased slowly but steadily since that time, climbing from 9.5 percent in 1995, to 13.6 percent in 2003, to 14.8 percent in 2007, to 15.2 percent in 2008. By 2008, almost all (86.8 percent) of the *Fortune* 500 companies had at least one woman on their boards, and 18.4 percent had three or more women directors. In a recent study (Joy 2008), Catalyst found a clear and positive correlation between the number of women directors companies had in 2001 and the number of women senior officers they had in 2006 (this study focused on women in top management generally, not just women CEOs).[3]

When the Hewlett-Packard board chose a new CEO in 1999, it appears that the dilemma it faced was not whether to choose a woman CEO but which woman CEO. In November 1998, John Markoff of the *New York Times* wrote that Ann Livermore, a sixteen-year veteran in the company, was "in a position to scale the peaks of one of the most male-dominated industries in America." Her recent promotion, he observed, "has made her a contender to succeed Lewis E. Platt, Hewlett's chief executive" (Markoff 1998, 2). Eight months later, however, the company instead chose Fiorina, an outsider, the only finalist with no direct experience in the computer business (she had been a president at Lucent, where her work concerned telephone equipment; Markoff 2005). Platt, the incumbent CEO, was especially sensitive to the issues that working women faced because back in the early 1980s his wife had died and he was left to provide the primary care for his nine- and eleven-year-old daughters. Platt subsequently advocated for flexible work schedules, for allowing employees to work at home, for the sharing of jobs, and even for yearlong unpaid leaves from the company. During his years as CEO, Hewlett-Packard was regularly on the annual *Fortune* magazine list of the 100 best companies to work for.

But why Fiorina, the outsider, instead of Livermore, the insider? According to a consultant who was asked by the Hewlett-Packard board to help evaluate Fiorina prior to its final decision, "they needed a new vision," and therefore, he explained, "I told the board that I thought that her style, in many ways, was a good fit for what they said they wanted" (Rivlin and Markoff 2005, 4). Khurana provides a similar explanation:

> According to a search consultant with knowledge of the H-P search, business analysts believed that the H-P culture had grown too soft, with too much emphasis on consensus decision-making, and H-P's board had increasingly adopted this view. The directors wanted someone to shake up the traditional culture, which worked to the detriment of inside candidate, Ann Livermore (the CEO of H-P's $14 billion Enterprise Computing division), who was said to be the outgoing CEO's choice. (Khurana 2002, 66)

Although the company's stock rose 2 percent the day Fiorina was appointed, things did not go well after that. Months after she was hired the technology bubble burst on Wall Street, which led her to push hard for a costly and controversial purchase of Compac, but Hewlett-Packard stock continued to drop. By the time she was fired, in February 2005, "an investor who bought stock on the day she was hired would have seen 55 percent of the investment vanish" (Norris 2005). After a two-day meeting in Chicago, Patricia Dunn, a director since 1998, was named to replace Fiorina as chair of the board. She announced that Robert Wayman, a thirty-six-year veteran of the company, and its chief financial officer, would serve as interim CEO.[4]

Carly Fiorina had been CEO for six years, twice as long as the average tenure for CEOs in 2005. She walked away with a $42 million severance package, so she wasn't exactly hurting. In the 2008 presidential campaign, she was a key advisor to John McCain, the Republican nominee for president (her official title was chairwoman of the "Victory '08 Committee"), and she was rumored at times to be a potential vice presidential running mate or a member of a McCain cabinet were he to win (Bumiller 2008). In November 2009 she announced that she was going to challenge Barbara Boxer, one of the two Democratic senators from California, for her seat, an election she subsequently lost.

Also noteworthy in these three appointments, and a forerunner of things to come, is that the companies that appointed Barad, Fiorina, and Jung were ranked higher than those headed by Graham, Wachner, and Sandler (the *Washington Post*, Warnaco, and Golden West ranked between #400 and #500 when they first made the *Fortune* 500 list). Hewlett-Packard, when it appointed Fiorina in 1999, was #13, Avon was #312 when it appointed Jung, and Mattel was #318 when it appointed Barad. Eight women have become CEOs of companies in the top 100 (with Hewlett-Packard, at #13 in 1999, the highest-ranking company at the time of a woman CEO appointment), and the others distributed throughout the top 500. Most have been closer to the top of the list than the bottom (the average ranking has been #238, and the median has been #208).

INSIDERS VERSUS OUTSIDERS

According to Khurana (2002, 248), choosing an outsider to become CEO of a *Fortune* 500 company was "virtually unheard of" before 1980 (this may have been true in the mid-twentieth century, but, as we pointed out in chapter 1, C. Wright Mills found that in 1870 fully six in ten top executives came to their positions from outside those companies; Mills 1956, 139). Khurana explains the reasoning for what had become the almost automatic selection of insiders in the following way:

> CEOs were chosen from inside the firm because this was the most efficient way to select them. CEOs require know-how and skills specific to a firm to run it most effectively. Moreover, when new employees join a firm, it is not clear in advance who will acquire the requisite know-how and be the best person to run the firm. Firms therefore use internal labor markets—which utilize training and promotions—both to impart firm-specific knowledge and to learn who is likely to be most effective in the CEO's job. (Khurana 2002, 46–47)

After 1980, however, more companies hired outsiders as CEOs. Khurana looked at the searches that had taken place in 850 firms from 1980 to 1996 and found that 27 percent involved outsiders (he defined outsiders conservatively—only if the newly hired CEO had no prior affiliation with the firm at all; some researchers, such as Richard Vancil [1987], have used broader definitions, including those who had been with the firm either for less than five years or for less than two years). Moreover, Khurana suggests that the number of outsiders had increased from 1996 to 2000. According to one expert that he interviewed, by the year 2000 close to 50 percent of all CEOs in large, publicly held companies were outsiders (Khurana 2002, 245 and 248).

Contrary to what we might expect based on Khurana's (2002) claims, most of those in our sample of twenty-eight women CEOs have been insiders, but seven (25 percent) were outsiders (we are using the same conservative definition of outsiders that Khurana used—people who had no prior affiliation with the company that hired them as CEOs). As we have noted, one of the outsiders was Carly Fiorina at Hewlett-Packard, chosen over the insider (also female) favored by the previous CEO. Another was Patricia Woertz, who in April 2006 became CEO of Archer Daniels Midland, a company that *Fortune* called "famously insular" (the subtitle of a *Fortune* article about her was "To Be Its CEO, Famously Insular ADM Picked Not Only a Woman But a Newcomer"; Birger 2006). Woertz had been at Chevron since 1984 and was considered a contender for the CEO spot there if it were to open; the CEO at Chevron, however, appeared to be years away from retiring, so in 2006, Woertz, then fifty-three, decided to leave Chevron and pursue CEO positions "as a full time job." When a headhunter from Spencer Stuart, one of the big four search firms, called her about the opening at Archer Daniels Midland, she eagerly pursued it.

Two months later she was hired, though not without opposition. There had never been an outsider CEO at the company, which had been run by the Andreas family for the previous thirty-five years. In 1997, the heir apparent, Michael Andreas, who was the son of the current CEO, Dwayne O. Andreas, was convicted of price-fixing. When Dwayne retired at age eighty, Michael was serving a three-year prison term, and the company chose as its new CEO Dwayne's nephew, fifty-five-year-old G. Allen Andreas, described by *Business Week* (July 9, 2001) as "an unassuming bean counter." Five years later, when G. Allen decided to retire, he made it known that he wanted the company to hire one of his deputies. The board, however, clearly looking for a change from the family that had controlled the company for many decades, chose Patricia Woertz, an outsider and a woman.

In a critique of the modern CEO search process, Khurana (2002, 155) argues that "in today's corporate folklore (which mirrors the psychologizing of public language in American society generally), charisma is often found to be rooted not so much in specific actions and accomplishments as in an individual's ability to overcome some personal handicap." He gives the example of former GE CEO Jack Welch, who overcame a stutter as a youngster, and John Chambers, of Cisco Systems, who had conquered dyslexia. Some of the portrayals of the women CEOs hired as outsiders very much stress their ability to overcome hardships. Consider the following excerpts, from an *Economist* story titled "One Tough Yahoo! Life Has Tested Carol Bartz Far More Than Even Running Yahoo! Will," explaining why in late 2008 the Yahoo board named Carol Bartz as its CEO:

> In fact, none of this reveals much about Ms. Bartz as a leader, nor about the real reason why Yahoo!'s board chose her. Her main qualification is that Ms. Bartz has been tested in life as few people in Silicon Valley have. Her trials have turned her into a hardened, disciplined, occasionally ruthless, but often inspiring boss—exactly the sort of leader, it could be argued, that Yahoo! now desperately needs.
>
> She was born in Minnesota but lost her mother when she was a child, so her grandmother raised her in a small town in Wisconsin. . . . Ms. Bartz then went to work at 3M, one of America's blue-chip companies, in the 1970s. But when

she requested a transfer to headquarters, she was told that "women don't do
these jobs." She walked straight out of 3M and into the computer industry. . . .
   Just as she began her new job, Ms. Bartz was diagnosed with breast cancer. She was 43 at the time, and decided to fight on all fronts. ("One Tough
Yahoo!" 2009).[5]

Most of the twenty-eight women CEOs, however, have been insiders, and
some worked for the same company for a long time. When Jill Barad became
CEO of Mattel in 1997, she had been with the company for fifteen years;
when Xerox appointed Anne Mulcahy CEO in 2001, she had been with the
company for twenty-six years; and, in 2002, when Pathmark named Eileen
Scott its CEO, she had been with the company for thirty years. In a few cases,
women had worked for a company for many years, left, and then returned
a few years later as CEO. This, as we have shown, was the case for Linda
Wachner, who came back as CEO at Warnaco after buying the company in
a hostile leveraged buyout. In a less hostile return, Patricia Russo, who had
worked for Lucent for eighteen years and had then left for two years, was
enticed back to be CEO; similarly, Irene Rosenfeld worked for Kraft for
twenty-two years, left to work for PepsiCo for three years, and was lured back
to Kraft to be its CEO.
   The women who have emerged as *Fortune* 500 CEOs clearly have broken
through the glass ceiling of gender. Do they differ from the men who have
gone before them in terms of their class background?

CLASS BACKGROUND

As C. Wright Mills and others have stressed, it is important to look beyond
the self-serving claims that corporate executives and their public relations
people make, for the Horatio Alger myth runs deep in American ideology
(e.g., Mills 1956, 91). The media very much assist in this process. For example, when Laurence Tisch, the former owner of Loews and CEO of CBS, died
in 2003, the *New York Times* proclaimed on its front page that Tisch, a "self-
made billionaire," had died, ignoring the fact that Tisch was from a wealthy
family that had started him off at the age of twenty-three with a gift that was
the equivalent of more than a million dollars in today's currency. Similarly,
when Roberto Goizueta, the Cuban-born former CEO of Coca-Cola died in
1997, almost all the media coverage, including the Associated Press and the
New York Times, emphasized how little money he was able to bring with him
when he left Cuba in 1960, but did not mention, or buried late in the stories,
that he, too, was from a family with considerable wealth (Zweigenhaft 2004).

In examining the class backgrounds of the twenty-eight women CEOs, it is therefore necessary to be cautious about the claims that they make, that their publicists make, and that are reported without any critical analysis in the media. In the spring of 2008, for example, when Carly Fiorina, the daughter of a federal judge and herself a Stanford graduate, was on the presidential campaign trail with John McCain, McCain frequently introduced her as an American success story "who began as a part-time secretary" (Bumiller 2008). Andrea Jung, whose Chinese parents immigrated to Canada but who were well-educated professionals (her father was an architect, her mother a chemical engineer), was asked if she thought that growing up as the daughter of immigrants had influenced her career. Her answer? "It has given me a global vantage point, being the daughter of immigrants from China, *who had nothing when they came here.* And now I am leading a company. It speaks to something deep in me, the concept that you don't have to start with anything" (Tarquinio 2008). Clearly we need to look beyond such self-serving assertions that ignore the enormous benefits of class privilege if we want to assess the class backgrounds of CEOs.

Sociologists who study class try to draw on multiple factors, including the education and occupations of parents, income, and, especially, family wealth. We were unable to obtain information about family wealth for most of the women who have become CEOs of *Fortune* 500 companies, but for almost all of them we were able to discover their parents' level of education and careers. Based on the information we could obtain for twenty-four of the twenty-eight women, the pattern is consistent with previous patterns for the men who were CEOs in 1900, 1925, 1950, and into the mid-1990s: seventeen of the twenty-four, or 71 percent, were from upper or upper middle class backgrounds, and seven were from middle class or working class backgrounds. Some, like Katharine Graham and Meg Whitman (the CEO of eBay from 1998 to 2007), grew up with considerable privilege, and their families were in what Gilbert (2011, 13–14) and many other sociologists call the capitalist class (about 1 percent of the population according to Gilbert). Many of the women CEOs, including Jill Barad, Carly Fiorina, and Andrea Jung, are from families in which the parents were doctors, lawyers, engineers, architects, or other professionals and were at least in the upper middle class, which, according to Gilbert, makes up about 14 percent of the population (if there was sufficient wealth in these families, they may actually have been in the capitalist class).[6] As was true for the CEOs of the past, only a minority (four of the twenty-four, or 17 percent) were from working class families: Eileen Scott, who rose through the ranks at Pathmark from clerk and part-time bookkeeper to CEO, is the daughter of a policeman; Brenda Barnes, the CEO at Sara Lee from 2005 to 2010, is the daughter of a factory worker[7]; Carol Bartz, the CEO at Yahoo since 2009, is the daughter of a mill worker; and Ursula Burns, CEO at Xerox since 2009, was raised in the projects by a single mother who took in ironing.

EDUCATION

Like the many women who preceded them as directors of *Fortune* 500 companies (Zweigenhaft and Domhoff 2006, 52), these women CEOs were quite well educated. All but two were college graduates. The first exception is Claire Babrowski, the daughter of a dentist, who started college at the University of Illinois, Urbana-Champaign, but dropped out and went to work for McDonald's. She rose through the ranks at McDonald's, and midcareer she was accepted into an executive MBA program at the University of North Carolina, from which she earned a degree in 1995 (thus, she has no BA but she has an MBA). Ironically, she subsequently became interim CEO at RadioShack when the CEO at that company was found to have lied about having earned two academic degrees (Norris 2006; see also George and Thomas 2006). The other exception, as far as we can tell, is Carol Meyrowitz, who was appointed CEO of TJX in 2006. We could find no evidence that she had attended college.

The remaining twenty-six women CEOs all earned bachelors degrees, and twelve of the twenty-six were from elite schools (including two from Princeton, two from Wellesley, and two from Harvard). Moreover, fifteen had earned higher degrees (eleven MBAs, one law degree, one PhD).[8]

ETHNICITY

Most, but not all, of the twenty-eight women are (or in the case of the two who have died, were) white. Andrea Jung, whose parents immigrated to Canada from China, is Asian American. Indra Nooyi grew up in India, and came to the United States to do graduate work at Yale (she is now an American citizen). Ursula Burns is African American. And the most recent addition to the list of women *Fortune* CEOs, Laura Sen, who became the CEO of BJ's Wholesale Club in February 2009 (BJ's was #269 in 2009), is the daughter of a Chinese father (who was a highway engineer) and an Irish mother (who was a secretary).

MARRIED WITH FAMILIES

Almost all (twenty-six of the twenty-eight) had married, some while in college, some after college, and some fairly late in their careers, and most (sixteen) had children (a few married men with children and some helped to raise stepchildren). A number are married to high-powered executives, and in some cases, to other CEOs. Compared with other women of their generational cohort, they do not seem to be less likely to have married or to have had children. Although one (Cinda Hallman) never married or had children, as a group they do not at all fit the stereotype of high-powered women executives who work so hard that they have no time for relationships or for families. A few do indicate that they have only been able to be successful in their careers because they have had husbands who have been willing to move to be with them or to provide primary care for their children.

CONCLUSION

In 1972, when Katharine Graham became the first women CEO of a *Fortune* 500 company, she was, obviously, one of five hundred CEOs, so women represented .2 percent of all *Fortune* 500 CEOs. Almost thirty years later, when she died in 2001, there were five women CEOs (1 percent). Back in 1998, when she became CEO of Mattel, Jill Barad predicted that within a decade 10 percent of the *Fortune* 500 CEOs would be women (Sellers 1998, 96). Barad joins many others who have made wildly optimistic predictions about the rate of progress for women as directors and as CEOs of *Fortune* 500 companies (see Zweigenhaft and Domhoff 2006, 59–60). In July 2009, when Catalyst published its annual report, there were fifteen women CEOs at *Fortune* 500 companies (3 percent). The doors have opened, and twenty-eight women have walked through those doors, but women continue to be woefully underrepresented in the CEO office.

Moreover, even though some women have made it to the CEO office, there are concerns about the extent to which there are women in the pipeline who will become future CEOs. For example, in one of the fastest growing sectors of the economy, high technology, there have been CEOs of *Fortune* 500 companies in Silicon Valley, the epicenter of that industry—Carly Fiorina at Hewlett-Packard, Meg Whitman at eBay, and Carol Bartz at Yahoo. At the same time, recent evidence indicates that women continue to be underrepresented in high-tech firms. Only 6 percent of the CEOs of the one hundred largest tech companies are women, and only 22 percent of the software engineers at tech companies are women. Although they are now in the majority at colleges, in law schools, and in medical schools, women are in a distinct minority when it comes to undergraduate and graduate degrees in math, engineering, and computer-related subjects. As a result, few women are hired in management positions at high-tech firms. As Carol Bartz observes: "As you look around the entry-level management positions, even just the ranks of engineers or product people, there just aren't many women. So, therefore, mathematically, it tells you it's impossible for them to move up and run something" (Miller 2010, 8).

Is there still a glass ceiling that prevents women in many corporations from making it to the top? Are there women in the pipeline? We will return to these questions in the final chapter. First, however, we turn to the experiences of African American CEOs, and then Latino and Asian American CEOs.

3

The African American *Fortune* 500 CEOs

On February 1, 1960, four black undergraduates at North Carolina A&T State University in Greensboro, North Carolina, sat at a segregated lunch counter at the downtown Woolworth's and refused to leave when they were denied service. Their protest received national publicity, and it inspired others to join them. Within days, there were similar demonstrations in Durham, Winston-Salem, Fayetteville, Charlotte, and Raleigh, and soon there were sit-ins and demonstrations in other states throughout the South, not only at Woolworth's stores but at other chains with similar policies, including Kress, S. S. Kresge, and W. T. Grant. As historian William Chafe writes, "In the long view of history, the Greensboro sit-ins will justifiably be seen as the catalyst that triggered a decade of revolt—one of the greatest movements in history toward self-determination and human dignity" (Chafe 1980, 137).

The effects of the movement were great and small, highly publicized and barely noticed. One of the quieter effects of the movement, eliciting only a brief article in the *New York Times*, was the appointment, in June 1964, of the first two blacks as directors of *Fortune* 500 companies. One of the two, Asa Spaulding of Durham, North Carolina, joined the board of W. T. Grant. Although the chairman of the board at W. T. Grant claimed that Spaulding's appointment had nothing to do with the massive demonstrations against his company, it is unlikely that anyone believed him. The other, Samuel R. Pierce, Jr., was appointed to the board of U.S. Industries, because the CEO of that company, John I. Snyder, Jr., was a longtime liberal maverick who was involved in civil rights work, was supportive of labor unions, and was a staunch Democrat, suggesting once again that there are some liberal leaders within a group that is mostly resistant to change and which narrowly focuses on the bottom line.

Over the next seven years, another nine blacks became directors at *Fortune* 500 boards (all were men, and most were from relatively privileged backgrounds). In May 1971, Patricia Harris, the former ambassador to Luxembourg, was asked to join two corporate boards (Scott Paper and IBM) and she became the only black woman among the thousands of men who were directors on *Fortune* 500 boards.[1] Over the next few decades, many companies added black directors to their boards, though few added more than one. By 2004, about 8 percent of the directors at *Fortune* 500 companies were African American, with slightly more at the larger companies than at the smaller ones (Zweigenhaft and Domhoff 2006, 92–96, 99–101).

Most of these black directors were outside directors rather than inside directors. That is, they had become prominent elsewhere—as lawyers, as college presidents, or in some cases as executives at or near the top at other companies—but they had not moved upward through the ranks of the company on whose board they sat. There was, therefore, a very small pipeline for African Americans to become CEOs if ever they were to be offered such positions. But it turned out there was a pipeline, and young African Americans who started out on the bottom rung of the corporate ladder in the 1960s and 1970s were slowly working their way to the top.

A BREAKTHROUGH YEAR: FRANKLIN RAINES AND LLOYD WARD

By the mid-1990s, a few African American men, and fewer African American women, had achieved senior-level positions in a handful of *Fortune* 500 companies, and periodically they received mention in the media as contenders for CEO positions at one *Fortune*-level company or another. It did not happen, however, until 1999 when two African American men became CEOs of *Fortune* 500 companies: Franklin Raines at Fannie Mae (#26 in 1999) and Lloyd Ward at Maytag (#379 in 1999).

Franklin Raines is a genuine rags to riches story. He grew up in Seattle, where his father worked at a variety of jobs, including as a custodian for the city of Seattle, and his mother worked as a cleaning woman at Boeing. During one especially difficult two-year stretch, when his father had to be hospitalized for an illness, the family was on welfare. Raines was a star at the local public high school on and off the field—he quarterbacked the football team, he was a state debate champion, and he was student body president. Few were surprised when he won a scholarship to attend Harvard. After completing his undergraduate degree, he spent a year in Oxford as a Rhodes scholar and then returned to Harvard where he earned a law degree.

Before making the big jump to become the CEO at Fannie Mae, Raines moved back and forth from government to industry in the classical fashion of those who become major power figures (Mills 1956; Salzman and Domhoff 1980; Useem 1984). He spent two years (1977–1979) working in government, mostly for the Office of Management and Budget (OMB). He then worked for Lazard Frères, the investment bank, for eleven years, and became a general partner. He left Lazard in 1991 to become vice chairman of Fannie Mae. At the start of Clinton's second term, Raines returned to government as the director of the Office of Management and Budget. Some thought that if Robert E. Rubin, the secretary of the Treasury, were to resign Raines would be his replacement. The CEO at Fannie Mae, however, unexpectedly decided to step down, and, as Raines explains, he was unable to pass up the offer: "Here was a company I knew. The board knew me. It's a job that opens up every 10 years or so. It was a case of being pulled to a once-in-a-lifetime opportunity rather than jumping or being pushed" (Stevenson 1998, 1).

Raines went from a government job with a good professional income (tens of thousands of dollars) to a compensation package that put him into a very different economic stratosphere (millions of dollars): at the White House he earned $151,500, and his initial contract at Fannie Mae paid him about $7 million. Fannie Mae, however, was an atypical corporation, and Raines became CEO at an especially difficult time. Fannie Mae, then called the Federal National Mortgage Association (FNMA), was established by Franklin Delano Roosevelt during the New Deal. Its mission was to ensure sufficient mortgage financing, especially for middle class families. It became a shareholder-owned corporation in the 1960s. In the 1980s and 1990s, Fannie Mae (and its lobbyists) was among those who encouraged Congress to eliminate some of the things that made buying a house difficult for lower-income people, such as high closing costs and discriminatory lending practices. At the time Raines took over Fannie Mae, the sale of homes was at 72 percent among white people but only 44 percent among blacks and 42 percent among Hispanics. The company had recently introduced a program that allowed lenders "to offer mortgages with down payments as low as 3 percent to people considered good credit risks" (Stevenson 1998, 10).

The company did not actually make the loans. Instead, it functioned as a mortgage insurance company; it bought the mortgages and it promised to pay off the loan if the borrower defaulted. The danger was that if it guaranteed the loans of borrowers who could not make their payments, it could end up holding a lot of bad mortgage. In 2000 the company announced that by 2010 it planned to buy $2 trillion in loans from low-income, minority, and risky borrowers.

In 2004, Raines was ousted from his position at Fannie Mae after two government agencies (the Office of Federal Housing Enterprise Oversight, or OFHEO, and the Securities and Exchange Commission) found that the company had violated accounting rules. The violations were substantial—the company was ordered to restate its earnings for the previous three years, which meant that about $9 billion previously declared as earnings were to be acknowledged as losses. Raines's compensation package, and that of other senior executives, included bonuses and other incentives that were based on meeting certain earnings goals. Over that three-year period, Raines had been paid $14 million in salary and bonus and another $25.6 million in incentive pay (Labaton 2004b). Over a five-year period, the company had paid out $245 million in bonuses (Labaton 2004a).

It is worth looking more carefully at Fannie Mae's board. Its eighteen members included Anne Mulcahy (then the CEO of Xerox), Ann Korologos (who, then named Ann McLaughlin, had been secretary of labor during Ronald Reagan's presidency), and H. Patrick Swygert, the president of Howard University (Swygert's son worked for Fannie Mae). Many on the Fannie Mae board were also on the boards of other organizations that had received substantial grants from the Fannie Mae Foundation. For example, Korologos was chair of the Aspen Institute, which had received $280,000 in grants over the previous few years. Howard University had received thirty-five different grants, totaling $555,186. As one institutional investors advisor put it, "This board has all the classic hallmarks of a cozy, friendly board" (Morgenson 2004, 6).

The board remained loyal to management even in the face of the bad news from the feds, and, in fact, only forced Raines out under pressure from the federal regulator. Even then they allowed Raines to "retire" rather than firing him, a distinction that meant millions of dollars to Raines (and to the company). Because he retired, he was still eligible for benefits and stock awards, including an annual pension of more than $1 million (Morgenson 2004, 1). The government subsequently sued Raines and two other top executives seeking $100 million in fines and $115 million in restitution from the bonuses that the government claimed were not earned. In 2008, without admitting wrongdoing, these three executives paid $31.4 million to settle the litigation (Morgenson 2009). When later that year the government bailed out Fannie Mae, with the collapse of the housing market, it inherited the company's legal defense bills for shareholder suits that had been brought against the company's top three executives. It had to spend $2.3 million to defend Raines (Morgenson 2009).

It was quite a fall from grace. Not only did Raines have an inspiring American Dream story of having risen from a working class family to become the

CEO of one of the largest companies in America, he had assumed many leadership positions (he had been the president of the board of overseers at Harvard and the cochairman of the Business Roundtable), and he was thought to be a contender for a cabinet position in a future Democratic administration. Most commentators, however, saw his ignominious departure from Fannie Mae as "the last chapter in a storied career" (Labaton 2004c, C4). In early 2009, when *Time* magazine ran its list of "the 25 people to blame for the financial crisis," they listed Franklin Raines #9, eight below Phil Gramm at #1, but three in front of Marion and Herb Sandler of Golden West (see chapter 2). Those who voted in *Time's* online poll ranked Raines even higher, at #5.

In mid-1999, months after Raines became CEO of Fannie Mae, Maytag (#379) named Lloyd Ward, a fifty-year-old African American who had been with the company since 1996 (prior to becoming CEO he had been the president and the chief operating officer at the company).

Ward, like Frank Raines, was from a poor family. He and his four siblings grew up about twenty miles west of Detroit in Romulus, Michigan, a small rural town, in a tiny three-room house with no running water. His father, who died suddenly of a heart attack during Ward's first year of college, worked during the day (in Detroit) as a postman and at night as a janitor at a movie theater. Like Raines, Ward was a good student and a multisport athlete—he was captain of the football team and such a good basketball player that he won a basketball scholarship to Michigan State University, where he played for four years and was captain of the team in his senior year (Leonhardt 1999).

At Michigan State, despite pressure from the athletic staff to drop the demanding courses he had enrolled in (organic chemistry, calculus) and take easy courses (health and "introductory basketball"), Ward, strongly influenced by his parents, who though not educated formally had a love of learning and were readers, took his academics seriously. (At the age of fifty, his mother went back to school and earned a bachelor's degree and then an MSW.) He initially planned to go into medicine, but when he was in a car accident he discovered that the sight of blood unnerved him, so he shifted to engineering.

When he graduated in 1970, he went to work for Procter & Gamble (P&G). One might think that as an engineering major who had captained the basketball team at a Big Ten school he would have no difficulty finding a good job, but P&G only hired him because the company had an affirmative action program (called a "qualifiable program"). As Ward later recalled, acknowledging the importance of such programs in the opportunities they provided for African American men and women: "They brought us in under the stigma of being 'qualifiable.' The idea was that there weren't qualified African

Americans. If it were not for the so-called affirmative action of the '60s and '70s, people like me may not have ever gotten the opportunity to provide the leadership that we have now been able to give" (Leonhardt 1999, 66). Sociologist Sharon Collins (1997) has provided many accounts of how badly black college graduates were treated by corporations prior to the disruptions that lead to affirmative action, and the stigma that they faced once affirmative action policies led to their being hired.

At P&G Ward was one of eight African American engineers in a department of about twelve hundred. He told one of his supervisors that his goal was to be CEO of a major American corporation (David Leonhardt, writing in 1999, observed that back in 1970 "a black CEO seemed as likely as a black President of the U.S."). Ward proceeded to climb the corporate ladder, first at P&G, then, starting in 1987, at PepsiCo, and subsequently, in 1996, at Maytag.

He only lasted fifteen months as CEO at Maytag. In November 2000, after a stretch in which profit growth declined and the company's share price dropped more than 60 percent from its peak in July 1999 (the time of Ward's appointment), he resigned, citing (in classic business lingo) "differences with the company's board." The sudden departure "stunned" Wall Street analysts (Barboza 2000). Ward left with a severance package of $1.7 million (Sandomir 2003).

After a stint as chairman and CEO of a used car website called iMotors .com, which did not make it, in November 2001 Ward became the chief executive of the U.S. Olympic Committee, a position that had seen considerable turnover (he was the fourth person to hold the CEO position in four years). A year later, Ward was accused of conflict of interest by having instructed a staff member to advance a $4.6 million proposal from a business run by his brother and a childhood friend to provide backup power for the Pan American Games that were to be held in the Dominican Republic in August 2003. Ward acknowledged that he had done so, calling it an error in judgment, and the ethics committee ruled that he had not violated the ethics code. However, five members of the ethics committee, including the chief ethics officer, and the USOC president, resigned over the failure to censure or fire Ward. Dissatisfaction with Ward increased after he refused to resign from Augusta National Golf Club, which discriminated against women (Ward was one of the club's few black members), and after reports emerged that he had authorized $35,000 in moving expenses for his newly hired chief marketing officer (on top of the $50,000 relocation payment that she had received). After two months of clinging to the job, he resigned (Sandomir 2003).

Ward has not returned to a *Fortune* 500 corporation, but instead has invested in entrepreneurial ventures and start-up companies. A month after he left the USOC, according to *Business Week,* he "bankrolled" and became chairman of BodyBlocks Nutrition Systems, an Atlanta-based company that makes nutrition bars and energy drinks (Arndt 2004). Since 2006, he has been chairman and general manager of Yuanzhen Org Dairy Co. Ltd., an Inner Mongolia Sino-American joint venture producing organic milk in China. And, since September 2006, he has been chairman and CEO of Cottonport-Monofill, a waste-tire processing facility founded in 1995 that seeks to keep scrap tires out of landfills (his brother Rupert is the president of the company).

THE ENTIRE GROUP OF FIFTEEN: RAINES, WARD, AND THE OTHER THIRTEEN AFRICAN AMERICAN CEOS

In 1999, the same year that Raines and Ward became CEOs, A. Barry Rand became CEO of Avis (Avis was not quite in the *Fortune* 500 in 1999 but was #465 on the list in 2000). The following year, in January 2001, Kenneth Chenault became CEO at American Express (he had been appointed to the number two position in the company and designated as the "apparent successor" as early as 1997 when Harvey Golub, then CEO, said that Chenault was "the primary internal candidate to succeed me when the time comes"; Hansell 1997, C2). As can be seen in table 3.1, Raines, Ward, Rand, and Chenault have been followed by another eleven African American CEOs of companies on the *Fortune* 500 list: Richard Parsons at Time Warner in 2001, Stanley O'Neal at Merrill Lynch in 2002, Aylwin Lewis at Kmart in 2004, Clarence Otis, Jr., at Darden Restaurants and James A. Bell (as interim CEO) at Boeing in 2005, Ronald A. Williams at Aetna in 2006, Rodney O'Neal at Delphi in 2007, and both John W. Thompson of Symantec and Roger W. Ferguson, Jr., of TIAA-CREF in 2008, Ursula M. Burns was appointed at Xerox in 2009, and, in January 2011, Kenneth C. Frazier became the CEO of Merck.

As we have indicated, in response to the sit-in movements of the previous few years, in 1964 two *Fortune* 500 companies became the first to name African Americans to their boards. Both of the new directors were men, and over the next seven years, another nine African American men were asked onto *Fortune* 500 boards. In 1971, when Patricia Harris was asked onto the boards of Scott Paper and IBM, she became the first female African American director at a *Fortune* 500 company.

The very same gender pattern played out when it came to African American CEOs of *Fortune* 500 companies. As we have shown, the first two African American CEOs—Franklin Raines and Lloyd Ward, both appointed in 1999—

Table 3.1. African American CEOs of *Fortune* 500 Companies, 1999–2011

Number	CEO	Born	First Year on List with African American as CEO, Ranking, and Company	Tenure as CEO
1	Raines, Franklin D.	1949	1999, #26: Fannie Mae	1999–2004
2	Ward, Lloyd D.	1949	1999, #379: Maytag	1999–2000
3	Rand, A. Barry	1944	2000, #465: Avis	1999–2001
4	Chenault, Kenneth	1951	2001, #74: American Express	2001–
5	Parsons, Richard D.	1948	2001, #35: Time Warner	2001–2007
6	O'Neal, E. Stanley	1951	2002, #36: Merrill Lynch	2002–2007
7	Lewis, Aylwin B.	1954	2004, #67: Kmart	2004–2008
8	Otis, Clarence Jr.	1956	2005, #386: Darden Restaurants	2005–
9	Bell, James A. (interim)	1948	2005, #25: Boeing	2005 (interim)
10	Williams, Ronald A.	1950	2006, #91: Aetna	2006–
11	O'Neal, Rodney	1954	2007, #83: Delphi	2007–
12	Thompson, John W.	1949	2008, #461: Symantec	1999–2009
13	Ferguson, Roger W. Jr.	1951	2008, #86: TIAA-CREF	2008–
14	Burns, Ursula	1958	2009, #147: Xerox	2009–
15	Frazier, Kenneth C.	1954	2011, #85: Merck	2011–

were followed by a string of subsequent African American CEOs, all men. A decade later, in 2009, Ursula Burns became the first African American woman CEO of a *Fortune* 500 company. Burns, who replaced Anne Mulcahy at Xerox, was also the first woman to replace another woman at a *Fortune* 500 company.

Born in 1958, Ursula Burns grew up on the Lower East Side in New York City. Her mother, Olga, raised Ursula, her brother, and her sister, making ends meet by taking care of neighborhood children, cleaning a doctor's office, and ironing shirts. Ursula attended a Catholic grammar school and then Cathedral High School, an all-girls school on East 56th Street, and she then received a bachelor's degree in engineering from the Polytechnic Institute (now a part of New York University). She was selected to participate in Xerox's graduate engineering program for minorities, which included a summer internship and which paid for part of her graduate work at Columbia, and when she completed her degree in 1981 she embarked upon a long career with the company.[2] In 1988, she married Lloyd Bean, a Xerox scientist twenty years older; they have two children, a son at MIT and a daughter still in high school (he is retired).

In 1990, Burns, described in a *New York Times* profile as "never shy about speaking her mind," came to the attention of a senior executive when, after a meeting, she challenged him on an answer he had given to a question about diversity initiatives. She became his executive assistant, traveling with him, sitting in on meetings, and learning the skills she would need as a senior executive. Among other things, he encouraged her to make people feel comfortable and not to intimidate them. While working for him, she sat in on the monthly meetings that Paul Allaire, the president of Xerox, held for top managers and their assistants. At one of those meetings she asked Allaire a pointed question about the contradiction between what he said and what he did ("I'm a little confused, Mr. Allaire. If you keep saying, 'No hiring,' and we hire 1,000 people every month, who can say 'No hiring' and make it actually happen?"). Impressed by her candor and her willingness to challenge him, Allaire asked her to be his executive assistant. He, too, mentored her, and she subsequently was appointed to a series of senior executive positions, including vice president for global marketing in 1999, senior vice president in 2000, and president in 2007 (Bryant 2010b).

Along the way, Burns worked closely with Anne Mulcahy, CEO at Xerox, and she received what the *New York Times* called "frank advice . . . about polish, patience, perspective and the importance of building 'followership' across the organization" from various prominent African Americans in the corporate world, including "power lawyer" Vernon Jordan and Kenneth Chenault, CEO of American Express. In July 2009, to the surprise of few people in Xerox, she became the CEO of the company.[3]

When Kenneth C. Frazier began as CEO at Merck (#85 on the *Fortune* 2010 list) in January 2011, he became the fifteenth African American CEO and, as the *New York Times* put it, "the first to run a global drug powerhouse" (Singer 2010). The son of a Philadelphia janitor, Frazier had attended Penn State and then the Harvard Law School before working for a Philadelphia law firm (Drinker, Biddle & Reath). Prior to his appointment as CEO, he had worked for Merck for eighteen years, at various times heading the corporation's public affairs department, its legal department, and its three largest divisions. He became president of the company in April 2010 (Hepp 2010).

INSIDERS VERSUS OUTSIDERS

Once again contrary to Khurana's (2002) predictions, only four of the fifteen (27 percent) came to their jobs as outsiders. One of these was A. Barry Rand who paid his dues as an insider by spending thirty-one years climbing the corporate ladder at Xerox, but when he saw that he was not likely to become the CEO there, he left to pursue CEO positions elsewhere, and, within a year, he was named CEO at Avis. Before Aylwin Lewis became CEO at Kmart in 2004, he had previously worked for thirteen years with Yum Brands (a company that operates or licenses fast food restaurants that include Taco Bell, Pizza Hut, and KFC). John W. Thompson became CEO at Symantec (in 1999, nine years before the company made it into the *Fortune* 500) after a career working for IBM. And, finally, Roger W. Ferguson came to TIAA-CREF in 2008 as an outsider having previously worked at McKinsey, the management consulting firm, the Federal Reserve, and Swiss Re.

The other eleven African Americans were insiders when they became CEOs. As was the case for Franklin Raines, some had worked for the company, gone elsewhere, and then returned as CEO. Some had started their careers elsewhere but when appointed CEO they had been at the company for a few years (for example, Lloyd Ward joined Maytag three years before he became CEO, and Ronald A. Williams was at Aetna for five years before he was appointed CEO). And some had been with the company for at least ten years and had worked their way up the corporate ladder (Kenneth Chenault had been with American Express for twenty years before he became CEO, Stanley O'Neal had been with Merrill Lynch for sixteen years before he became CEO, and, as we have indicated, Ursula Burns began to work at Xerox in 1980, twenty-nine years before she became CEO).

CLASS BACKGROUND

As we have indicated in the previous two chapters, various scholars have found that throughout the twentieth century about two-thirds of the senior executives at the country's largest companies came from the upper or upper middle classes. Based on Gilbert's current model of the class system, which we are drawing on, this means they were from about the top 15 percent in the socioeconomic class structure.[4] This held true for the twenty-eight women CEOs, 70 percent of whom were from those two highest classes, but it does not hold for the fifteen African American CEOs, many of whom come from poverty or working class backgrounds. Only two come from relative privilege—Kenneth Chenault's father was a dentist and Roger Ferguson's father was a cartographer for the U.S. Army, although Ferguson also described him as an "avid investor" who periodically traveled to the Federal Reserve Bank in Richmond to buy Treasury securities (Ferguson's grandfather had been an architect). Their relative privilege can be seen in the fact that during their high school years neither simply went to whatever public school was closest to their homes—Chenault went to a private Waldorf school in New York, and Ferguson was a student at Sidwell Friends (a private Quaker day school that has educated the sons and daughters of the

Washington elite for generations, including the children of Theodore Roosevelt, Richard Nixon, Bill Clinton, Al Gore, and Barack Obama).

The others come from middle class or working class backgrounds, and many, like Franklin Raines and Lloyd Ward, are from families that at times had to struggle to earn enough money to put food on the table.[5] The fathers of a number of the CEOs worked as janitors, as parking lot attendants, in factories, and for the post office. The mothers cleaned houses, did childcare, took in ironing, were manicurists, and some were school teachers. These CEOs came from working America, many were among the working poor, and at times some of their families were on welfare and lived in public housing. Although many were economically disadvantaged, they seem to have come from loving families that emphasized hard work and education, and many did not experience their childhoods as deprived. Richard Parsons, the former CEO of Time Warner (2001–2007) and now the chairman at Citigroup, gave the following explanation when asked if he grew up in a "disadvantaged background":

> I personally would answer that question no. But if you looked at the demographics, you would say yes. I was born in the Bedford-Stuyvesant part of Brooklyn, raised in what's called South Jamaica, Queens, both of which are heavily minority communities. I went to the New York City public schools, had a one-income family—but an intact family, and that's an important thing. My father probably never earned more than $7,500 a year when I was a kid, but at the time I had absolutely no idea that we were statistically working poor. We were like everybody else on the block; it didn't seem so bad to me. (Green 1998)

If there is a group that reflects the American dream of rising from the working class to the very top, most (though not all) of these African American CEOs are in that group.

EDUCATION

As we have noted, the two CEOs from relatively privileged backgrounds attended excellent secondary schools. At least two of the others went to private Catholic schools (A. Barry Rand and Ursula Burns). The others went to public high schools. All went to college, and four did their undergraduate work at prestigious private schools (two at Harvard, one at Williams, one at Bowdoin). All but one of the fifteen earned advanced degrees—among them they have four MBAs, five law degrees, and one PhD. Many of these graduate degrees are from elite institutions (five from Harvard, three from Stanford, two from MIT, and one each from Columbia and Johns Hopkins). This is an exceptionally well-educated group, certainly a group with far more impressive educational credentials than most CEOs, a pattern that corresponds to what we found when we compared the educational credentials of African American directors of *Fortune* 500 companies with those of other directors (Zweigenhaft and Domhoff 2006, 103–4).

There are two striking patterns related to their school experiences. First, at least four were presidents either of their high school student body or their high school class (Franklin Raines, Barry Rand, Kenneth Chenault, and James Bell). We say "at least" because we only happened upon mention of this in the many articles we read, and others may have held these offices without our discovering it. Still, the fact that four of the fifteen were class or student body presidents reveals that by high school they had demonstrated the capacity for leadership.

More striking was the fact that many of the men were high school athletes, some participated in sports at the college level, and all of those who were athletes were multisport athletes. Raines, as we have noted, was not only student body president but quarterback and captain of his high school football team, and Ward, who played both football and basketball in high school, was a good enough basketball player to play for four years at Michigan State (he was captain of the team his senior year). Rand was a three-sport athlete at his Catholic high school in D.C. (he was "all-metropolitan" in all three sports, no mean feat), and he went to Rutgers to play football. Chenault was the captain of the basketball, soccer, and track teams in high school, and he started college at Springfield College on an athletic scholarship (he transferred to Bowdoin, where he played soccer and ran track). Parsons, who is six feet four, played football, basketball, and baseball in high school, and, after being wait-listed at Princeton, decided to go to the University of Hawaii, where he played basketball (he was only sixteen years old when he started college). Aylwin Lewis was captain of his high school football team, and Clarence Otis played football and tennis in high school.

Many critics have expressed concern about the amount of time that young African American males spend on sports, often motivated by dreams that they will someday play in the NBA or the NFL. Sport sociologist Harry Edwards has argued for decades that because so many youngsters dedicate so much time and energy to sports and put so little time and energy into academics, they end up with nothing when their playing careers come to an end, which in almost all cases happens long before they make the NBA or the NFL (Edwards 1983, 2000). The odds are much greater that they could become doctors, lawyers, or dentists than professional athletes. As Henry Louis Gates points out, there were only fourteen hundred black athletes playing professional basketball, football, and baseball in the year 2000, compared with thirty-one thousand black physicians and surgeons, thirty-three thousand black lawyers, and five thousand black dentists (Gates 2004).

On the other hand, as Robert Sellers and his colleagues have argued, athletic scholarships, for African American men in the past, and for both African American men and women more recently, have provided the opportunity for many African Americans to obtain college educations who otherwise would not have been able to do so (Sellers, Chavous, and Brown 2002; Sellers, Kuperminc, and Damas 1997). Arne Duncan, Obama's secretary of education, who played basketball at Harvard and in the Australian professional league, supports Sellers's analysis. At a speech he gave at a convention of the National Collegiate Athletic Association (thus he was preaching to the choir), Duncan asserted that "outside of the Army, the NCAA may be the biggest producer of leaders this country has" (Brady 2010). Although only a few of the African Americans who became CEOs went to college on athletic scholarships (most notably, Lloyd Ward), their participation in sports seems to have served them well and does not seem to have hindered their educational accomplishments.

All of the African American CEOs were born between 1944 (Rand) and 1958 (Burns), which means that they were in high school in the 1960s and 1970s. Not only were those who participated in sports multisport athletes (unlike so many youngsters today, who focus on a single sport and play it year-round), they participated in other extracurricular activities. Franklin Raines was the quarterback of his high school football team, the president of the student body, and he was also an all-state debater. He remembers a conflict he faced between a Friday night football game and important out-of-town debate tournament, and how it was resolved (it does not appear to have been up to him):

> One Friday, there was an out-of-town debate and a football game. In very dramatic fashion, my debate coach and football coach held a meeting to decide what to do. They treated it like a summit meeting and picked a neutral spot. They decided that I'd attend the debate, and that I was expected to win! We did, though the football team lost. The two of them really cared what happened to me. It showed me the importance of thinking about consequences. That, and you had better succeed. (Raines 2002, 14)

Though a few describe themselves as less than committed to academic work when they were in high school, or even in their first year or two of college, most seem to have taken their schoolwork seriously. Lloyd Ward, who played more than one sport in high school but did focus on a single sport, basketball, at Michigan State, resisted the pressures from coaches and others in the athletic department to avoid difficult courses. Instead, he majored in engineering and prepared himself for work beyond the world of organized sports.

When an interviewer asked Clarence Otis if anything in his background had prepared him for the "art of building a team," Otis made no mention of having played football and tennis in high school but spoke about another extracurricular activity: theater. "The thing that prepared me the most," he replied, "was theater, which I did a lot of growing up—in high school, during college, law school and even for a couple of years after law school. I would say that probably is the starkest lesson in how reliant you are on others, because you're there in front of an audience. It's all live, and everybody's got to know their lines and know their cues, and know their movement, and so you're totally dependent on people doing that" (Bryant 2009, 2).

Only with the passage of Title IX did many women begin to have access to high school sports experiences comparable to those of males, and there is evidence that women executives who have reached the higher levels of the corporate world fairly recently are much more likely to have participated in organized sports than those who preceded them.[6] For example, Ellen Kullman, who became the CEO at DuPont in 2009, at five feet nine was the center and the captain of the basketball team at the prep school she attended, the Tower Hill School, and she played two years of Division III college basketball at Tufts (Yearick 2009). According to one study, executive women are more likely to participate in organized sports after elementary school than other women their age (Jones 2002).

However, participation in competitive sports may mean that some women athletes, like some male athletes, learn to behave in ways that are not so positive. When she was the CEO of eBay, Meg Whitman, who is six feet tall and who played three sports in high school and was a member of the squash and lacrosse teams at Princeton, became angry and shoved Young Mi Kim (height unknown), a Korean American employee who was briefing Whitman for an interview. Kim threatened to sue, Whitman and Kim went through mediation supervised by a private dispute resolution service, and the company allegedly settled for "around $200,000" (Stone 2010b, A13).

Many in the corporate world have acknowledged that a lot of important business decisions take place on the golf course, and some women in the corporate world have lamented that they have been excluded from these outings (and sometimes from the golf courses themselves; see Chambers 1995; Driscoll and Goldberg 1993; Scott 1998; Benoit, 2007, 35–38). Some women executives, like Hazel O'Leary, the vice president of an energy company before she became secretary of labor during the Clinton administration, took up golf when they perceived that not playing golf would hurt their careers

(Zweigenhaft and Domhoff 2006, 56). At least one of the African American male CEOs has been sensitive to this issue. Aylwin Lewis, when he was chief operating officer of the KFC and Pizza Hut divisions of Yum Brands, issued a decree that there could be no discussion of business matters on the golf course because that left out those who did not play the sport (Brennan 2005).

Lewis's policy would have been fine with Ursula Burns who broke the mold in yet another way by refusing to take up golf. Not long after she became the "apparent heir" at Xerox, one *New York Times* profile of her began: "Ursula M. Burns doesn't play golf. She doesn't belong to the local country club. Small talk is not her strong suit. And she insists on being home on weekends. She sounds like an unlikely climber on the Xerox corporate ladder" (Deutsch 2003).

SKIN COLOR AND "BABYFACENESS"

In the mid-1990s, as we read hundreds of articles, academic and popular, while writing *Diversity in the Power Elite* (Zweigenhaft and Domhoff 1998), we observed that many of the African American men and women who had become part of what C. Wright Mills called the power elite seemed to have very light skin tone. We decided to test this systematically. We gathered photographs of some of the African American men and women we had identified as members of the power elite and a group of "control" photographs of other prominent African American men and women. We put these photos in random order and then asked some students to rate them in terms of skin color (on a scale that ran from 1, very light, to 10, very dark). The African Americans in the power elite were rated as having significantly lighter skin than other prominent African Americans, and this was especially true of the African American women (Zweigenhaft and Domhoff 1998, 110–13).

We interpreted these findings as part of a larger pattern: the less different people were from the white male norm that was dominant in the power elite, the more likely they were to be deemed acceptable. This included not behaving in radically different ways, but it also included not looking dramatically different. In the case of African Americans, the darker skinned they were, the more different they appeared, and, for women, who were already different in terms of gender, being both female and dark skinned had a double whammy effect. Moreover, since many whites see black males as threatening, we suggested that lighter-skinned black males were perceived as less threatening. After summarizing the findings from our study of the skin color ratings of photographs, we quoted Colin Powell, then a former chairman of the Joint

Chiefs of Staff (and now a former secretary of state) explaining why he was so popular among whites:

> One, I don't shove it in their face, you know? I don't bring any stereotypes or threatening visage to their presence. Some black people do. Two, I can overcome any stereotypes or reservations they have, because I perform well. Third, thing is, I ain't that black. . . . I speak reasonably well, like a white person. I am very comfortable in a white social situation, and I don't go off in a corner. My features are clearly black, and I've never denied what I am. It fits into their general social setting, so they do not find me threatening. (Gates 1995, 70)

In this current research on African American *Fortune* 500 CEOs, we have again been struck by how many of them seem to have light skin tones, so, again, we decided to test this systematically. Whereas in the mid-1990s we simply cut out photographs from magazines and showed them to raters, for this study we used Google Images to find head and shoulder portraits of the African American CEOs on our list (this study was done prior to the appointment of Kenneth C. Frazier at Merck, so he was not included). Most of the photos we selected were those distributed by the corporation for which they worked, and others were from business magazines or newspapers like *Business Week, Forbes*, or *Fortune*. For the black "control group," we randomly selected twenty male college presidents whose schools were included on "The White House Initiative on Historically Black Colleges and Universities" (HBCUs). Our reasoning for this choice was that African American men who had become college or university presidents were well educated and highly successful, but, unlike the CEOs of *Fortune* 500 companies, they had not had to rise through the ranks of predominantly white institutions (and thus were not as likely to need to be light skinned). At the same time, we know that blacks favor light-skinned blacks (e.g., Herring 2004; Glenn 2009), so we assumed that the differences could be small.

We performed two studies (for a more detailed account of the methods used, and the statistical analyses that we performed, see appendix 2). The first study included photos of 65 males: 13 African American *Fortune* 500 CEOs, 12 Latino *Fortune* 500 CEOs, 20 white male *Fortune* 500 CEOs (randomly selected from the white male CEO control group described in the final chapter of this book), and 20 presidents of historically black colleges and universities. The second included a total of 107 photos: these 65 photos plus another 42 photos (18 of Asian American CEOs and 24 of white women CEOs).

In the first study, ten college students, working individually, were asked to rate the 65 photos, randomly assorted. In the second study, another twenty college students, again working individually, rated the 107 photos, randomly assorted. Each student was seated in front of a computer screen (and each student was paid $5 for his or her participation). The students were asked to rate the skin color of the person in each of the photos on a scale from 1 to 10, with 1 as the lightest and 10 as the darkest. Table 3.2 shows the results for the ratings of the photos of the white male CEOs, the Latino CEOs, the African American CEOs, and the male presidents of historically black colleges and universities (the ratings for these four groups did not differ in the two conditions, so the means reported here are based on the combined scores for all thirty raters). As can be seen in table 3.2, for both sets of photos, the African American college presidents were rated as having significantly darker skin color (a mean score of 7.04 on the ten-point scale) than the African American CEOs (a mean score of 6.33). The ratings of the Latinos (a mean score of 2.86) were much closer to those of the white male CEOs (2.27) than those of the African American CEOs; we'll say more about the skin color ratings of the Latino and the Asian American CEOs in chapter 4, and the statistical details of our study are provided in appendix 2.

As we expected, the African American CEOs were rated as lighter skinned than the presidents of HBCUs who are highly accomplished but who work in predominantly black settings. We also asked the students who rated the photographs to answer another question about each photo: in the case of the 65-photo task, we asked them to identify the person as African American, Latino, or white; in the case of the 107-photo task, we asked them to identify the person as African American, Asian American, Latino, or white. The accuracy rate was quite high for whites (over 94 percent), for the African American college presidents (over 95 percent), and for the black *Fortune* 500 CEOs (over 94 percent), lower for Asian Americans (55 percent), and the lowest for the Latinos (30 percent). When we looked separately at the ratings for the

Table 3.2. Skin Color Ratings of White Male, Latino, and African American CEOs, and Presidents of Historically Black Colleges and Universities (HBCUs)

	Photos of White Male CEOs (n = 20)	*Photos of Latino CEOs (n = 12)*	*Photos of African American CEOs (n = 13)*	*Photos of Presidents of HBCUs (n = 20)*
Mean rating =	2.27[a,b,c]	2.86 [b,c,d]	6.33 [a,c,d]	7.04 [a,b,d]
St. dev. =	(.653)	(.698)	(.862)	(.778)
Number of raters	30	30	30	30
F =	419.88			
df =	3			
p <	.001			

a = significantly different (p < .05) from the ratings for the Latino CEOs
b = significantly different (p < .05) from the ratings for the African American CEOs
c = significantly different (p < .05) from the ratings for the presidents of HBCUs
d = significantly different (p < .05) from the ratings for the white male CEOs

thirteen African American CEOs, we found that all but one were correctly identified as African American by 90 percent of the raters or more, but one of the African American CEOs, Rodney O'Neal, was only identified accurately as an African American by 70 percent of the raters (twenty-one of the thirty).

Interestingly, Rodney O'Neal did not receive the lowest ratings for skin color (Kenneth Chenault, Richard Parsons, and Barry Rand all received lighter skin color ratings than did O'Neal). Clearly, then, other factors, such as facial features, eye color, and texture of hair, are at play in the perception of ethnicity. As Thompson and Keith (2004, 47) point out: "Skin color is highly correlated with other phenotypic features—eye color, hair texture, broadness of nose, and fullness of lips. Along with light skin, blue and green eyes, European shaped noses, and straight as opposed to 'kinky' hair are all accorded higher status, both within and beyond the African American community."

A recent study by Robert W. Livingston and Nicholas A. Pearce (2009a), both at the Kellogg School of Management at Northwestern University, used photos of CEOs to look at something psychologists have called "baby-faceness." A body of research in social psychology has revealed that some adults are seen as "baby-faced," as opposed to most adults who are seen to have "mature" faces (in this literature, a person has a "baby face," but is "baby-faced," and researchers study "babyfaceness"). Those seen as baby-faced are also perceived as more warm, trustworthy, and innocent than mature-faced adults, and they are treated with greater patience, compassion, and sensitivity (see Zebrowitz 1997). Whereas previous studies have shown that having a baby face works against white males in positions of leadership, Livingston and Pearce (2009a) hypothesized that having a baby face might help African Americans in leadership positions because they would be perceived as less threatening. They presented 40 photos of CEOs to a group of students. Their photos included 10 current and former African American male *Fortune* 500 CEOs, 10 white males who have been CEOs at the same companies, 10 white female CEOs of *Fortune* 500 companies, and 10 more white male CEOs randomly sampled from the remaining *Fortune* 500 companies. They found that raters perceived the black CEOs as significantly more baby-faced than the white CEOs (they were also rated as having darker skin than the other three groups, but Livingston and Pearce did not include a control group of other black leaders, so one can't tell from their study if they were lighter skinned than other blacks).

In their study, Livingston and Pearce report that there was no significant relationship between babyfaceness and skin color (2009a, 1234). Using a four-point scale, with 1 as the lightest and 4 as the darkest, the photographs that they used of black CEOs did receive higher ratings on skin color (a mean score of 3.12, on a four-point scale) than did the photos of white CEOs

(1.79).[7] After the participants in our study rated the Google image photos that we used, we asked them to rate twenty of the photos that Livingston and Pearce used in their study (ten of African Americans, ten of white CEOs), which they had converted to grayscale. There was a clear positive correlation between the ratings of the ten African American CEO photos used in Livingston and Pearce's study and the ten photos we used of the same ten men.[8]

Livingston and Pearce draw a conclusion about babyfaceness that is quite similar to the one we have drawn based on skin color: "Babyfaceness is a disarming mechanism that facilitates the success of Black leaders by attenuating stereotypical perceptions that Blacks are threatening" (Livingston and Pearce 2009a, 1229). We can conclude, then, that the very few black men who become CEOs of *Fortune* 500 companies are likely to be lighter skinned than other successful blacks, and likely to be more baby-faced; both features contribute to their being perceived as less threatening than other black men.[9]

CONCLUSION

As of January 2011, eight of the fifteen African American CEOs were no longer CEOs of *Fortune* 500 companies. Lloyd Ward only lasted for fifteen months at Maytag. In 2001, A. Barry Rand left Avis when Cendant acquired it (in March 2009 Rand became the CEO of AARP).[10] Franklin Raines left Fannie Mae in 2004 as a multimillionaire but with his reputation battered, and he has not held a major corporate or government position since. James Bell, who served as interim CEO at Boeing in 2005, remained there as chief financial officer after the company completed its search for a CEO, and since June 2008 he has been the company's corporate president. In 2007 Richard Parsons retired at age sixty as CEO of Time Warner (he remained chairman of the board at Time Warner until he became chairman of the board, but not CEO, at Citigroup in January 2009). Stanley O'Neal was forced out at Merrill Lynch in 2007. Although he was ousted after the company announced its biggest quarterly loss in its ninety-three-year-old history, O'Neal had a golden parachute worth $161.5 million, at the time the fifth-largest exit pay package for any U.S. executive (Moran 2007).[11] In January 2008 Aylwin Lewis stepped down as CEO at Kmart (which merged with Sears Holdings in 2005); six months later he became CEO of Potbelly Sandwich Works. John Thompson left Symantec in 2009, and Ronald Williams stepped down at Aetna in November 2010.

The door that opened in 1999 when Raines and Ward became *Fortune* 500 CEOs has remained open. Still, more than a decade later, only thirteen other African Americans have gone through that door, and only six are now

CEOs. These six African American CEOs (Chenault at American Express, Otis at Darden Restaurants, Williams at Aetna, Rodney O'Neal at Delphi, Ferguson at TIAA-CREF, Burns at Xerox, and Frazier at Merck) make up 1.2 percent of the *Fortune* 500 CEOs, which means that white women and African Americans together make up only 3.4 percent of those who hold the most senior position at a *Fortune* 500 corporation at the beginning of 2011.

Are there more African Americans climbing the corporate ladder with real possibilities of becoming CEOs in the future? We will return to this question in considerable detail in our final chapter. First, though, let us take a look at Latino and Asian American CEOs to see if these two immigrant groups have fared as well as or better than the women CEOs we looked at in chapter 2 and the African American CEOs we have looked at in this chapter.

4

Going Global

Latino and Asian American *Fortune* 500 CEOs

In 1971, Coca-Cola ran an ad that featured a large multiethnic group of young people, standing on a hill outside Rome, Italy, singing about Coca-Cola. The key phrase was: "I'd like to teach the world to sing, in perfect harmony, I'd like to buy the world a Coke and keep it company." The ad was so popular that it was converted into a full-length song (with no direct mention of Coke), recorded by a group called the New Seekers, and it became a number one hit in the United Kingdom (and number seven in the United States). Turning good publicity into even better publicity, Coca-Cola waived all the rights to royalties and donated them instead to UNICEF.

The ad foreshadowed the efforts in the 1980s and 1990s by Coca-Cola, and many other *Fortune* 500 companies, to place much greater emphasis on marketing and selling products globally. As early as 1926, Coca-Cola had established a "foreign department," and it began to sell Cokes in Germany in 1929. By 1939 it had five overseas bottling plants. During World War II, Robert Woodruff, the CEO of Coca-Cola for almost sixty years (1923 to 1980), issued an order to make Cokes available to "every man in uniform," and in 1943 General Dwight David Eisenhower sent three million bottles to the allies in North Africa. Coke thus supported the troops and spread its markets (by 1945 there were sixty-four overseas bottling plants). It was only, however, with the emergence of a new CEO in 1981, Roberto Goizueta, the first Latino CEO of a *Fortune* 500 company, that Coke really saw the entire world as its market. As David Greising, the former Atlanta bureau chief of *Business Week* magazine and the author of a biography on Goizueta, observes, "Goizueta broadened and deepened Coke's presence in almost every country on the planet" (Greising 1998, xvii).

Although it is at times difficult to determine if a person is African American or not, Latinos (or Hispanics) pose even greater challenges. In fact, the very terms *Latino* and *Hispanic* are seen by some as controversial—some (especially on the East Coast) prefer the term *Hispanic*, some (especially on the West Coast) prefer the term *Latino*, and studies have shown that the majority of people who are of Cuban, Mexican, or Puerto Rican backgrounds don't like either term, but prefer labels that reflect their specific background (de la Garza, De Sipio, Garcia, Garcia, and Falcon 1992; Oboler 1995). Moreover, the countries of origin for Hispanics (or Latinos) vary tremendously, including the United States, the Caribbean, Central America, all of South America, and Spain. Those who came to the United States from these countries left very different cultures and they left very different political and economic environments. The link that binds, to the extent that these disparate individuals are bound, is the fact that Spanish is the native language in all these countries. Acknowledging the heterogeneous nature of this category, and the sensitivity of the terms, we will use *Latino* and *Hispanic* interchangeably, and, when possible, we will use specific ethnic identifications.[1]

In addition to geographical differences in preferences for the term *Latino* or *Hispanic*, there are also changes over time and changes by generation. In a fascinating study that includes follow-up interviews of a 1965 sample, and also includes interviews with a sample of the children of the original interviewees, Telles and Ortiz show that preferences for various ethnic identifications changed based on location and by generation, and changed over time, as did the reasons for those preferences (see Telles and Ortiz 2008, 212–18, 236–37).

Similarly, the term *Asian American* refers to a heterogeneous category that includes Japanese Americans, Chinese Americans, and Korean Americans, as well as those who came, or whose families came, from various other countries throughout Asia. They, too, left varying cultural and economic circumstances. Unlike Latinos, they do not speak the same language (and in some cases there has been great enmity between their countries of origin). Despite the obvious limitations of these categories (Latinos, Asian Americans), we believe that they are useful in helping us to see that things have changed in the CEO suites of *Fortune* 500 companies: not only are there some women who are CEOs today, and some African Americans, but there are CEOs who differ from those we are calling "the old CEOs" in some other ways, including country of origin, the ability to move comfortably from one culture to another, and fluency in more than one language. As of January 1, 2011, there had been fifteen Latino and twenty Asian American *Fortune* 500 CEOs (because of their notable presence as *Fortune* 500 CEOs since 1995, we have included those born in India among the Asian Americans). Fifteen of the twenty in the category we are calling "Asian Americans" were born outside the United States, and twelve of those fifteen have become U.S. citizens; our use of the term *Asian American*, in this chapter and throughout the book, therefore, is mostly accurate, though we are aware that three of those we are including in this category are citizens of India, Pakistan, and South Korea (and thus, not technically Asian Americans).

LATINO *FORTUNE* 500 CEOS

The Cuban Americans

In 2000 Latinos became the largest racial-ethnic group in the United States, surpassing African Americans (12.5 percent vs. 12.1 percent). Of the 35.3 million Hispanics, 20.6 million (59 percent) were of Mexican background, and only 1.2 million (3.4 percent) were of Cuban background (www.census .gov). However, five of the fifteen Latino *Fortune* 500 CEOs have been Cuban Americans and only two have been Mexican American. At least four of the five Cuban Americans came from families with education and economic privilege before the revolution; in contrast, both Mexican Americans grew up in working class families.

Three of the first six Latinos to become CEOs of companies that were at the time on the *Fortune* 500 list (or were already CEOs of companies that then made it onto the list) were Cuban exiles. Roberto Goizueta, appointed CEO of Coca-Cola in 1981, was the first, and he remained the only Latino CEO of a *Fortune* 500 company until 1995, when two more Latinos became *Fortune* 500 CEOs (see table 4.1).[2] Born in 1931, he was the son of wealthy parents. His father was an architect and real estate investor, and his mother was a sugar heiress (both sets of grandparents were light-skinned Basques who had immigrated to Cuba from Spain in the late nineteenth century when Cuba was a Spanish colony). From the first grade through twelfth grade he attended the Belen Academy, described by Greising as "a veritable fortress of wealth and power for the aristocratic class of prerevolutionary Cuba" (1998, 8). (Fidel Castro, four years older than Goizueta, attended the same school.) Then, because he wanted to work on his English to make sure he could get into a top Ivy League school, he spent a year at the Cheshire Academy, a boarding school just outside New Haven.[3] From Cheshire he went to Yale, where he majored in chemical engineering (and made almost daily phone calls back to his father in Cuba). After he received a BA in 1953, he got married (his wife was from a family even wealthier than his—it was thought to be one of the dozen wealthiest in Cuba; Greising 1998, 2) and started to work in his father's business. About a year later, however, in an attempt to establish

Table 4.1. Latino CEOs of *Fortune* 500 Companies, 1981–2010

Number	CEO	Year Born, Country of Birth	First Year on List with Latino as CEO, Ranking, and Company	Tenure as CEO
1	Goizueta, Roberto	1931–1997, Cuba	1981, #56: Coca-Cola	1981–1997
2	Cantu, Carlos	1933–2003, USA	1995, #376: ServiceMaster	1994–1999
3	White, Tony L.	1946, Cuba	1995, #429: Perkin-Elmer	1995–2008
4	Osorio, Claudio	1959, Venezuela	1998, #320: CHS Electronics	1993–
5	Gutierrez, Carlos M.	1953, Cuba	1999, #246: Kellogg	1999–2004
6	Trujillo, Solomon	1951, USA	1999, #135: US West	1995–2000
7	Belda, Alain	1943, Morocco	1999, #96: Alcoa	1999–2008
8	Ruiz, Hector	1945, Mexico	2002, #424: Advanced Micro Devices (AMD)	2002–2008
9	Diaz, Paul J.	1961, USA	2004, #479: Kindred Health-care	2004–
10	Perez, Antonio M.	1945, Spain	2005, #153: Eastman Kodak	2005–
11	Alapont, Jose Maria	1951, Spain	2005, #326: Federal-Mogul	2005–
12	Perez, William D.	1947, USA	2006, #482: Wrigley	2006–2008
13	Conde, Cristobal	1959, Chile	2006, #495: SunGard Data	2002–
14	Aguirre, Fernando G.	1958, Mexico	2007, #488: Chiquita Brands	2004–
15	de Molina, Alvaro G.	1957, Cuba	2008, #78: GMAC Financial Services	2008–2009

some independence, he applied for and accepted a job with the Coca-Cola bottling company in Havana (he had seen an ad for a "bilingual chemical engineer or chemist"). His father, with the advice that "You shouldn't work for someone else, you should work for yourself," gave young Roberto $8,000 to buy a hundred shares of Coca-Cola stock (Greising 1998, 18).[4]

The stock was later to come in handy. After the revolution, those Cubans who were able to leave often did so with little or none of their material wealth. In August 1960, slightly more than a year and a half after Castro took power, Goizueta and his wife Olga left for what they said was to be a two-week vacation in Miami (their three children were already in Miami, staying with his parents and his in-laws, who had already left Cuba). Roberto and Olga had the clothes they had brought with them, some cash (some reports said $20, others said $40, and some said $200), and they had the one hundred shares of Coca-Cola stock.[5] Goizueta spent most of the next ten years overseeing bottling plants throughout the Caribbean, and in 1964 he moved to the corporate headquarters in Atlanta. In 1979 he became one of six senior executives thought to be contenders for the CEO position. After what was apparently a fierce internal battle, he emerged as Robert Woodruff's choice to succeed him as CEO in 1981.

In Greising's analysis, it was not only Goizueta's bilingualism and potential for strengthening Coca-Cola's international reach, but his aristocratic background that appealed to the Southern white men who ran the company, and especially Woodruff. As he puts it:

> After he moved to Atlanta, rose through Coke's ranks, and ultimately vied for the top job, Goizueta's Cuban upbringing became a useful tool that helped improve the trajectory of his career path. His Cuban roots had an exotic appeal to the old-line Southerners running the company as they began focusing on the need to internationalize Coke's management to match the global growth of the business. And his aristocratic breeding gave him an aura that very early on served as a passport into Coke's upper echelon of managers, especially Robert W. Woodruff, the longtime Coca-Cola chieftain who liked to surround himself with people of high social and political standing. (Greising 1998, 5)

Goizueta immediately placed emphasis on expanding markets globally. Early in 1981 he took a two-week tour of operations in six of Coke's largest South American markets. He hired a Brazilian consultant to help the company focus on global opportunities and to help him plan organizational change. He put together a senior management team that included an Egyptian financier, a Mexican marketing whiz, and an Argentine who ran the United States operation. "We're a kind of United Nations," claimed Goizueta (Greising 1998, 79).

In 1991 he received a highly controversial compensation package of nearly $86 million in pay and bonuses, at the time the largest CEO compensation package ever. It was not only controversial because of its size, but because it was explained to shareholders in proxy materials in a way that Greising calls "insultingly sneaky . . . designed to mislead" (Greising 1998, 189–90; see also Schwartz 1997). By the time he died, Goizueta was a very wealthy man. According to the *CNN* obituary, "He owned nearly 16 million Coke shares worth roughly $1 billion, making him America's first corporate manager to achieve billionaire status through owning stock in a company he didn't help found or take public" ("Coke CEO" 1997). When he died, *Forbes* magazine listed his worth at $1.3 billion, #120 on its list of the richest Americans (Jones 1999).

Given his name and his Southern drawl, few people would know that Tony L. White was born in Cuba in 1946.[6] His is a story of the blending of two cultures, a story that is less unusual in the era of Barack Obama. In the mid-1940s, his father, who was from the mountains of North Carolina, traveled to Cuba where he met and married White's mother, a young woman from a wealthy family. After running the Cuban subsidiary of an American oil company, her father had become a millionaire as a real estate developer—among other things, he bought beach property and sold it to Americans (Pollack 2002; Jones 1999). White describes himself as "half Cuban, half hillbilly" (Jones 1999, 3B). After the revolution, the millionaire grandfather, the young couple, and their son Tony fled Cuba and headed for the mountains of North Carolina, where the grandfather went to work, at first pumping gas and then as an accountant, and Tony, a young teenager, began to develop his Southern drawl.

Tony's father, who he describes as "a mountain type," went from job to job, and left the family when Tony was fifteen. After graduating from Western Carolina University, White married his high school sweetheart and went to work for Baxter, a manufacturer of health care products. He started selling surgical gloves and intravenous supplies to hospitals and worked his way up through the company. After twenty-six years, he was a senior executive within the corporation, but it did not appear that he would become the company's CEO. As he told one interviewer: "Maybe I didn't have the right pedigree, I hadn't been to business school, my father hadn't been a big CEO. Or maybe I was too aggressive and just didn't have the style" (Warsh 2000). In 1995, when Perkin-Elmer came calling, seeking a president and CEO (the company was #429 on the *Fortune* list in 1995), he decided to leave Baxter. Through various mergers and acquisitions, Perkin-Elmer became Applera, which in turn became Applied Biosystems, and Tony White remained the CEO of the company until his retirement in 2008. In 2002, White was ranked #11 on *Business Week*'s list of the CEOs with the highest compensation—his salary and bonus that year was $1.7 million, but his long-term capital compensation was $60.2 million, giving him a total of $61.9 million (Lavelle 2002).

In 1999, when he was named CEO at Kellogg, Carlos Gutierrez became the third Cuban-born CEO of a company on the *Fortune* 500 list. Born in 1953, Gutierrez's family lived in an upscale Havana suburb, in a spacious home shaded by mango and banana trees (Llorente 2004). "My father," he wrote in a column for the *New York Times*, "owned a pineapple business and the family was part of Cuba's high society, but the Cuban Revolution changed all that" (Gutierrez 2001, C6).

About a year after Fidel Castro came to power, shortly before Carlos's seventh birthday, his father was detained for a few days ("Men in olive-green uniforms took my father away. He was gone a couple of days"). A few days after his father returned to the family, they left the country and settled in Miami. He, his parents, and his older brother were allowed to take $2,000 each and their clothes (they took thirty-one bags of clothes). The rest they left behind. As was true of Tony White's grandfather, and many other wealthy men who left Cuba during or after the revolution, Gutierrez's father at first took any work he could get (in his case it was parking cars), but he and the family soon moved to Mexico where he worked for the Heinz Company and then started his own business. When the business ran into trouble, Gutierrez's father moved to Queens where he became a middle manager for an apparel company.

Unlike almost all of the other CEOs we have considered so far (the twenty-eight women and the fifteen African Americans), Gutierrez did not complete college. While living in Mexico, and working part time for his father, he enrolled at the Monterrey Institute of Technology, where he began to study business administration. In 1975, however, at the age of twenty-two, he dropped out and went to work for Kellogg ("Kellogg de Mexico"), driving a cereal delivery truck. His outstanding performance at various sales and marketing assignments led to his transfer in 1982 to the company's corporate headquarters in Battle Creek, Michigan. After a few years there, supervising all of Kellogg's Latin American services, he returned to Mexico, at the age of twenty-nine, as general manager of Kellogg de Mexico. After turning around the Mexico operation, he was also named general manager of Kellogg Canada. By 1990 he was back in Battle Creek, and in 1999, after twenty-four years with the company, he became, at age forty-three, the youngest CEO in Kellogg's history.

Gutierrez was Kellogg's CEO until 2004 when he joined George W. Bush's cabinet as secretary of commerce. He remained in that position until January 2009, and since then he has been a news commentator on CNBC, a scholar in residence at the University of Miami's Institute for Cuban and Cuban American Studies, and a member of three corporate boards (Corning, Occidental Petroleum, and United Technologies).

The youngest of the fifteen Latinos on our list, Paul Diaz, is a Cuban American born in Miami. Diaz's grandfather was a surgeon in Cuba, and his mother worked in the business office of a Miami hospital. He went to

American University, and then Georgetown Law School, before investing in a retirement home that led to a career in health care. He became the COO and president of Kindred Healthcare in 2002, and the CEO in 2004.

In 2008 a fifth Cuban American became the CEO of a *Fortune* 500 company when Alvaro G. de Molina was selected as the CEO of GMAC Financial Services (until 2006, it was a subsidiary of GM). Born in Cuba in 1957, de Molina and his family left three years later and settled in Queens. He did his undergraduate work at Fairleigh Dickinson, and then received a master's degree from Duke and an MBA from Rutgers. He worked for the Bank of America for seventeen years before taking a job with GMAC in 2007 as chief operating officer. A year later he became the CEO.

The Other Ten Latino CEOs

As can be seen in table 4.1, the other ten Latinos who have become CEOs of *Fortune* 500 companies are a varied group geographically. Two are Mexican Americans born in the United States (Carlos Cantu and Solomon Trujillo), and another was born in Akron, Ohio, but raised in Colombia (William Perez); two were born in Spain (Jose Alapont and Antonio Perez), two were born in Mexico (Hector Ruiz and Fernando Aguirre), and the other three are from Chile, Morocco, and Venezuela. One, like the four Cuban-born *Fortune* 500 CEOs, left his home country because of political events there: Cristobal Conde, CEO of SunGard, came to the United States after the 1973 U.S.-backed military coup in Chile toppled the democratically elected Allende government. The Latino CEOs also vary in age. Carlos Cantu, the CEO of ServiceMaster from 1994 through 1999, was born in 1933, just two years after Roberto Goizueta; five were born in the 1940s, six were born in the 1950s, and one (Paul Diaz) was born in 1961. So far, all of the Latino CEOs have been male.

Insiders versus Outsiders

Ten of the fifteen were promoted to the CEO position from within their companies. At least three began to work for their companies in countries outside the United States, using their proficiency speaking Spanish. We have seen that Roberto Goizueta's first job with Coca-Cola was in Havana, and that he gained valuable experience after he moved to Miami when he oversaw Coke's Caribbean bottling operations. Similarly, we have seen that Carlos Gutierrez started working for Kellogg when he lived in Mexico, and that his success running Kellogg de Mexico, and then both the company's Mexican and Canadian divisions, were key elements in his path to the CEO office.

Alain Belda provides yet another example of work that initially took place outside the United States leading to the role of CEO in an American-based *Fortune* 500 company. Born in Morocco to a Spanish businessman father who specialized in turning underperforming companies around, and a Portuguese mother, Belda's family moved to Brazil when he was thirteen, and not long after that to Canada. His father died when he was seventeen, and the family returned to Brazil where he became a citizen and attended college. While working in the finance office for the German chemical company BASF, he went to visit his younger brother, Ricardo, who worked for Alcoa Aluminio. Alcoa was recruiting, so he applied for a job, and he was offered twice the salary he was making at BASF. He went to work for Alcoa in what turned out to be a forty-year career with the company. He started, in 1969, in finance and planning and after working there for ten years he was promoted to president of Alcoa Aluminio (he was the first person from outside the United States to hold that position). Within a few years he headed all of the Latin American operations. In 1994 he left Brazil to live in Pittsburgh where he became the executive vice president, and in 1999 he became the company's CEO, a position he held until 2008 (in 1999, the year Belda became CEO, Alcoa was #96 on the *Fortune* list—as can be seen in table 4.1; of the fifteen companies that Latinos have headed, only Coca-Cola and GMAC have been ranked higher).

When Belda became president of Alcoa in Brazil, it was a $100 million business. By the time he left for Pittsburgh, it was a $1 billion dollar division. Business for Alcoa was growing internationally, and the company saw Belda—who speaks five languages—as the right choice to continue its global outreach. The company moved its headquarters from Pittsburgh to New York City. "By the time we moved," Belda told one interviewer, "40% of the business was international. Soon it will be 60%. So to be near our international partners, we had to move here" (Berman 2004). A year later, in an interview with *Industry Week* magazine, Belda described the Alcoa workforce, providing further evidence of the extent to which the company had gone global: "Our top management is 40% foreign-born, and over 50% international, if we consider Americans that have lived long periods abroad. We have shared business systems and a common infrastructure applied across a globally connected workforce. We also strive to put Alcoa's strategies in line with meaningful global trends" (Vinas 2005).

A few of the Latinos became CEOs of companies that acquired companies they previously worked for. Carlos Cantu, for example, worked first for Terminex, where he became president, and then, after ServiceMaster purchased it, he became the CEO at ServiceMaster. Cristobal Conde founded Devon Systems, which SunGard acquired, and then Conde became CEO of SunGard.

Some of the Latino CEOs hired from the outside had previously spent long careers at other companies. Tony White, as we have noted, spent twenty-six years with Baxter before he became CEO at Perkin-Elmer, and Antonio Perez spent twenty-five years at Hewlett-Packard before he became CEO at Eastman Kodak in 2005. William Perez worked for S. C. Johnson for thirty-four years, running their operations in Spain and Latin America before he became CEO of Wrigley. Before joining Chiquita Brands as CEO in 2004 (it did not make the *Fortune* 500 list until 2007), Fernando Aguirre spent twenty-three years with Procter & Gamble (P&G); while with P&G, he improved the profitability of business units in both Brazil and Mexico, and he became vice president of P&G's global snacks and food products as well as president of global feminine care. Aguirre is convinced that Chiquita—with headquarters right down the street from Procter & Gamble in Cincinnati—hired him because of his international experience. "Whereas people who only have worked in the United States think about expanding a particular project to eventually cover all of this country," he told an interviewer, "the foreign-born executive will say, 'OK, we can do that in the U.S., or we can also do things in China and Europe and Latin America and so on.' Obviously, that gets you to much bigger goals" ("World Class" 2004).

Class Background

We do not have the family background details we would like for all of the Latino CEOs, and eleven of the fifteen were born outside the United States, which means that the class structures varied country to country. Still, based on the metric we have used so far—that throughout the twentieth century about 70 percent of the top executives and CEOs were from the upper middle or capitalist classes (which in recent years means the top 15 percent of the class structure)—it appears that about two-thirds of the Latino CEOs began their lives in families within the top 15 percent of the class structures in their home countries.[7] As we have seen, three of the Cuban exiles (Goizueta, White, and Gutierrez) came from economically privileged families (and Paul Diaz's grandfather was a surgeon in Cuba, though it appears that his mother in Miami did not have it so easy, raising as she did three sons while working in the business office of a hospital); we have not found information about de Molina's class background. So, too, did Alain Belda come from economic privilege (he was born in Morocco but his family moved from country to country because his father, a successful businessman, specialized in rebuilding failing companies). William Perez's father was not a college graduate, but he became the manager of the Goodyear plant in Cali, Colombia, and then he managed all of Goodyear's Latin American operations. For high school, the family sent Perez back to the states to attend the Western Reserve Academy, a prestigious Midwest prep school. And Cristobal Conde, whose family left Chile after the military coup in 1973 when he was fourteen and who has a degree in astronomy and physics from Yale, came from a highly educated and professional family—his mother, who majored in economics at Mt. Holyoke, became the head of a statistics unit for an agency of the United Nations, and his father, trained as an engineer, taught statistics at the University of Chile before the military coup (after the coup he became head of the Statistics Division of the Organization of American States in Washington, D.C.).[8]

At least two of the Latino CEOs (one from Mexico, one from Spain) are from middle class families. Hector Ruiz, the CEO of Advanced Micro Devices since 2002 (#424 on the *Fortune* list in 2004), explained his class background in the weekly *New York Times* column titled "The Boss": "Within Mexican society, I guess, we were considered middle class. My mother was the secretary of an export company, and my father prepared documents for the same company. Eventually, they bought a small building and opened a bookstore. To this day, my mother runs the bookstore. I have four sisters, and all five of us received quite a bit of schooling, with tremendous assistance from our parents" (Ruiz 2003, 10). The other, Antonio Perez, who became CEO of Eastman Kodak in 2005, grew up in a small Spanish fishing village where his father ran a fish merchandising business. Perez worked for his father every summer, and ultimately decided not to take over the family business (Perez may have been part of what we'd consider the upper middle class in that small village, or in Spain, but, lacking the information we would need to make that distinction, we are assuming that the family was middle class rather than upper middle class).

Both Mexican-American Latinos came from working class families. Carlos Cantu, the former CEO of ServiceMaster, was the son of Mexican immigrants. His father, a sharecropper's son, sold auto parts for a Ford dealer. When he was a student at Texas A&M University, Cantu worked as a custodian to help him pay his way through school (he later gave $1 million to the school for the study of Hispanic high school dropouts). Solomon Trujillo, who became CEO of US West in 1995 (it made the *Fortune* list in 1999, #135, and then was purchased by Qwest), is the son of a railway laborer.

Education

With the exception of Gutierrez, who did not complete college, all the Latino CEOs are college graduates. Two attended Yale and the rest earned their degrees from colleges throughout the United States (Western North Carolina, Texas, Southern Illinois, and Washington, D.C.) and abroad (in Spain, Brazil, and Venezuela). Three have MBAs, two have master's degrees, one has a law degree, and one has a PhD. All in all, they are a well-educated group, though far less so in terms of degrees and attendance at elite schools than either the women CEOs or the African American CEOs.

Skin Color

When we examined the skin color of African American CEOs and presidents of historically black colleges and universities (see chapter 3), we also asked students to rate the skin color of twelve Latino males who have been CEOs of *Fortune* 500 companies (we were only able to attain acceptable photographs for twelve of the fifteen Latino CEOs). The first of the two studies used 65 photos and included a control group of white male CEOs; the second study, which had a total of 107 photos, also included pictures of Asian American CEOs and white women CEOs. As we showed in table 3.1, which summarized the data from the two studies on three groups of CEOs (African Americans, Latinos, and white males) and presidents of historically black colleges and universities (HBCUs), the mean skin rating scores for the Latinos indicated that they were seen as significantly darker than the white CEOs and significantly lighter than the two African American groups. Notably, the ratings for the Latino CEOs were much closer to the ratings of the white CEOs than they were to the ratings of the black CEOs.

In addition to rating the 65 or 107 photographs, we asked the undergraduate raters to identify the ethnicity of the person in each photo (in the 65-photo study, they were given three choices: African American, Latino, or White; in the 107-photo study, they were given four choices: African American, Asian American, Latino, or White). This task, of course, is not based solely on skin color, as eye color, hair texture, and other phenotypic features may influence the identification of ethnicity (Thompson and Keith 2004, 47). Although the student raters were accurate more than 90 percent of the time when asked to identify the ethnicity of the black CEOs, the black college presidents, and the white CEOs, they were only accurate 57 percent of the time for the Asian CEOs, and they were the least accurate for the Latino CEOs (33 percent of the time in the 65-photo condition, and 21 percent of the time in the 107-photo condition—adding the Asian American CEOs in the 107-photo version apparently made it even more difficult to identify the Latinos, some of whom were misidentified as Asian American). Not only were the student raters unlikely to identify the Latino CEOs as Latinos, there was great variability in accuracy for the twelve Latino photos. Four of the twelve Latinos were identified as Latinos by more than half of the raters (Alain Belda, Carlos Gutierrez, Hector Ruiz, and Solomon Trujillo), but the raters had much more difficulty identifying the other eight Latinos, and none correctly identified Fernando Aguirre or William Perez as Latinos. In almost all cases, when errors were made, the Latinos were misidentified as whites, not as African Americans or as Asian Americans.[9] (For a detailed account of the study that we did on skin color and CEOs, see appendix 2.)

These findings demonstrate just how light skinned and Anglo-looking most of the Latino CEOs are, and, in fact, it reminds us that one can be both Latino and white (those who have struggled with the wording of the questions on the national census every ten years are well aware that race and ethnicity are not one and the same). In fact, new census data reveal that 87 percent of the Americans born in Cuba, and 53 percent of those born in Mexico identified themselves as white (Roberts 2010). Though we did not include a control group of prominent Latinos, as we did in our previous study of Latino corporate directors (Zweigenhaft and Domhoff 1998, 129–31), we think it is safe to conclude that these Latino CEOs are lighter skinned than most other Latinos and that this is related to the fact that many are from privileged class backgrounds. This claim is supported by research in the Latino community in general, with large sample sizes (Telles and Murguia 1990; Arce, Murguia, and Frisbie 1987; Murguia and Forman 2003).

ASIAN AMERICAN *FORTUNE* 500 CEOS

What could be more American than Mom, apple pie, Coke, and Pepsi? It is striking, therefore, that as of 2008 both Coke and Pepsi had CEOs who came to the United States from other countries. Indra Nooyi, the CEO of Pepsi since 2006, was born and raised in India, and Muhtar Kent, the CEO of Coke since 2008, is Turkish (technically he is Turkish American, as he was born in 1952 in New York City—at the time, his father was the Turkish consul-general).

Table 4.2 lists the names, dates of birth, and companies of those *Fortune* 500 CEOs we are considering "Asian American" (broadly defined). As can be seen, five are Chinese American, three are Japanese American, eight are from India, one is from Pakistan, and the other three are from South Korea, Sri Lanka, and Turkey. Seventeen of the twenty are male (the three women are Andrea Jung, Indra Nooyi, and Laura Sen).

Chinese Americans

The Chinese American *Fortune* 500 CEOs, or their parents, like the Cuban Americans, left a country that had experienced a revolution. All were from

Table 4.2. Asian American CEOs of *Fortune* 500 Companies, 1986–2010

Number	CEO	Year Born, Country of Birth	First Year on List with Asian as CEO, Ranking, and Company	Tenure as CEO
1	Tsai, Gerald	1929–2008, China	1986, #140: American Can (then Primerica)	1986–1987
2	Nishimura, Koichi (Ko)	1938, USA	1994, #399: Solectron	1992–2003
3	Wang, Charles B.	1944, China	1996, #474: Computer Associates Int.	1976–2000
4	Ayer, Ramani	1947, India	1997, #105: Hartford Financial Services	1997–
5	Hassan, Fred	1945, Pakistan	1997, #196, Pharmacia; 2003; became Schering-Plough	1997–2009
6	Nakasone, Robert C.	1947, USA	1998, #143: Toys "R" Us	1998–1999
7	Gangwal, Rakesh	1953, India	1998, #146: US Airways	1998–2001
8	Gupta, Rajiv L.	1945, India	1999, #408: Rohm and Haas	1999–2009
9	Jung, Andrea	1959, Canada	1999, #312: Avon	1999–
10	Kumar, Sanjay	1962, Sri Lanka	2000, #315: Computer Associates	2000–2004
11	Mohapatra, Surya N.	1950, India	2004, #366: Quest Diagnostics	2004–
12	Park, Chong S.	c. 1948, South Korea	2004, #423: Maxtor	2004–2006
13	Inouye, Wayne	1953, USA	2004, #484: Gateway	2004–2006
14	Yang, Jerry	1968, Taiwan	2006, #412: Yahoo	1994–2008
15	Nooyi, Indra	1955, India	2006, #63: PepsiCo	2006–
16	Pandit, Vikram	1957, India	2007, #8: Citigroup	2007–
17	Jha, Sanjay K.	1963, India	2008, #65: Motorola (co-CEO)	2008–
18	Kent, Muhtar	1952, USA	2008, #83: Coca-Cola	2008–
19	Sen, Laura	1956, USA	2009, #269: BJ's Wholesale Club	2009–
20	Banga, Ajay	1960, India	2010, #411: MasterCard	2010–

educated professional families. Gerald Tsai, the first on our list, was born in 1929 and came to the United States at the age of eighteen in 1947. He started college at Wesleyan University, but having lived in Shanghai he found Middletown, Connecticut, to be an alarmingly small town ("You stand at one end of Main Street and you can see the other"). After one semester he transferred to Boston University (how you gonna keep them down in Middletown after they've seen Shanghai?). In the 1960s and 1970s he pioneered the creation of performance funds and started a mutual fund company that he sold to CNA Financial Corporation in 1968, a sale that brought him profits of more than $30 million. By the mid-1980s he was the CEO at the American Can Company (soon to become Primerica, which, in turn, was then to become a key component of Citigroup). American Can made the *Fortune* list in 1986 when Tsai was CEO, so even though he had been a multimillionaire since 1968, we have designated 1986 as the first year an Asian American was the CEO of a *Fortune* 500 corporation. Both Tsai's grandfather and his father had been educated in the United States. Before the communist revolution his father was the Shanghai district manager for Ford Motor Company, and his mother had made a fortune speculating in stocks, currencies, silver, and gold. "We had servants, cars, a chauffeur," he says about his childhood (Leinster 1987; see also Brooks 1999).

The next two Chinese Americans named as *Fortune* 500 CEOs are Charles Wang and Andrea Jung. Wang (pronounced "wong"), like Tsai, was born in Shanghai, and he, too, was educated in the United States (his family moved to New York when he was eight years old, and he graduated from Queens College where he majored in math). In 1976 he founded a company, Computer Associates, which then, through a series of more than sixty takeovers of smaller businesses over a twenty-year period, grew tremendously (Barry 1997). Computer Associates first made the *Fortune* list in 1996, though Wang was quite wealthy long before 1996. From 1997 to 2000, Computer Associates paid Wang more than $700 million, including a $670 million bonus in 1998 that was issued shortly before its stock dropped 31 percent in a single day. The company was the subject of a five-year federal investigation that resulted in several executives pleading guilty to securities fraud (the company agreed to pay $225 million to a shareholder fund to settle the investigation).

In 1996, Wang announced that he was giving between $20 and $25 million to create an Asian American cultural center at SUNY at Stony Brook, then the largest gift the school had ever received (it subsequently increased to $40 million; Berenson 2002). After the company faced criminal investigations, however, questions were raised about that gift because Shirley Kenny, the president of the school, had been on the board of Computer Associates, and she was one of only three board members on the audit committee. She was not the only Computer Associates board member who appeared to have benefited from Wang's contributions. Alfonse D'Amato, former senator from New York, also was a board member, and Wang gave $25,000 toward D'Amato's unsuccessful bid for the Senate in 1998. That same year, Wang also contributed $100,000 to the National Republican Senatorial Committee and $10,000 to the Republican National Committee.

Though harshly criticized in a 390-page report released by the Computer Associates board in 2007, Wang has not faced criminal charges. In fact, as the owner of the New York Islanders, which he bought for $188 million in 2000 with the man who succeeded him as CEO of Computer Associates, Sanjay Kumar (from Sri Lanka, also on our list of Asian American CEOs, and now serving time), he remains a highly visible, influential, and controversial figure (Sandomir 2000; Berenson 2007).

Andrea Jung, as we indicated in chapter 2, was born in Canada to well-educated Chinese immigrants with professional positions in architecture and engineering. The family moved from Toronto to Massachusetts when she was two, and she went to Princeton from which she graduated in 1979 with a major in English literature (she also speaks Mandarin). She worked for Bloomingdales, I. Magnin, and Neiman Marcus before moving to Avon, where, in 1999, she became CEO. Like so many of the foreign-born CEOs, Jung is given credit for having taken the company global: by 2001 Avon products were sold in over 143 countries, and nearly 40 percent of the company's profits were international ("Andrea Jung" 2007).[10]

Jerry Yang, the cofounder of Yahoo, was born Jerry Chih-Yuan Yang in Taiwan in 1968. His mother, Lily, taught English and drama at the university level (his father, who had come to Taiwan from China, died when he was two). In 1978, his mother, her father, Jerry, and his younger brother came to live in San Jose, California. Yang learned English quickly, and by his senior year in high school he was the valedictorian, the president of his class, and a member of the tennis team. He received a bachelor's degree from Stanford, and stayed there to work on a PhD in electrical engineering. He never finished, however, because a project he was working on turned out to be the start of Yahoo, the search engine website. The company was incorporated in 1995, it was #502 on the *Fortune* list in 2005, and by the time it made it onto the *Fortune* 500 list in 2006 (#412) Yang was a millionaire many times over (Yang was #773 on *Forbes* magazine's 2010 list of "The World's Billionaires").

The newest Chinese American arrival to the *Fortune* CEO ranks is Laura Sen, who is the daughter of a Chinese father and an Irish mother. She grew up in Massachusetts, where her father was a highway engineer and her mother worked as a secretary. After completing her BA at Boston College, she worked for Jordan Marsh and for Zayre's, and then for BJ's Wholesale Club from 1997 to 2003. She was a contender for the CEO position at BJ's in 2002, but she was not chosen and she did not get along with the person the board selected. When she was "asked to leave" (as she puts it in a column in the *New York Times*), she went out on her own (Sen Retail Consulting). When the CEO hired by BJ's eventually resigned three and a half years later, she returned to the company as an executive vice president, and two years later, in 2009, she became CEO (Sen 2009).

Japanese Americans

The three Japanese American *Fortune* 500 CEOs were all born in the United States. Koichi (Ko) Nishimura, the oldest of the three, was born in 1938 and, he, his parents, and siblings were among the 120,000 Japanese Americans placed in "relocation centers" during World War II. Nishimura's father studied engineering at Berkeley, but after the war he was unable to find work and ended up working in a fruit stand. Ko, a football star in high school, went to Pasadena Junior College to play football, but got hurt. He transferred to San Jose State, where he switched his major from physical education to engineering, earned BS and MS degrees, and then went to Stanford for a PhD in engineering (more specifically, in materials science). He worked for IBM for twenty-three years, and then went to work for Solectron in 1988 as its COO, and by 1992 became the CEO (Saito 2003). Solectron first made the *Fortune* 500 list in 1996.

Robert Nakasone, the former CEO of Toys "R" Us, was born in 1947. His parents had been sent to an internment camp in Idaho during World War II. After the war, the family moved to Chicago (where Robert was born), and then to Seattle and later to Southern California. Nakasone was a three-sport athlete and student body president at Verdugo Hills High School, the public school he attended in the San Fernando Valley; he then received degrees from Claremont Men's College (a BA in economics) and the University of Chicago (an MBA). He went to work for Toys "R" Us in 1985 and became the CEO in 1998.

Wayne Inouye, the former CEO of Gateway, was born in 1953. His parents, too, had been incarcerated in internment camps during the war, and after the war they bought a farm in Yuba City, a desert town an hour north of Sacramento. As he recalls, "Farming was a tough life. We'd have money one year and be flat broke the next" (Weintraub 2003). He started college at Berkeley, but joined a blues band, dropped out, and managed to pay the rent by working in music stores and selling guitars. He was good at it (he sold guitars to Joni Mitchell, to the Beach Boys, and to the Grateful Dead), and ultimately held various management positions at audio stores and then at Best Buy. He became CEO of eMachines in 2001, and CEO of Gateway in 2004 (Weintraub 2003).

Indians

Eight of the twenty on the Asian American list (see table 4.2) were born in India. The first three became CEOs between 1996 and 1998 (Ramani Ayer at Hartford Financial Services, Rakesh Gangwal at US Airways, and Rajiv Gupta at Rohm and Haas). The other five became CEOs between 2004 and 2010 (Surya Mohapatra at Quest Diagnostics, Indra Nooyi at PepsiCo, Vikram Pandit at Citigroup, Sanjay Jha at Motorola, and Ajay Banga at MasterCard).

Nooyi's appointment at PepsiCo was a breakthrough, not only because she is the first Indian American woman to become the CEO of a *Fortune* 500 company, but because it is such a major company: PepsiCo was #63 on the *Fortune* list in 2006 when she became CEO. Nooyi, from a well-off Brahmin family, received her undergraduate degree in chemistry and a master's degree in business administration from schools in India, and then she came to the United States to study for a master's in public and private management (an MPPM) from the Yale School of Management. As she explains, it was quite unusual for an Indian female of her class background to travel, on her own, to study in America: "It was unheard of for a good, conservative, south Indian Brahmin girl to do this. It would make her an absolutely unmarriageable commodity." She stayed in the states, working first for Boston Consulting Group, then Motorola, and then, starting in 1994, PepsiCo (she did get married, to Raj Nooyi, an Indian man who is a management consultant—her maiden name was Indra Krishnamurthy).

A year later, another Indian was named CEO at a company even higher on the *Fortune* list: Vikram Pandit became CEO of Citigroup (#8 on the 2007 list). Pandit, like Nooyi, and like most of the Indians on the list, is from an affluent family (his father was an executive director at a chemical company).[11] He came to the United States to attend college and received BS, MS, MBA, and PhD degrees, all from Columbia University (he now sits on the board at Columbia). After teaching economics at Columbia and finance at Indiana University, he left academia to work for Morgan Stanley from 1994 until 2005. In 2005, after months of internecine battling for power within the company in which the sitting CEO concluded that Pandit and others were plotting against him, Pandit was fired. He started a hedge fund called Old Lane Partners along with some other Morgan Stanley refugees. In 2007, the company was purchased by Citigroup for $800 million (Pandit's profits were estimated at $165 million), and in December 2007, Pandit was named CEO of the company. In 2008, Pandit received $38,237,437 in compensation. In 2009, after Citigroup received $45 billion in a federal bailout, President Obama publicly rebuked Pandit for having ordered a new $50 million jet for the company.

As we noted in chapter 1, in our previous studies of the women and the men of color who became directors of major corporations, we emphasized the need for identity management. There are various ways that corporate directors signal that they can work effectively with the white men they are about to join on boards of directors. We drew on some memorable anecdotes that described such behavior: one woman director told a story about how she had smoked cigars with the guys at her first board meeting as a way to let them know she was one of them, and another explained that when she became a senior executive at an energy company she realized that she had to take up golf. In terms of appearance, we concluded that African Americans were unlikely to wear dashikis and Jews were unlikely to wear yarmulkes (Zweigenhaft and Domhoff 2006, 233–34).

We therefore found it of interest when Ajay Banga was named to become the new CEO of MasterCard as of July 1, 2010 (#474 on the *Fortune* 500 list in 2009 and #411 in 2010). Banga, a native of India who received his bachelor's degree in economics from Delhi University and an MBA from the Indian Institute of Management, worked for Nestle, Kraft, and then Citigroup. While at Citigroup, he managed the company's overseas credit card and banking businesses, and he oversaw the bank's operations in Asia. Given that seven other Indians had become *Fortune* 500 CEOs, and given his considerable experience with Citigroup, Banga's appointment did not surprise us. We did, however, take careful notice of his photograph in the *New York Times*, which shows him wearing a turban. As the *New York Times* explains, Banga is "a Sikh and wears the turban that distinguishes worshipers of his religion" (Martin and Dash 2010). His appointment, therefore, suggests another breakthrough at the top, one that signals that appearance no longer needs to conform quite so rigidly to the dominant white male (and Christian) model to which we have become so accustomed.

The reason that Ajay Banga's strikingly atypical appearance was more acceptable to the MasterCard board became clear late in 2010. Just one day after India announced that it planned to give identity cards to its 1.2 billion citizens, Banga arrived in Mumbai in the hopes of securing a contract for the company to implement such a massive undertaking. Born, raised, and educated in India, and, as we have noted, having previously held management-level jobs in that country at Nestle's and PepsiCo, Banga knows the country and the culture. Although there was no guarantee that MasterCard would get this lucrative contract, as the *New York Times* explains, "MasterCard hopes that Mr. Banga's ability to glide among cultures, languages and borders gives it an edge" (Bajaj and Martin 2010).

In addition to the identity card account, Banga hoped that millions of middle class Indians would choose MasterCard for their credit cards, or their prepaid debit cards, or other mobile payment systems. He knows that future business growth for MasterCard will depend on winning battles for the growing middle classes in countries like India. As he notes, estimating the size of the emerging global middle class over the next five years, "Whether it's 200 million or 400 million, it's a lot of millions" (Bajaj and Martin 2010).

Banga, perhaps more than any of the other newly appointed Latino and Asian American CEOs, demonstrates the increasingly global nature of the *Fortune* 500 and the potential benefits of appointing a new CEO who is "not from around here."

The Other Four

In addition to the five Chinese American CEOs, the three Japanese American CEOs, and the eight CEOs from India, four more CEOs are on our list: Chong S. Park from Korea, Fred Hassan from Pakistan, Sanjay Kumar from Sri Lanka, and Muhtar Kent from Turkey (including Turkey admittedly stretches our definition of Asian, so perhaps we should use a more encompassing term such as "Near and Far East"). Park was born in Seoul, Korea, and received both BS and MA degrees there before coming to the University of Chicago for an MBA (he subsequently earned a PhD from Nova Southeastern). He was president and CEO of Hynix Semiconductor before he joined the board of Maxtor in 1994. He became president of the company in 1995 and was CEO from 2004 to 2006.

Fred Hassan was born in Pakistan in 1945, where his father was the country's first ambassador to India. Hassan did undergraduate work in chemical engineering at the University of London and then received an MBA from Harvard. Hassan started his career with Sandoz Pharmaceuticals, where he worked for seventeen years before joining another pharmaceutical company, Wyeth, as a vice president. In 1997 he became CEO of yet another pharmaceutical company, then called Pharmacia & Upjohn (which a few years later merged with Monsanto, and was known as Pharmacia). In 2003, he became CEO of Schering-Plough (that company merged in November 2009 with Merck, and Hassan, at age 63, left the company, though he still sat on a number of corporate boards; see Rubenstein 2009).

Sanjay Kumar, born in Sri Lanka, is the only CEO of the seventy-four we have looked at who is now in jail, serving a twelve-year sentence for orchestrating a $2.2 billion accounting fraud. Kumar's father was an animal husbandry researcher and his mother a school administrator when the family left Sri Lanka in 1976 due to political unrest there. He started college at Furman University but never completed his degree. Instead, in 1987, in his midtwenties, he went to work for Charles Wang at Computer Associates. He became Wang's protégé, and in 2000 he became CEO of the company (Kumar was Charles Wang's partner when he purchased the New York Islanders hockey team for $188 million in 2000). Two weeks before his trial was to begin, Kumar pleaded guilty to charges that included conspiracy, securities fraud, and obstruction of justice. He admitted that he had used illegal accounting practices to meet bonus goals in 1999 and 2000 and then lied to investigators about it. He also admitted to having paid $3.7 million to a potential witness in an effort to buy the witness's silence, and to having backdated contracts. He and Charles Wang received huge bonuses as a result of the company apparently reaching the 1999 and 2000 goals, though Wang was never charged and claimed that it was all Kumar's doing. Kumar agreed to repay $800 million to the victims of the fraud (the company's shareholders; Berenson 2007).

As we have mentioned, Muhtar Kent, the CEO of Coca-Cola since 2008, is a Turkish American born in New York City when his father was the Turkish consul-general. He did his undergraduate work, and a master's degree, in England, served in the Turkish military, and in 1978 came to the United States where he lived with an uncle and went to work for Coca-Cola. By 1985 he was the general manager of Coca-Cola Turkey and Central Asia (living in Istanbul), by 1988 he was the vice president of Coca-Cola International (living in Vienna), and by 1995 he was general manager of Coca-Cola Amatil-Europe. For six years he left Coca-Cola to work in Turkey, and then returned in 2005 where he was responsible for all of Coke's operations outside North America. In 2008 he became the company's CEO.

Insiders versus Outsiders

Strikingly, seventeen of the twenty Asian American *Fortune* 500 CEOs have been insiders. One founded his own company, some had been with their companies for decades, and others had come fairly recently to the companies as senior executives and then emerged as CEOs. As we have mentioned, Vikram Pandit came to work for Citigroup when the company bought Old Lane, the hedge fund group he formed after he was fired from Morgan Stanley. After merely six months with the company, he became its CEO. Thus, he too, like sixteen other Asian CEOs, was an insider, but he had not been on the inside of Citigroup for long, and he had no experience running a large public company. Apparently he was very much the choice of Robert E. Rubin (former head of Goldman Sachs, former secretary of treasury under Bill Clinton, and the chairman of the board at Citigroup at the time the company bought Old Lane and brought Pandit on board). Some claimed that Rubin had agreed to pay way too much for Old Lane as a means of persuading Pandit to work for Citigroup (Dash 2007).

Class Background

Most of the Asian Americans for whom we were able to obtain information came from upper or upper middle class families. This was especially the case for the Chinese Americans and the Indians. Gerald Tsai, for example, born in 1929 in Shanghai, was the son and grandson of men who were educated in the United States. His father, a graduate of the University of Michigan, was the Shanghai district manager for the Ford Motor Company. Charles Wang, also born in Shanghai (in 1944), was the son of Kenneth Wang, a former law school professor, judge, and college president who fled communist China in 1952 and then taught law for thirty years at St. John's School of Law in New York. Andrea Jung, born in Toronto in 1959, is the daughter of an architect (her father, born in Hong Kong) and a chemical engineer (her mother, born in Shanghai). So, too, are a number of the Indian CEOs from quite prominent families, including Vikram Pandit, whose father was the executive director of Sarabhai Chemicals, and Indra Nooyi, whose father was a banker (and whose aunt was a noted classical musician). Fred Hassan's father was the first Pakistani ambassador to India, and Muhtar Kent's father an ambassador from Turkey to the United States. Of the twenty men and women of Asian backgrounds on our list, only a few seem to be from middle or working class backgrounds (we were unable to find relevant information for a few of them).

Education

Even though two of the twenty Asian and Asian American CEOs started but didn't finish their undergraduate degrees (Kumar and Inouye), they are quite well educated as a group, with fifteen of the twenty having completed postgraduate degrees of one type or another (seven completed PhDs). Eight attended elite schools in the United States (including Princeton, Columbia, Cal Tech, and the University of Chicago) and some attended elite schools in the countries in which they grew up, especially the Indians, three of whom are graduates of the Indian Institute of Technology, a school that is "more difficult to get into than MIT, Yale, or Harvard" according to one writer (Heenan 2005, 96). The Asian Americans, then, like the women and the African Americans, but not the Latinos, appear to be far better educated in terms of degrees from prestigious universities than most white male CEOs.

Skin Color and Recognition of the Asian American CEOs

As we have indicated in the chapter on African Americans, and earlier in this chapter, we asked twenty undergraduates to rate photographs of African American, Latino, Asian, and white CEOs (men and women), as well as a control group (for the blacks) of presidents of historically black colleges and universities. As can be seen in table 4.3, which lists the mean skin color ratings for each of the six groups, and in figure 4.1, the photos of the Asian

Table 4.3. Skin Color Ratings of White Women, White Male, Latino, Asian American, and African American CEOs, and Presidents of Historically Black Colleges and Universities (HBCUs)

	Photos of White Women CEOs (n = 24)	Photos of White Male CEOs (n = 20)	Photos of Latino CEOs (n = 12)	Photos of Asian American CEOs (n = 18)	Photos of African American CEOs (n = 13)	Photos of Presidents of HBCUs (n = 20)
Mean rating =	1.97 [b,c,d,e,f]	2.12 [a,c,d,e,f]	2.68 [a,b,d,e,f]	3.47 [a,b,c,e,f]	6.27 [a,b,c,d,f]	7.06 [a,b,c,d,e]
St. dev. =	(.551)	(.661)	(.755)	(.724)	(.960)	(.850)
Number of raters	20	20	20	20	20	20

F = 281.50
df = 5
p < .001

a = significantly different (p < .05) from the ratings for the white women CEOs
b = significantly different (p < .05) from the ratings for the white male CEOs
c = significantly different (p < .05) from the ratings for the Latino CEOs
d = significantly different (p < .05) from the ratings for the Asian American CEOs
e = significantly different (p < .05) from the ratings for the African American CEOs
f = significantly different (p < .05) from the ratings for the presidents of HBCUs

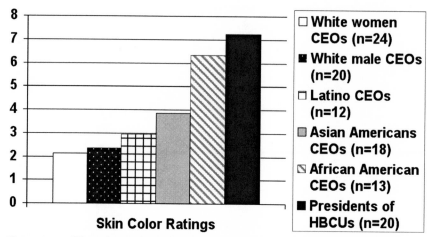

Figure 4.1. Skin Color Ratings of White, African American, Latino, and Asian American CEOs, and Presidents of Historically Black Colleges and Universities (HBCUs)

American CEOs were rated as darker than those of the whites or the Latinos, but lighter than those of either group of blacks. The ratings of the Asian Americans were much closer to those of the Latinos and whites than they were to those of the blacks (the differences among all six groups were statistically significant from one another).[12]

The undergraduates also were asked to identify the ethnicity of those in the photographs, and they were much more accurate for whites and African Americans (well over 90 percent accuracy rate for all four of these groups) than for Asian Americans or Latinos. The accuracy rate for Asians was much lower, 57 percent (though not as low as it was for Latinos, 31 percent). A closer look at accuracy rates for the Asian CEOs reveals that the raters were 100 percent accurate for six of the eighteen Asians, all of whom are Japanese Americans or Chinese Americans (Inouye, Jung, Nakasone, Tsai, Wang, and Yang), and 100 percent inaccurate, or close to it, for another six of the Asians, including three Indians (Gupta, Nooyi, Gangwal), the two men from Pakistan and Turkey (Kent and Hassan), and Laura Sen, whose mother is Irish and whose father is Chinese.

In terms of skin color and the accuracy of identifying their ethnicity, therefore, the Asian CEOs fall into two distinct subgroups: the Chinese Americans and Japanese Americans, whose skin color ratings were, on average, 4.30, and who were identified as Asians 96 percent of the time, and the others (the Indians, and the CEOs from Pakistan, Turkey, and Sri Lanka) whose skin color ratings were, on average, 3.11, and whose Asian ethnicity was accurately identified only 32 percent of the time.[13]

GENERAL CONCLUSIONS ABOUT THE
LATINOS AND ASIAN AMERICANS

As we look at the lives and career patterns of these thirty-five Latinos and Asian Americans (almost all of whom have become *Fortune* 500 CEOs in the last fifteen years), two clear patterns emerge. The first is that many of them made tremendous strides in their careers working outside the United States and that their international expertise contributed to their ascendance as CEOs because so many companies were looking for ways to improve their global outreach. This included, but was not limited to, proficiency in languages. Time and time again we saw how these CEOs developed their skills managing a company's operation in Colombia, or Venezuela, or all of Latin America, or east central Europe.

We have seen that Ajay Banga of MasterCard flew to India the day after that country announced that it was planning to develop identity cards for its 1.2 billion residents. MasterCard sees the future, and it is not primarily in the United States. In fact, for many *Fortune* 500 companies, the future is now, for many of their employees, and the bulk of their profits, are outside the United States as well. Citigroup, for example, whose CEO, Vikram Pandit, is Indian, has 260,000 employees, two-thirds of whom work outside the United States. Almost three-fourths of the company's profits in the first nine months of 2010 came from Europe, Asia, and Latin America (Cassidy 2010, 54). Appointing CEOs who were born outside the United States, therefore, is not the radical act it might once have been. It may be, in fact, a shrewd investment in the future.

Second, at least half of these men and women come from economic privilege. Here it is important to acknowledge the different subgroups. Of the four Latinos and three Japanese Americans born in the United States, only one comes from the upper middle or upper class (William Perez, whose father managed the Goodyear plant in Colombia and then managed all their plants throughout Latin America). On the other hand, of those men and women born outside the United States, at least seventeen were from upper middle or upper class backgrounds, and there are probably more. Most (and perhaps all) of those whose families left Cuba and China were from educated, professional, and in some cases quite wealthy families.

As the *Fortune* 500 have added Latino and Asian CEOs to their ranks, therefore, they have followed the general pattern observed by C. Wright Mills and others before and after him: a disproportionately high percentage come from privilege, though it does not appear to be as high as 70 percent, which it was for most of the twentieth century, and which it is for the women CEOs of *Fortune* 500 companies. These men and women have helped these companies to become global in their operations.

They are not the only foreign-born CEOs to have served the *Fortune* 500 this way. As of 2007, there were fifteen foreign-born CEOs leading *Fortune* 100 companies, up from nine in 1996. These included men who were born in Ireland (David O'Reilly of Chevron, and Edmund Kelly of Liberty Mutual), Britain (Martin Sullivan of American International Group, and George Buckley of 3M), and Canada (R. Kerry Clark of Cardinal Health, and Ronald Sugar of Northrup Grumman), as well as a handful from more distant locations (e.g., Louis Camilleri from Egypt; Story 2007). We have focused on Latinos and Asians, not only because many of them, even though born elsewhere, have become American citizens, but also because for many their ability to speak more than one language has been central to the work they have done.

Nor is it a new pattern for a small minority of American corporate executives to be born into middle-level or well-to-do families in foreign countries and rise to the top. This pattern was notable in a study of 303 American corporate executives for the years 1870 to 1879 in the seventeen largest railroads (by far the biggest companies in the country), the thirty largest steel companies (the newest large-scale industry at the time), and the thirty largest textile companies (the oldest large-scale industry in the country); 10 percent of the men were born outside the United States. Of the five foreign-born executives among the 101 railroad leaders, three came from established professional families, one was the son of a "well-to-do farmer," and one was already a lawyer when he arrived; six of the ten foreign born among 100 steel executives were from "substantial middle-class backgrounds," with the most important exception being the famous robber baron Andrew Carnegie; and two of four foreign born among the 102 textile executives on whom information could be found were the sons of "a man of fair estate" (Gregory and Neu 1962, 197–98). A very similar pattern was discovered in a study of 190 presidents and board chairmen in a wider range of large businesses—manufacturing and mining, railroad, public utilities, and finance—for the years 1901 to 1910, all of them "career men" in business organizations, not business founders. Once again, 10 percent were foreign born, and once again, "scarcely two or three" could be characterized as low-income individuals who made good (Miller 1962, 322).

However, the most important and dramatic example of an immigrant who became a top executive was the very first one, Samuel Slater, who is often called "the father of American manufactures" or "the father of the American factory system" in historical biographies (Cameron 1960). An expert machinist in London in the 1780s, Slater came to America in reaction to handbills distributed throughout England's textile districts by American investors offering big rewards to anyone who could memorize or smuggle out closely guarded plans for textile machinery, which would be necessary for the United States to develop its own textile industry. In fact, any British citizen suspected of knowing enough to help the Americans was refused emigration, but Slater managed to slip through the net with the key features of the intricate machinery stored in his head. In 1790 he joined with the wealthy Brown family of Rhode Island, the first benefactors of Brown University, who already had made their fortunes in the rum and slave trade, to build one of the first water-powered cotton mills in the country. Slater soon became a partner with the Browns and then went on to build his own mills and make an even larger fortune.

Let us now turn, in the fifth chapter, to some bigger issues related to these twenty-four white women, fifteen African Americans, fifteen Latinos, and twenty Asian Americans. Does it matter that there is such diversity in the *Fortune* 500 CEO suites? In what ways are they similar to, and in what ways do they differ from, the white men who hold most such positions?

5

Where Do They Fit in the Corporate Elite, and How Do They Compare with White Male CEOs?

In the last three chapters we have presented the players—the men and women who have become CEOs of *Fortune* 500 companies (twenty-eight women, fifteen African Americans, fifteen Latinos, and twenty Asian Americans, the sum of which totals seventy-eight, but because four of the women appear on more than one list the total is actually seventy-four). Our focus in the previous three chapters was on their stories—where they were from, their backgrounds, where they were educated, and the trajectory of their careers. In this chapter we shift our focus to *where* and *how* they fit in the corporate elite, and to how they compare with our previous findings on corporate directors, top government appointees, and military leaders on the four factors that we mentioned in chapter 1: class background, education, skin tone, and "style," which we can more broadly consider under the concept of cultural capital. We will attempt to answer six questions.

The first question is, which companies have appointed women, blacks, Latinos, and Asian Americans? Are they a random sample of the *Fortune* 500, or are they bigger companies, or smaller companies, and are they more likely to fall in certain industrial sectors than others?

After locating these seventy-four CEOs in the constellation of *Fortune* 500 corporations, we then turn to our second question, which has to do with how these *Fortune* 500 CEOs connect to other *Fortune* 500 CEOs, both through outside directorships that they hold and by membership on certain policy planning groups. Mills (1956), Domhoff (2010), Useem (1984), and others have shown that CEOs are typically connected to other companies by sitting as outside directors on their boards, and some CEOs are part of what Useem has called "the inner circle." As of 1975, more than 85 percent of the CEOs of the top 800 *Fortune*-level boards sat on other *Fortune* boards as outside directors, and most sat on two to three (Useem 1984, 48). More recently, according to Domhoff (2006, 30), "approximately 15 to 20 percent of all present-day directors sit on two or more corporate boards. . . . This percentage has proved to be very stable over time."

Although asking if a CEO holds multiple board memberships is a helpful starting point in identifying those in the inner circle, other factors are at play as well, including membership on the councils of business associations that provide a "forum for the discussion and articulation of policies affecting most large companies, regardless of sector or region," such as the Business Roundtable, the Business Council, the Council on Foreign Relations (CFR), the Committee for Economic Development (CED), and the Conference Board (Useem 1984, 70). "The inner circle, then," concludes Useem (1984, 75), "refers not just to the company executive directors who constitute its membership, but also to the networks that constitute its internal structure. It is the power of these internal networks that propel members of the inner circle into leadership roles on behalf of the entire corporate community." To address the second question about inner circle status, we will look at both outside directorships and membership on one or more of the five policy planning groups we just named.

A third question asks whether or not this cohort of seventy-four new CEOs supports Khurana's (2002) claims that corporations, because they are looking for "corporate saviors" when they choose CEOs, now are more likely than in the past to seek outsiders rather than insiders. Have the new CEOs been mostly outsiders, have they been brought in to save the companies that chose them, and, correspondingly, as Khurana argues, have the outsiders been offered huge compensation packages (even larger than those of other CEOs)?

A fourth question has to do with compensation more generally for these new CEOs. As we noted in the first chapter, the compensation of CEOs has skyrocketed over the last few decades, and it is not unusual for CEOs to receive millions of dollars per year even when their companies have lost money. In the previous few chapters, as we profiled many of the women, blacks, Latinos, and Asian Americans who have become CEOs, we have mentioned individuals who received immense paychecks for the work they did. In this chapter, we will look more systematically at compensation for the new CEOs and ask if their compensation has been comparable to that of other *Fortune* 500 CEOs.

The fifth question that we will address in this chapter concerns the campaign contributions made by these new CEOs. People who ascend to the top of America's corporate ladder tend to be conservative in outlook and politics. There are, of course, wide variations among the corporate elite in terms of their civic involvements, political affiliations, philanthropic activities, and leadership styles within their firms, but in general it is fair to say that the top corporate leaders are not prone to rock the boat, and they tend to support Republicans or moderate Democrats. For example, a survey of 751 CEOs conducted by *Chief Executive Magazine* shortly before the 2008 election found that 80 percent favored John McCain over Barack Obama ("Job Creators" 2008; see also Sasseen 2008).[1] Are the new CEOs as likely to support Republicans as CEOs have been in the past?

The sixth question we will address in this chapter has to do with the companies they work for: how have they been rated by some of the many watchdog groups that evaluate corporations in terms of such matters as their environmental policies, the ways they treat their employees, including gay, lesbian, bisexual, and transgender employees, and in terms of the opportunities they provide for women executives?

As we ask these questions about the women, African American, Latino, and Asian American CEOs, we include two additional groups for purposes of comparison. The first is a set of Jewish CEOs. Jews have been well represented in the corporate elite for much longer than women, blacks, Latinos, or Asian Americans, though it is often harder to know who is Jewish than who is in these other categories. Still, using self-references in *Who's Who in America*, previous investigations of Jews in the power elite (Zweigenhaft and Domhoff 1982, 1998, 2006), and various other credible sources that we were able to find in print or on the Internet, we have identified a sample of thirty-one Jewish men who are or who have been CEOs of *Fortune* 500 corporations (some Jewish CEOs, like Laurence Tisch of Loews, rose to the top of companies that they themselves founded; others, like Irving Shapiro, former CEO of DuPont, and Michael Eisner of Disney, became CEOs of companies founded by non-Jews).

There is some overlap among the women and Jews in our sample. More specifically, at least two of the women in our sample (Marian Sandler, CEO of Golden West, and Irene Rosenfeld, CEO of Kraft since June 2006) are also Jewish.

Our second comparison group is a set of non-Jewish white males. We started with the *Fortune* rankings of the companies of the black, women, and Jewish CEOs, and then selected the CEO from a company on the *Fortune* list that had a very similar ranking (unless it too had, or previously had, a black, woman, or Jewish CEO, in which case we skipped to another company nearby on the list). For example, Carly Fiorina was CEO of Hewlett-Packard from July 1999 through February 2005. Hewlett-Packard was ranked #14 in 2007. We therefore selected the 15th ranked company in 2007, which was IBM, and added the CEO of that company (Samuel J. Palmisano) to the comparison group.

QUESTION #1: WHICH COMPANIES, WHICH SECTORS?

We compared the four target groups in terms of where the corporations they worked for ranked on the *Fortune* 500 list (we used the year each became a CEO, or the first year the company made the list after they became CEOs). The average ranking for the four groups was women, #238; African Americans, #169; Latinos, #306; and Asian Americans, #253. Given that the median ranking for the *Fortune* 500 is #250, the African American CEOs (of whom there have been the fewest) have been more likely to head larger corporations than the CEOs in the other three groups, and the Latinos have been more likely to head smaller corporations.[2] As another way to look at these findings, 60 percent of the African American CEOs headed *Fortune* 100 companies, compared to 25 percent for the other three groups.[3]

In order to determine whether companies in different sectors of the economy were more or less likely to appoint women, African Americans, Latinos, and Asian Americans as CEOs, we drew on the thirteen categories provided on the website maintained by the Center for Responsive Politics (Opensecrets.org). These thirteen sectors are (1) Agribusiness; (2) Communications/Electronics; (3) Construction; (4) Defense; (5) Energy & Natural Resources; (6) Finance, Insurance, and Real Estate; (7) Health; (8) Ideological/Single Issue; (9) Labor; (10) Lawyers & Lobbyists; (11) Miscellaneous Business (which includes "retail sales"); (12) Other; and (13) Transportation.

We found that four-fifths of the CEOs have worked for companies that fell in one of four sectors: Agribusiness, Communications/Electronics, Finance, and Miscellaneous Business (the other 20 percent of the CEOs worked for companies that were distributed among the other nine sectors). As can be seen in table 5.1, the CEOs in the four groups did not hold jobs in the same sectors: the women CEOs were most likely to be in the Miscellaneous Business sector (with only two of the twenty-eight in Finance), the African American CEOs were especially likely to be in Finance (with none in Agribusiness), the Latino CEOs were especially likely to be in Communications/Electronics and Agribusiness (with only one in Finance), the Asian Americans were especially likely to be in Communications/Electronics, the Jewish CEOs were most likely to be in Communications/Electronics and Finance, and the non-Jewish white male CEOs were most likely to be in the other nine sectors.

We also determined the location of the headquarters for the companies that have appointed new CEOs. In a previous study that focused on Atlanta's role in the national power elite, we found that corporations headquartered in Atlanta were less likely to have appointed women, African Americans, and Latino members to their boards, and less likely to have appointed women, African Americans, and Latinos as CEOs, than corporations headquartered

Table 5.1. Sectors of the *Fortune* 500 CEOs' Companies

	Agribus	Comms/ Elec	Finance	Misc. Bus	Other	Total
Women	5 (18%)	7 (25%)	2 (7%)	10 (36%)	4 (14%)	28 (100%)
African Americans	0 (0%)	3 (21%)	5 (36%)	3 (21%)	3 (21%)	14 (100%)
Latinos	4 (27%)	6 (40%)	1 (7%)	1 (7%)	3 (20%)	15 (100%)
Asian Americans	2 (11%)	8 (42%)	2 (11%)	5 (26%)	2 (11%)	19 (100%)
Jews	0 (0%)	14 (45%)	9 (29%)	6 (19%)	2 (6%)	31 (100%)
White gentile men	11 (16%)	6 (9%)	14 (21%)	14 (21%)	23 (34%)	68 (100%)
	22	44	33	39	35	All
	$x^2 =$ 10.97	$x^2 =$ 21.18	$x^2 =$ 9.66	$x^2 =$ 5.54	$x^2 =$ 12.72	$x^2 =$ 47.21
	$df = 5$	$df = 5$	$df = 5$	$df = 5$	$df = 5$	$df = 20$
	$p < .05$	$p < .001$	$p < .08$	ns	$p < .03$	$p < .001$
	$r = .02$	$r = .12$	$r = .10$	$r = .08$	$r = .14$	$r = .10$

in New York, but more likely to have done so than companies headquartered in Houston (at the time, New York, Houston, and Atlanta were the cities with the most *Fortune* 500 companies; Zweigenhaft 2007). We therefore expected to see some geographic differences when we looked at the locations of the headquarters of the companies that had hired the new CEOs, and this indeed is what we found. As can be seen in table 5.2, which lists the twenty states with the largest number of *Fortune* 500 corporate headquarters in 2009, the new CEOs were more likely to have been appointed by companies with headquarters in some states, and less likely to have been appointed by companies with headquarters in other states. For example, although only 2.2 percent of the *Fortune* 500 had headquarters in Connecticut, 8.2 percent of the new CEOs were appointed by companies with headquarters in that state. Similarly, although 12.8 percent of the *Fortune* 500 companies had headquarters in the state of Texas, only 1.4 percent of the new CEOs headed companies based in Texas. Although these differences for Connecticut and Texas were statistically significant, most of the comparisons for individual states were not. Combining states, however, reveals the regional patterns quite clearly. For example, the three states of New York, New Jersey, and Connecticut were the headquarters for 17.6 percent of all *Fortune* 500 companies in 2009, but 34.2 percent of the new CEOs were appointed by companies with headquarters in those three states. Similarly, the eleven states that were all part of the Confederacy (in the order in which they seceded: South Carolina, Mississippi, Florida, Alabama, Georgia, Louisiana, Texas, Virginia, Arkansas, Tennessee, and North Carolina) housed 27.8 percent of

Table 5.2. Geographic Locations of the Headquarters of the Companies That Have Appointed New CEOs

	Percentage of F500 Companies with Headquarters in the State (2009)	Percentage of New CEOs Appointed at Companies with Headquarters in the State*	Z	h <	p <=
1. TX	12.8	1.4	**3.95**	**.50**	**.01**
2. NY	11.2	16.4			
3. CA	10.2	13.7			
4. IL	6.4	9.6			
5. OH	5.4	1.4			
6. PA	4.8	8.2			
7. NJ	4.2	9.6			
8. MI	4.2	4.1			
9. MN	3.8	1.4			
10. VA	3.6	0			
11. FL	2.8	2.7			
12. GA	2.6	4.1			
13. NC	2.6	0			
14. MA	2.4	0			
15. CO	2.2	2.7			
16. CT	2.2	8.2	**2.25**	**.28**	**.05**
17. WI	2.0	0			
18. MO	1.6	0			
19. MD	1.4	0			
20. IN	1.2	0			
NY, NJ, and CT	17.6	34.2	**3.05**	**.38**	**.01**
Confederate states	27.8	8.4	**4.10**	**.52**	**.01**

Note: These data are based on seventy-two rather than seventy-three companies that appointed new CEOs since Xerox has appointed two new CEOs (Anne Mulcahy and Ursula Burns). We only counted Xerox once. (Nor was the appointment of Kenneth Frazier as CEO by Merck in 2011 included.)

the *Fortune* 500 companies in 2009, but only 8.4 percent of the new CEOs were from companies with headquarters in those states.

QUESTION #2: ARE THE NEW CEOS IN THE INNER CIRCLE?

Slightly more than one-third (38 percent) of the CEOs in our sample sat on two or more corporate boards.[4] As can be seen in table 5.3 (which has slightly smaller samples in some cases because we did not include those CEOs who have died), the African Americans were most likely to be interlocking directors—11 of the 14 were on two or more boards (79 percent). Slightly more than half of the women CEOs were interlockers (14 of 26). In contrast, only 5 of the 13 Latinos (38 percent), 5 of the 17 Asian Americans (29 percent),

Table 5.3. Inner Circle Status: CEO Interlocks and Membership on Key Policy Groups

	Two or more Fortune Boards	Business Council	Business Roundtable	Committee for Economic Development (CED)	Conference Board	Council on Foreign Relations (CFR)	At Least One of the Five Policy Groups
Women (n = 26)	14 (54%)	4	4	0	0	0	6 (23%)
African Americans (n = 14)	11 (79%)	4	2	1	1	0	5 (36%)
Latinos (n = 13)	5 (38%)	1	2	0	1	0	3 (23%)
Asian Americans (n = 17)	5 (29%)	3	4	0	0	0	6 (35%)
Jewish (n = 29)	6 (21%)	3	2	0	0	1	5 (17%)
Non-Jewish white men (n = 68)	23 (34%)	12	10	4	0	0	19 (28%)
	$x^2 = 17.63$ $df = 5$ $p < .003$ $r = .20$	$x^2 = 3.81$ $df = 5$ ns	$x^2 = 2.54$ $df = 5$ ns	$x^2 = 5.98$ $df = 5$ ns	$x^2 = 10.13$ $df = 5$ $p < .07$ $r = .10$	$x^2 = 4.64$, $df = 5$ ns	$x^2 = 3.49$ $df = 5$ ns

6 of the 29 Jewish CEOs (21 percent), and only 23 of the 68 non-Jewish white males (34 percent) were interlockers. These statistically significant results[5] very much correspond to earlier findings that in recent years corporate boards have sought blacks and women as corporate directors in their efforts to diversify. Once a black or a woman is on one corporate board, he or she is likely to be asked onto other boards, and previous findings have indicated that black women on corporate boards hold more directorships than black men (Zweigenhaft and Domhoff 2006, 100); in this sample, there is only one black woman, Ursula Burns, the CEO of Xerox, who as of 2009 sat on three *Fortune* 1000 boards (Xerox, American Express, and Boston Scientific).

The African American CEOs and the Asian American CEOs were only slightly more likely than the CEOs in the other groups to be members of the councils of the business and policy groups that we examined, and the differences were not statistically significant. Five of the 14 African Americans (36 percent) sat on at least one of the five policy groups, and 6 of the 17 Asian Americans (35 percent), compared to 19 of the 68 non-Jewish male CEOs (28 percent), 8 of the 26 women (31 percent), 3 of 13 Latinos (23 percent), and 5 of the 29 Jews (17 percent).

If we combine two variables—whether or not they hold interlocking directorships and whether or not they sit on at least one of the five policy boards—to create a single variable assessing inner circle status, then the new CEOs (the women, African Americans, Latinos, and Asian Americans) score significantly higher than the "old" CEOs (the Jews and the non-Jewish white males). The African American CEOs have the highest score, the women CEOs second highest, followed by Asian Americans, Latinos, gentile white men, and finally, the Jewish CEOs.[6] In general, then, the "new CEOs" are more likely than the Jewish and non-Jewish white male CEOs to be in the inner circle, and this is especially the case for the African American and women CEOs.

QUESTION #3: INSIDERS VERSUS OUTSIDERS?

In chapter 1, we summarized Rakesh Khurana's (2002) argument that in the modern era of investor capitalism, the flawed system of searching for CEOs has contributed to futile attempts to find external "corporate saviors." As a result, he claimed, far more outsiders were being hired as CEOs than in the past. In a sample of 850 CEO appointments between 1980 and 1996, he found that 27 percent selected outsiders. Writing in 2002, he suggested that by the year 2000 this 27 percent figure had grown, and was perhaps as high as 50 percent (Khurana 2002, 248). In a study of CEO turnover in the five hundred largest public companies during 1997 and 1998, Margarethe Wiersema found that 36 percent of those brought in to replace CEOs were outsiders. Despite this 36 percent figure (which was, after all, a statistical minority), she went on to write, "The desire to please (or appease) the investment community leads board members to choose a candidate who promises a quick fix, usually an outsider they hope will magically turn the company around. They barely consider internal candidates" (Wiersema 2009, 21, 27).

Khurana also argued that part of the flawed process that leads corporations to hire what they hope will be corporate saviors is that corporations buy into the mythology that they have to pay exorbitant amounts of money to attract them. In Khurana's view, both the selection process itself increases the bargaining power of outsiders, and so too does "the deferential treatment that candidates receive" (Khurana 2002, 179). If he is right, we would expect the outsiders to have received greater compensation than the insiders in our sample. How do our findings compare with his claims? Have the new CEOs mostly been outsiders, as the claims of Khurana (2002) and Wiersema (2009) suggest, and have the new CEOs who were appointed from the outside been compensated more than those appointed from the inside?

The large majority of the men and women who fall in one of our four groups of new CEOs have been appointed from the inside, not the outside (71 percent). The others (29 percent), however, have been hired from the outside, a figure that is quite similar to what Khurana found in his sample of the CEO searches in 850 companies from 1980 to 1996, and less than Wiersema found in her 1997–1998 sample. Since the large majority of the CEOs in our sample were appointed after 1997, this suggests that either the frequency with which companies appointed external CEOs did not continue to climb as Khurana predicted, or it did so but not for women, African American, Latino, and Asian American CEOs. There were no differences between the insiders and the outsiders in terms of how high the company ranked on the *Fortune* lists, or in terms of race, gender, or ethnicity.

When we compared the new CEOs who came to their positions from outside their companies with those who were appointed internally in terms of compensation, there were no meaningful differences. That is, we did not find, as suggested by Khurana's claims about the way the search process works, that those CEOs appointed from the outside have been paid more than those recruited from the inside. As Khurana does note, the very fact that the procedures for finding CEOs have driven up compensation packages for some CEOs works to inflate those packages for all CEOs. He may be correct that the process of searching for CEOs currently employed by many companies has contributed to the inflated compensation packages for external CEOs and for those hired from the inside.[7]

QUESTION #4: WHAT ABOUT COMPENSATION?

Not only do the new CEOs appear to be mostly insiders, not outsiders, who are very much a part of the inner circle, there is evidence that they are at least as well compensated as their non-Jewish white male counterparts. That is to say, they too are paid millions of dollars, and in some cases, many millions of dollars, on an annual basis.

We looked at three sets of figures on CEO compensation. We looked at the information reported in an April 5, 2009, special section in the *New York Times* on executive pay (April 5, 2009); at *Business Week*'s website; and on *Forbes*'s website. All three analyses are skewed by the enormous compensation packages of a few CEOs (for example, according to the *New York Times*, in 2008 Sanjay Jha, the CEO of Motorola, hauled in $104,000,000, and Larry Ellison, the CEO of Oracle, was paid $84,600,000), and by the few incredibly rich CEOs who symbolically received very small compensation packages (in 2008, for example, John Mackey, CEO of Whole Foods, was compensated only $33,831 and Richard Kinder, CEO of Kinder Morgan, received only $1).

Therefore, we have looked at median incomes as well as mean incomes. Even though the three data sets used slightly different formulas and different dates by which they determined estimated value of stocks, they were highly correlated.[8] For the analysis reported here, we have used the data from *Business Week* because that data set included the largest number of CEOs in our sample ($n = 86$).

As can be seen in table 5.4, all three groups received hefty compensation packages in 2008. The thirty new CEOs had a mean compensation package of $10,130,000, and the median was $9,570,000; the Jewish CEOs had a mean

Table 5.4.   Compensation (in millions of dollars), *Fortune* 500 CEOs, *Business Week* 2008

	Business Week, *2008*
Women ($n = 14$)	$9,310,000
African Americans ($n = 6$)	$12,970,000
Latinos ($n = 6$)	$7,180,000
Asian Americans ($n = 7$)	$11,850,000
All New CEOs ($n = 30$)	$10,120,000
Jewish CEOs ($n = 12$)	$17,060,000
White gentile male CEOs ($n = 41$)	$10,290,000
Mean CEO pay	$11,170,000
New vs. Jewish vs. white gentile men	$F = 2.61$
	$df = 2$
	$p < .08$

compensation package of $17,060,000, and a median of $13,750,000; the gentile males mean was $10,290,000, and the median was $7,240,000.

Therefore, whether one uses the mean compensation or the median compensation, the Jewish CEOs seem to receive the most compensation. Although these differences approach statistical significance when one uses the means, they do not when we do the same analyses based on the medians or when we do comparisons without the outliers. We therefore conclude that the 2008 compensation for the new CEOs was comparable to that of both white male control groups.

QUESTION #5: WHICH POLITICAL CANDIDATES HAVE THEY SUPPORTED?

Laws require that campaign donations be disclosed, so it is possible to know the names of those who contribute more than $200 to political candidates. Moreover, with the growth of the Internet, numerous search engines now post reports provided by the Federal Election Commission (FEC) that make it possible to monitor these contributions relatively easily. We used three of these, Newsmeat.com, Opensecrets.org (maintained by the Center for Responsive Politics), and fundrace.huffingtonpost.com (maintained by the Huffington Post), to examine the campaign contributions of the women, African American, Latino, and Asian American CEOs of *Fortune* 500 companies (we did not include the few CEOs who had died by November 2008, the time of Obama's election), and the comparison groups of Jewish and white male non-Jewish CEOs.

We examined the CEOs on these search engines and classified each in one of four categories: (1) those who had given primarily to Democrats (70 percent or more of their contributions); (2) those who had given primarily to Republicans (70 percent or more of their contributions); (3) those who had given to both parties, but no more than 69 percent to either party; (4) those who had not given enough money to be included in the public FEC reports. We were especially interested in contributions to candidates for president, but also to candidates for the Senate and the House. We knew that some CEOs were likely to contribute to local politicians, whatever their party, and to senators and congresspersons who sat on committees that had jurisdiction over policies that affected their companies, so we not only noted how much they gave to each party, but to which House, Senate, or presidential campaigns (for a study that focuses on donations to congressional campaigns, see Francia, Green, Herrnson, Powell, and Wilcox 2005). In addition, we noted whether these CEOs had contributed to the campaigns of the three candidates who ran in the 2008 primaries for the Democratic presidential nomination who were not white males, and thus were path breakers—Barack Obama (an African American), Hillary Clinton (a woman), and, to a lesser extent, Bill Richardson (he self-identifies as a Latino: his mother was Mexican and his Anglo father was a banker; he attended an elite New England boarding school and is also very much an upper class white male).

As can be seen in the top half of table 5.5, which shows the campaign contributions of the new CEOs, the Jewish CEOs, and the gentile male CEOs, the new CEOs and the Jewish CEOs were four times as likely to give predominantly to Democrats as the gentile male CEOs, and, correspondingly, the white gentile males were more than twice as likely as those two groups to give predominantly to Republicans. The new CEOs were least likely to fall in the "Both" category, and the Jewish CEOs were least likely to fall in the "Neither" category.

When we look just at the four groups that make up the new CEO category (shown in the middle section of table 5.5), we see that the African Americans were by far the most likely to support Democrats (71 percent); the Asian Americans were second at 50 percent, followed by the women at 32 percent and the Latinos at 15 percent. The African Americans were ten times as likely to support Democrats as Republicans, the Asian Americans were three times as likely, the women were equally likely to support Democrats as Republicans, and the Latinos were three times as likely to support Republicans.

It is revealing to compare these figures with the voting patterns for these same groups in the 2008 presidential election. Exit polls revealed that 95 percent of African Americans voted for Obama, 78 percent of Jewish voters, 67 percent of Latinos, 62 percent of Asian Americans, and 53 percent of women (only 43 percent of non-Hispanic white men voted for Obama, the only group of the six we have focused on who preferred McCain; see Limonic 2008). Therefore, the African American CEOs and the Jewish CEOs follow the same patterns as the demographic groups to which they belong, but they were less pronounced in their tendency to support Democrats. The Asian American CEOs, the white women CEOs, and the Latino CEOs were less likely to support Democrats than Asian American voters, white women voters, and Latino voters. We think it is likely that the African American and Jewish CEOs, despite the tendency for people in general to support the Republicans as they become more affluent, will support the Democrats as long as the Republican right is perceived as the home of racists and anti-Semites, showing once again that class and economic interests are not necessarily the primary determinant of voting and campaign donation patterns.

Also notable in table 5.5 is the fact that about one in five of the white non-Jewish male CEOs, and about one in four of the Jewish CEOs, fell in

Table 5.5. Campaign Contributions of the New CEOs, Jewish, and Non-Jewish White Male CEOs

	Democrats	Republicans	Both	Neither	
All new CEOs ($n = 67$)	28 (42%)	17 (25%)	7 (10%)	15 (22%)	100%
Jewish CEOs ($n = 29$)	13 (45%)	7 (24%)	7 (24%)	2 (7%)	100%
Non-Jewish white male CEOs ($n = 68$)	7 (10%)	37 (55%)	13 (19%)	11(16%)	100%
x^2	**20.29**	**14.75**	3.35	3.50	
df	**2**	**2**	2	2	
p <	**.001**	**.001**	.19	.17	
r	**.32**	**.27**	.11	.07	
New CEOs, looked at separately					
White women CEOs ($n = 22$)	7 (32%)	7 (32%)	1 (4%)	7 (32%)	100%
African American CEOs ($n = 14$)	10 (71%)	1 (7%)	2 (14%)	1 (7%)	100%
Latino CEOs ($n = 13$)	2 (15%)	6 (46%)	2 (15%)	3 (23%)	100%
Asian American CEOs ($n = 18$)	9 (50%)	3 (17%)	2 (11%)	4 (22%)	100%
$x^2 =$	**10.18**	6.63	1.38	3.00	
df =	**3**	3	3	3	
p <	**.02**	.08	ns	ns	
r =	**.04**	.05	.09	.06	
Regression analyses					
R =	.41	.37	.25	.37	
df =	7	7	7	7	
F =	**3.56**	2.83	1.15	**2.84**	
p <	**.002**	.01	.34	**.009**	
Woman CEOs		Beta = -.15 (p < .10)	Beta = −.22 (p < .02)	Beta = .26 (p < .004)	
African American CEOs	Beta = .35 (p < .001)	Beta = -.25 (p < .01)			
Latino CEOs					
Asian American CEOs		Beta = .24 (p < .01)		Beta = .19 (p < .04)	
Jewish CEOs	Beta = .18 (p < .06)	Beta = -.18 (p < .06)			
Sector	Beta = .15 (p < .08)				
Inner circle status					

the "Both" category. That is, they contributed to Democrats and Republicans, and neither party received 70 percent or more of their contributions. For example, Ron Sargent, the CEO of Staples (since 2002) and Thomas J. Wilson, the CEO of Allstate (since 2007), each of whom was among the white non-Jewish male CEOs on our list, contributed to various Republican and Democratic candidates over the years, and each contributed to the 2008 presidential campaigns of both John McCain and Barack Obama. In contrast, few of the new CEOs adopted this donation strategy: only two of the African American CEOs, two of the Latino CEOs, two of the Asian American CEOs, and only one of the white women CEOs fell in the "Both" category.

The bottom of table 5.5 includes regression analyses performed on each of these four outcome measures (70 percent or more given to Democrats, 70 percent or more given to Republicans, Both, or Neither). It makes use of seven potentially predictive variables: whether or not the CEO was female; whether or not the CEO was African American; whether or not the CEO was Latino; whether or not the CEO was Asian American; whether or not the CEO was Jewish; the percentage of contributions given to Democrats in the sector in which the CEO's company fell; and the measure that we used of "inner circle status" that combined whether or not the CEO sat on at least two *Fortune* 1000 boards and whether or not the CEO sat on any of the five policy boards. As can be seen, neither corporate sector, inner circle status, nor being a Latino was a meaningful predictor of whether they gave campaign contributions to Democrats, Republicans, Both, or Neither. However, gender, whether or not they were African American, Asian American or Jewish, did predict certain of these categories of campaign contributions.

A more focused look at each of the CEO groups is informative. The women CEOs were divided in two ways—first, only fifteen of the twenty-two made large enough contributions to appear on the FEC list (and, thus, on the websites that make this information available to the public), and, second, seven gave mostly or exclusively to Democrats, and seven gave mostly or exclusively to Republicans. Four of the women CEOs contributed to Hillary Clinton's presidential campaign: Jill Barad, former CEO of Mattel (1997–2000), S. Marce Fuller (CEO of Mirant from 1999 to 2005), Anne Mulcahy (CEO of Xerox from 2001 through 2009), and Ursula Burns (who became CEO of Xerox in 2009). Only two of the women CEOs contributed to Obama's campaign—Brenda Barnes (CEO of Sara Lee from 2005 to 2010) and Ursula Burns. Some of the women CEOs gave most of their money to Republicans, and some became key advisors to Republican presidential aspirants. Carly Fiorina, former CEO of Hewlett-Packard (1999–2005), gave $4,400 to McCain and became a key McCain advisor before and after he won the Republican nomination. Over the years, Meg Whitman, who was the CEO of eBay from 1998 until early in 2008, gave $158,000 to Republicans and $10,000 to Democrats, and during the Republican primaries she campaigned first for Mitt Romney, her friend and former colleague at a consulting firm, Bain & Company, and then for John McCain. During the second presidential debate in 2008, McCain said she would be considered as secretary of the Treasury if he were to be elected (Bohan 2008).

In February 2009, Whitman announced that she was planning to seek the Republican nomination for governor of California in the 2010 race (Otterman 2009), and nine months later Fiorina announced that she was running for the Republican nomination for Senate, also in California. By mid-June 2010, when they both won their Republican primaries, Whitman, a billionaire, had spent $71 million of her vast personal fortune on her campaign, and Fiorina, whose worth was estimated as "only" about $100 million, had given herself loans that totaled $5.5 million (Steinhauer 2010, A19; Stone 2010a, A20). Both lost (by the time of the election Whitman had set records by spending more than $150 million on her campaign; McKinley 2011).

Only one of the women CEOs fell into the "Both" category (Ellen Kullman, CEO of DuPont since 2008), though a few made token contributions to candidates of their less preferred party. For example, S. Marce Fuller, who gave money to Hillary Clinton's Senate campaigns in 2004, 2005, and 2006 and to her presidential campaign in 2008, and to John Kerry's presidential campaign in 2004, also contributed $1,000 to Saxby Chambliss, a Republican senator from her home state of Georgia. Similarly, Angela Braly, the CEO of WellPoint since June 2007, gave $10,000 to the Republican Senatorial Committee in 2008, and $2,000 to support Republican Mitch McConnell (R-KY) in 2007, and earlier in the decade she contributed to the campaigns of George Bush and John Ashcroft, but in 2007 she also gave $1,000 to support Ken Salazar (D-CO).

In a study performed in August 2008, Jones (2008) used Opensecrets.org to look at the campaign contributions of the 191 African American directors of the 250 largest companies. He found 99 who had made contributions. Of those 99, 95 percent had contributed either to Obama or Clinton's campaigns, and 83 percent had contributed to Obama's. These African American directors, therefore, like African American voters, strongly supported Democrats.

So, too, were the African American CEOs much more likely to support Democrats than Republicans: ten of the fourteen (71 percent) gave primarily to Democrats. Ken Chenault, CEO of American Express since 2001, for example, by the end of 2008 had given $50,000 to Democrats, but only $3,000 to Republicans. Franklin Raines, former CEO of Fannie Mae (1999–2004), had given $68,500 to Democrats, and $6,000 to Republicans. By the time the 2008 election took place, eight of the fourteen had given to Obama: James

A. Bell (interim CEO at Boeing in 2005), Ursula Burns of Xerox, Ronald Ferguson (CEO at TIAA-CREF, since 2008), Stanley O'Neal (former CEO at Merrill Lynch, 2002–2007), Clarence Otis (CEO of Darden Restaurants since 2005), Richard Parsons (CEO at Time Warner from 2001 to 2007, and now chairman of the board at Citigroup), A. Barry Rand (CEO at Avis, 1999–2001), and John W. Thompson (CEO at Symantec, from 1999 through 2009). Ursula Burns and Stanley O'Neal gave money both to Clinton's campaign and to Obama's, and John Thompson went for the trifecta: he not only hosted a fund-raiser for Obama (as the *New York Times* put it, "in his secluded house in Woodside, Calif."), he also contributed to the Clinton campaign and to Bill Richardson's campaign (Flynn 2007, C1, C4).

Only one of the African American CEOs gave primarily to Republicans, but he is a very heavy hitter: Richard Parsons, the former CEO of Time Warner and current chair of the board at Citigroup. A relatively rare African American Republican (he told one interviewer: "I wasn't born a Republican. I became a Republican"), over the years Parsons has given $259,850 to Republicans (including a $1,500 contribution in 2007 to John McCain, and a $25,000 contribution in May 2008 to the "McCain Victory Committee"), and he gave what for him was small change to a few Democrats. Notably, in August 2008, he gave $6,900 to "Obama for America." Perhaps as a result of his late but meaningful support of Obama, Parsons became part of Obama's Transition Economic Advisory Board. His name was among those mentioned as a possible choice as Obama's secretary of commerce (Lloyd and Lowery 1994; Arango 2009).[9]

As of a few months before Obama's election, three of the African American CEOs were in our Both category. One was Clarence Otis, CEO of the Florida-based Darden Restaurants, who gave 62 percent to the Democrats and 38 percent to the Republicans. In March 2007 he contributed $2,300 to McCain's campaign, and in February of 2008 he contributed the same amount to Obama's campaign. Similarly, in previous years he had supported Democrats, including Al Gore and Bill Bradley, but also Republican senators, including Lauch Faircloth (R-NC) and Bill McCollum (R-FL). By mid-2008, however, in the months before the election, Otis saw the Obama light: he gave $28,500 to Obama's campaign in August 2008 and another $2,300 in September 2008. He, therefore, shifted from the Both category to the Democrat category.

Stanley O'Neal, the former CEO of Merrill Lynch, was one of the two African Americans who remained in our Both category. He supported Democrats, but he also supported Republicans, including right-wingers like Rick Santorum (R-PA), Richard Shelby (R-AL), and Phil Gramm (R-TX). He supported Obama when he ran for the Senate in 2003 and during his presidential campaign ($2,300 in April 2007). The financial services industry was in big trouble in 2008 and federal regulation of that industry was a major campaign issue. Whoever won was going to play a big role in regulating or bailing out or otherwise shaping the future of Merrill Lynch, so O'Neal was apparently quite strategic in contributing to both parties. Interestingly, the other African American CEO in the Both category was Rodney O'Neal, CEO of Delphi since 2007 and Stanley O'Neal's cousin.

The fifteen Latino CEOs were distributed almost equally among the four categories (two gave predominantly to Democrats, six to Republicans, two to Both, and three to Neither). The Latino CEO who has given the most money is one of the five Cuban Americans, Paul Diaz, the CEO of Kindred Healthcare since 2004. Over the years he has given $64,200 to Democrats and $47,200 to Republicans (placing him in the Both category). Second on the Latino CEO list is another of the Cuban Americans, Carlos Gutierrez, former CEO of Kellogg (and secretary of commerce under George W. Bush), who gave $20,100 to Republicans, including a $1,000 contribution to McCain's campaign (he contributed once to a Democrat—back in 1998 he gave $250 to a Democrat who was running for the House of Representatives from Battle Creek, Michigan, the corporate home of Kellogg). It does not clarify matters much to subdivide the Latinos based on their countries of origin; the three who gave predominantly to Democrats were born in Venezuela, Spain, and Chile, and those who gave predominantly to Republicans were born in Cuba, Mexico, and the United States.

Half the Asian American CEOs (nine) gave mostly to Democrats, three times the number who gave predominantly to Republicans (three). The two biggest Asian American donors, however, have been Republicans, not Democrats. The biggest donor is Fred Hassan, formerly the CEO of Pharmacia and Schering-Plough, who has given $93,500 to Republicans and $13,300 to Democrats. The second largest Asian American CEO donor has been Charles Wang, founder of Computer Associates (and owner of the New York Islanders, a hockey team), who has given $90,000 either to Democratic candidates or to the Democratic Party, but who has also given $7,000 to some Republicans, including (smart New Yorker that he is) Rudolph Giuliani, mayor of New York City. The third biggest donor has been Jerry Yang, co-founder and longtime CEO of Yahoo, who has given $61,600 to Democrats and $2,000 to Republicans.

Jews made it into the corporate elite well before, and in larger numbers, than either women or African Americans (Zweigenhaft and Domhoff 1982, 1998, 2006). The Jewish CEOs were the most likely of the six groups of CEOs to fall in the Both category. John Hess, the chairman and CEO of Amerada Hess since 1995 (he is the son of Leon Hess, the founder of the company), provides a nice example. He has given money to many Democrats and many Republicans, candidates for the House and the Senate, but his donations to presidential campaigns are especially revealing. He contributed to the 2008 presidential campaigns of McCain ($2,300 in May 2007, and another $28,500 in June of 2008), Richardson ($2,300 in December 2007), Obama ($2,300, March 2007), Dodd ($2,300, March 2007), and Giuliani ($2,300, February 2007). With the exception of Hillary Clinton—that apparently was where he drew the line—Hess seemed willing to support anyone who had a chance to become president.

Even those Jewish CEOs who gave mostly to Democrats often covered their bets. Between 2000 and 2008, Paul Jacobs, the CEO of Qualcomm (in 2005 he took over that position from his father, who founded the company in 1985) gave 91 percent of his political contributions to Democrats. Still, he gave $2,300 to McCain (and the same amount to Clinton), and in the 2004 campaign he made contributions both to Kerry and to Bush (and to Kucinich, though only $250).

For the most part, there were fewer large donors among the new CEOs than among the Jewish and the non-Jewish white male CEOs. Only one of the women (Meg Whitman of eBay) gave more than $100,000, and only three of the African American CEOs (Parsons, Thompson, and Chenault), one of the Latinos (Diaz), and one of the Asian Americans (Hassan). At least eight of the Jewish CEOs, and at least eight of the white non-Jewish male CEOs, have contributed more than $100,000, and some have given far more than that (for example, as of the end of 2008, Richard Kinder, the CEO of Kinder Morgan, had given more than $800,000 in campaign contributions, as had Michael Dell of Dell; James Dimon, CEO of J. P. Morgan Chase, had given about $600,000, and James Sinegal, CEO of Costco, had contributed $540,000).

QUESTION #6: ARE THE COMPANIES THAT HAVE HIRED NEW CEOS RATED BETTER THAN OTHER COMPANIES?

In this section, our focus is on the companies, not the CEOs. In a number of cases, the same company has hired two CEOs from our various groups. For example, Xerox has hired two women CEOs (Anne Mulcahy and Ursula Burns), two of the Jewish men in our sample have been CEOs of MetLife (Robert Benmosche and Harry Kamen), and two other Jewish men have been CEOs of Loews (Laurence Tisch and James Tisch). As a result, the sample of companies for the analyses to follow is slightly smaller than the sample of CEOs that we have been looking at (for example, there are twenty-eight women who have been *Fortune* 500 CEOs, but only twenty-seven companies have hired women).

We looked to see if the companies that at some point had appointed women, African Americans, Latinos, or Asian Americans as CEOs were more likely to have been rated positively on each of five different evaluations of corporate behavior than the companies that hired the Jewish male CEOs and the non-Jewish white male CEOs. As is the case with any set of ratings, each has its limitations. Still, the following five sets of ratings, individually and collectively, provide a rough look at how magazines and organizations concerned about corporate behavior have assessed these companies.

1. *The 100 Best Companies for Women.* Since 2002, *Working Mother* magazine has provided an annual rating of the "100 Best Companies for Women." Companies submit applications, and then *Working Mother* hires an independent survey research firm to validate the applications and tabulate scores. We used the ratings for 2007 and 2008, which were based on the following seven categories: workforce profile, compensation, child care, flexibility, time off and leaves, family friendly programs, and company culture.

2. *The 100 Best Corporate Citizens.* *Corporate Responsibility* magazine (formerly *Business Ethics* magazine), published by the Corporate Responsibility Officers Association (CROA), includes an annual list of "The 100 Best Corporate Citizens" based on the "corporate responsibility efforts" in eight categories: climate change, employee relations, environment, financial, governance, human rights, lobbying, and philanthropy. The list, which began in 2000, is based on public information about companies on the "Russell 1000 Index" (an index of 1,000 component stocks, not unlike the Dow or Standard & Poor's—it is one of the benchmarks frequently used by money managers).[10]

3. *The CEI.* Each year since 2002, the Human Rights Campaign's Workplace Project has rated companies based on their "policies and practices" pertinent to lesbian, gay, bisexual, and transgender employees. The group publishes a "Corporate Equality Index" (CEI), which they subtitle "A Report Card on Lesbian, Gay, Bisexual and Transgender Equality in Corporate America." The number of companies that achieved a 100 percent rating on the index has increased from 13 in 2002 to 260 in 2009. We used the 2008 and 2009 lists of companies that had achieved a 100 percent rating.

4. *The 100 Best Companies to Work For.* *Fortune* magazine publishes an annual list of the best companies to work for. Conducted by a global research and consulting firm, the list is based on a survey sent to more than a hundred thousand employees at more than four hundred companies asking them about such things as "the management's credibility, job

satisfaction and camaraderie," and another survey sent to the companies asking about such things as demographic makeup, pay and benefit programs, management philosophy, methods of internal communications, and diversity efforts.

5. *The NAFE 50 Top Companies for Executive Women.* Drawing on applications from private or public profit firms with at least a thousand employees and at least two female directors on their boards, the National Association for Female Executives (NAFE) selects the top companies for executive women. Based on the 250-item questionnaire they are asked to complete, corporations are rated on three components: representation of women at the higher levels of management, especially those positions that "occupy profit and loss jobs"; policies and programs to advance women within the corporation; and programs to help women balance their work and family responsibilities.[11]

With the exception of the NAFE 50, which first appeared in 2009, we used the two most recent sets of ratings (2008 and 2009) for the CEI, *CR, Fortune,* and *Working Mother* lists. We looked to see if the companies on our lists that have appointed women, African American, Latino, Asian American, or Jewish CEOs, and those companies on our control group list that have appointed only gentile white male CEOs, have been included on any of these five lists of "good companies to work for." The findings, shown in table 5.6, also include (in the far right column) cumulative totals based on whether companies appeared on at least one of the five lists.

As can be seen in the upper half of table 5.6, the companies that had appointed Jewish CEOs were the most likely to have appeared on at least one of the five lists (62 percent), the companies that had appointed new CEOs were next (51 percent), and the companies that have appointed only gentile white males were least likely to have done so (40 percent), a finding that approached but did not reach statistical significance. Much to our surprise, the only rating of the five on which there was statistical significance was the one done by *Working Mother*, but the companies that appointed new CEOs were the least likely of the three groups to be on that list.

Comparisons based on all six groups of CEOs, as shown in the bottom half of table 5.6, indicate that the companies that have hired Latino CEOs were the least likely to appear on at least one of the lists (33 percent), with those that have hired African Americans (69 percent), Asian Americans (62 percent), and Jewish CEOs (62 percent) the most likely. Another finding that stands out in table 5.6 is that the companies that have hired African American CEOs have been more likely to receive high ratings than other companies on the

Table 5.6. Ratings of Companies That Have Hired Women, African American, Latino, and Asian American CEOs Compared to Companies with Jewish and Non-Jewish White Male CEOs

	CEI^a	CR^b	Fortune[c]	$NAFE50^d$	Working Mother[e]	Any of the Five
New CEOs (n = 75)	27 (36%)	21 (28%)	5 (7%)	10 (13%)	9 (12%)	38 (51%)
Jewish CEOs (n = 29)	13 (45%)	10 (34%)	3 (3%)	6 (21%)	10 (34%)	18 (62%)
Non-Jewish white male CEOs (n = 68)	18 (26%)	15 (22%)	4 (6%)	12 (18%)	15 (22%)	27 (40%)
x^2	3.37	1.71	.63	.99	**7.04**	4.38
df	2	2	2	2	**2**	2
p <	.18	.43	.73	.51	**.03**	.11
r =	.09	.06	.02	.05	**.12**	.10
Women CEOs (n = 27)	8 (30%)	7 (26%)	3 (11%)	5 (19%)	4 (15%)	14 (52%)
African American CEOs (n = 14)	9 (64%)	4 (29%)	1 (7%)	2 (14%)	3 (21%)	9 (69%)
Latino CEOs (n = 15)	2 (13%)	3 (20%)	0 (0%)	1 (7%)	1 (7%)	5 (33%)
Asian American CEOs (n = 19)	8 (42%)	7 (37%)	1 (6%)	2 (11%)	1 (6%)	10 (62%)
Jewish CEOs (n = 29)	13 (45%)	10 (34%)	3 (3%)	6 (21%)	10 (34%)	18 (62%)
Non-Jewish white male CEOs (n = 68)	18 (26%)	15 (22%)	4 (6%)	12 (18%)	15 (22%)	27 (40%)
x^2	**12.64**	3.02	2.55	2.13	8.77	7.27
df	**5**	5	5	5	5	5
p <	**.03**	Ns	ns	ns	.12	.20
r =	**.06**	.02	.04	.03	.10	.08
African Americans and Jews (n = 45)[f] **vs. all others** (n = 127)	49% vs. 28% $x^2 = 6.27$ df = 1 p < .01 r = .19	ns	ns	ns	31% vs. 16% $x^2 = 4.95$ df = 1 p < .03 r = .17	62% vs. 43% $x^2 = 4.76$ df = 1 p < .03 r = .17

[a]Corporate Equality Index, published by the Human Rights Campaign
[b]*Corporate Responsibility* magazine's annual list of "The 100 Best Corporate Citizens"
[c]*Fortune* magazine's "100 Best Companies to Work For"
[d]National Association for Female Executives (NAFE) top companies for executive women
[e]*Working Mother* magazine's "100 Best Companies for Women"
[f]For these analyses, we have included the two Jewish women (Rosenfeld and Sandler) with the Jewish CEOs; the same analyses are significant whether or not they are included.

CEI, the Human Rights Campaign's assessment of how companies treat their gay, lesbian, bisexual, and transgender employees.

When we combined the companies that have hired African American CEOs and companies that have hired Jewish CEOs—keeping in mind that African Americans and Jews are the two groups most likely to vote Democratic, and thus the two most likely to be liberal—and compared them with all of the other companies in our sample, some significant patterns emerged, as can be seen in the bottom row of table 5.6. For the CEI ratings, for *Working Mother*'s "Best Companies for Women," and for the summary measure based on whether or not a company appeared on any of the five lists, the companies that have hired either African American CEOs or Jewish CEOs scored significantly better than the other companies. It is important to stress that the higher ratings for these companies may not be due to the actions of the African American and Jewish CEOs, but rather their having been appointed as CEOs may be part of a larger pattern of tolerant or inclusive thinking on the part of the boards of these companies, and perhaps simply a more tolerant corporate culture at those companies. Given that—as we have noted— African Americans tend to vote Democratic (95 percent in 2008), as do Jews (78 percent in 2008), the willingness to appoint either an African American CEO or a Jewish CEO may reflect a greater acceptance of liberal values, and this may manifest itself in, or contribute to, better treatment of employees.

It was quite surprising that the companies that have hired women as CEOs did not score better in general, and, especially, on the two ratings that focused on the treatment of women employees, including the opportunities for advancement. In a 2008 study performed by Catalyst, the organization mentioned in chapter 2 that has monitored the progress of women in the corporate world for many years, the researchers found that the more women directors a company had in 2001, the more women corporate officers there were in 2005 (Joy 2008). Based on such findings, we expected that the presence of a woman CEO would lead not only to the promotion of more women corporate officers, but also to the kinds of policies that would result in high scores in the annual ratings done by *Working Mother, Fortune*, and the National Association for Female Executives, but this was not the case. The fact that the companies that had hired women CEOs were no different than other companies is supported by the study that we cited in chapter 1 that found a relationship between CEO compensation and "meanness" (Desai, Brief, and George 2010a, 2010b). In that study, gender was not a meaningful predictor in the regression analysis that the authors performed. That is, just as we find that the companies that have hired women are no more and no less likely to be rated as "good corporate citizens," they found that the 11 companies in their sample (of 261 companies) that had women as CEOs were no more and no less likely "to behave meanly toward those lower down in the hierarchy" (by which they mean these companies were no more likely to have had a history of poor employee relations, including, for example, a history of poor union relations and violations of health and safety standards).

At the least, this finding is consistent with what we know of the women CEOs we have studied, who seem to be as likely to behave badly as other CEOs. As we noted in chapter 2, Linda Wachner, former CEO of Warnaco, was known for her autocratic and abusive behavior toward subordinates (she was labeled by one journalist as "hell on high heels"). Similarly, observers described Yahoo CEO Carol Bartz as "hardened" and "occasionally ruth-less," and *Esquire*, emphasizing both her harshness and her proclivity for off-color language, titled an article it ran about her in May 2010, "Hi, I'm Carol Bartz . . . Are You an Asshole?" And, as we noted in chapter 3, after she became so angry that she shoved a Korean American employee, former eBay CEO Meg Whitman went through mediation and settled out of court for an alleged $200,000 to avoid a lawsuit. In short, we conclude that the women CEOs are not all that different from the men CEOs.

CONCLUSION

The new CEOs, still relatively few in number, and more likely to be found in some business sectors than in others, are very much a part of the white gentile male corporate establishment that has populated the CEO offices of major corporations for more than a century. They are part of the inner circle, especially the African American and women CEOs who are highly sought as corporate directors on boards of other *Fortune* 500 companies. Like their white gentile CEO counterparts they are paid millions of dollars per year (they are not paid quite as much as the CEOs in our Jewish sample). They are no more, and no less, likely to be hired as outsiders than other CEOs. In these ways, the new CEOs are much like the old CEOs.

When it comes to the campaign contributions they have made and the rat-ings of their companies by outside organizations in terms of good corporate behavior, the new CEOs differ from the old CEOs, and they differ depending on which group they are in. On both these dimensions, the salient grouping seems to be African Americans and Jews compared to the others: the African American and Jewish CEOs were far more likely to support Democrats (just as African Americans and Jews in general are far more likely than any other groups to vote for Democrats), and the companies that have appointed Afri-can American and Jewish CEOs have been more likely to receive favorable ratings for the ways they treat their employees.

Why is this? For the African American CEOs, we think a key factor is that they are the least likely to have come from economically privileged backgrounds. A much lower percentage of the African American CEOs than the women, Latino, or Asian American CEOs were born into economic privilege. Fully 71 percent of the women CEOs for whom we found information on class background came from the upper 15 percent of the class structure, and so, too, did a fairly high proportion of the Latinos and Asian Americans (many were born into elite families in other countries). In striking contrast, only two of the African American CEOs came from economic privilege—the large majority came from middle or working class families.

The Jewish CEOs, like the women, Latinos, Asian Americans, and white gentile male CEOs, were born to economic privilege (73 percent of the Jewish CEOs for whom we could find clear information on class background had grown up in economically privileged circumstances). Despite this, and despite the fact that Jews have been among the most successful groups in America in terms of economic achievement, which typically would lead to a tendency to support Republicans rather than Democrats, they continue to be consistently politically liberal, especially on social issues.

However, the fact that blacks from low-income backgrounds and Jews from higher-income backgrounds both continue to favor the Democrats despite their differing class backgrounds suggests that something else may be going on as well. We think that something else involves the continuing social exclusion and stigmatization that both groups experience, reminding them that highly conservative and populist forces remain virulently opposed to them. For example, both groups have been excluded from high-status social clubs and country clubs in many cities (Zweigenhaft and Domhoff 1982, Kendall 2008). They are also lumped together and excoriated in white supremacist literature and media as inherently evil and accused of not being true Americans, including on dozens of white supremacist websites on the Internet (Burris 2000).

Our findings on CEO women surprised us in some ways. We were not surprised to find that the CEO women, who had to traverse organizational structures controlled by conservative white men, are not especially liberal politically. It is not a big shock that when Meg Whitman, the former CEO of eBay, decided to run for governor of California, she did so as a Republican, nor is it a shock that when Carly Fiorina, the former CEO of Hewlett-Packard, decided to run for the Senate in California, she, too, did so as a Republican. Nor were we surprised that Angela Braly, the CEO of WellPoint, and as we have noted a big Republican campaign contributor, was against the health care legislation that passed in March of 2010. However, we were somewhat surprised that as the battle over health care legislation raged, her company raised rates by 39 percent on some policy holders, leading one journalist to suggest that President Obama should send the company a thank you note for providing him and the Democrats a classic example of why it was important to pass the legislation (see Carlson 2010). WellPoint, in fact, has been targeted by health care proponents as an insurance company with especially egregious practices, "the poster child for why reform is needed" (Dreier 2009). In the face of such criticism, and questions raised by Congress and by President Obama, Braly remained combative and unapologetic: "I'm not a politician. I'm a businessperson" (Abelson 2010, 6). Wealthy white women born to privilege, like wealthy white men born to privilege, tend to be conservative and they tend to be Republicans. Braly's tone-deaf responses aside, we were most surprised that the companies that had hired women as CEOs did not do better on the various ratings we looked at, especially those that focused on the treatment of female employees.

Enlightened treatment of employees can stem from many causes. Recall, from chapter 2, that by the time Lewis Platt, the Jewish CEO of Hewlett-Packard, was planning to retire, he had been sensitized to the dilemmas faced by single parents in the corporate world. His wife had died, and he had been the primary caregiver for his two daughters. He proceeded to install many worker-friendly policies, such as flextime, shared jobs, and extended unpaid leaves, and by the time he retired the choice of a new CEO came down to one of two women (Ann Livermore or Carly Fiorina). It was Platt, the Jewish man, who seems to have played a key role in establishing a humane work setting at Hewlett-Packard, not Fiorina. (Perhaps Platt's liberal values had yet another effect: one of his daughters became a lawyer who represents prisoners on death row. She explained her work in the following way: "My job is to find the hurt, vulnerable, sad or angry side of the person, and to argue that they need help, not execution"; Tatelli 1999.)

So, too, can unenlightened treatment of employees stem from many causes. One of these is the pressure to achieve the largest possible returns for the company's shareholders. Another is to receive the largest possible payoff for one's own work. As we noted in chapter 1, a September 2010 study showed that in 2009 the CEOs whose companies had laid off the most employees were paid more than other CEOs. This study found that those CEOs whose companies eliminated the most jobs earned 42 percent more in compensation than other *Fortune* 500 CEOs (Anderson, Collins, Pizzigati, and Shih 2010, 4). Moreover—and very much in line with the general conclusion of this chapter, that the new CEOs do not differ in meaningful ways from the old CEOs—the list of "the 50 top recession layoff leaders" included five new CEOs: Fred Hassan, who made $50 million while Schering-Plough laid off 16,000 employees, Kenneth Chenault, who made $16.8 million while

American Express laid off 4,000 people, Ellen Kullman, who made $8.3 million while DuPont eliminated 4,500 jobs, Andrea Jung of Avon ($7.1 million to her, 3,242 layoffs), and Vikram Pandit (of Citigroup, 52,00 layoffs; because the bank had received billions of dollars in federal bailout money, and because of all the bad publicity surrounding huge CEO salaries, Pandit informed the board that he would accept only a token amount until the bank returned to profitability; by 2010, however, that token amount, just $1, was back up to $1.75 million; Craig 2011).

Now that we have shown how the new CEOs do and do not differ from their white male counterparts, we turn to a more detailed analysis of a question that we raised in the first chapter. What made it possible for this diverse group of women and people of color to have the opportunity to rise in the corporate hierarchy?

6

Why Now, and What's Next?

The emergence of seventy-four new CEOs, most of them appointed in the last twelve years, adds a new dimension to earlier studies of diversity in the business world. The white males who dominate corporate boards might feel pressure to include at least one woman, African American, or member of another previously underrepresented group in their midst, or even believe they might be useful as tokens, buffers, or political ambassadors. But we don't think they would appoint a woman, an African American, a Latino, or an Asian American as the CEO of one of the corporations they direct if they thought such a choice would jeopardize profit margins. The decision to ask someone to be CEO, unlike the decision to ask someone to be one of ten or fifteen directors who sit on a board that meets four to ten times a year, is too important to the financial health of the company to be made on the basis of a "diversity" argument. We have to believe that the corporate boards that appointed these seventy-four women, African American, Latino, and Asian American CEOs thought that they were the best available people for the job at the time of those appointments.

Some of those who were the first to be CEOs of *Fortune* 500 companies, such as Katharine Graham, the former CEO of the *Washington Post*, and Marion Sandler, the former cochair of Golden West, had close family connections to the companies they managed. Most of the more recently appointed new CEOs, however, worked their way up in the corporate world and, as we have shown, most were hired as insiders, or previously were employees of the companies that appointed them as CEOs. As they rose through the corporate ranks, they proved themselves to the white male executives above them and, ultimately, to the predominantly white male corporate boards that appointed them. Correspondingly, many of those appointed as outsiders spent many years climbing the corporate ladder at a single company. A. Barry Rand, for example, was an outsider when he was appointed CEO at Avis, but he had previously worked for thirty-one years at Xerox.

Why, then, did this dramatic breakthrough happen when it did? And how is it that so many were appointed during one of the most conservative presidential administrations in modern history and during a period when there was very little pressure from the outside for such appointments?

SOCIAL PROTEST, URBAN UNREST, THE GOVERNMENT, AND THE CORPORATIONS: FROM "AFFIRMATIVE ACTION" TO "DIVERSITY"

As we noted at the beginning of chapter 3, the sit-in movement in the early 1960s led directly in 1964 to the appointment of the first two African American directors of *Fortune* 500 companies. Nine more African American men were appointed as directors of *Fortune* 500 corporations before the first African American woman, Patricia Harris, was asked to sit on the boards of both Scott Paper and IBM in May 1971. By the early 1980s, according to one report, there were sixty-seven African American men and five African American women on the boards of more than a hundred "major U.S. companies" (Moskowitz 1982, 54). The door to the boardroom had opened, though the newly arrived African Americans made up less than 1 percent of the directors at *Fortune* 500 corporations.[1]

In 1961, John F. Kennedy issued an executive order (EO 10925) that called for federal contractors to use "affirmative action" to end discrimination based on "race, color, creed, or national origin." Four years later, in another executive order (EO 11246), Lyndon Johnson extended that to apply to "all work done by contractors and subcontractors (not merely contracted work)" and, in 1967, in yet another executive order (EO 11375), Johnson added sex to the list of protected categories. These orders were to be carried out by the Office of Federal Contract Compliance (OFCC). They were greeted with criticism and grumbling by white male workers and their local union leaders, especially in the building trades, a portent of things to come (Sugrue 2001, 2008).

After Kennedy's assassination in 1963, Lyndon Johnson, who had been the Senate majority leader prior to becoming Kennedy's vice president, used his considerable political skills to guide the Civil Rights Act of 1964 through Congress. Title VII of that act prohibited not only racial and religious discrimination in employment, but gender discrimination as well, even though there had been no agitation or lobbying on gender issues. But a ban on sex discrimination was added at the last minute by a segregationist Southern Democrat at the urging of the few remaining leaders from the National

Women's Party of the Progressive Era, many of them highly conservative by that time. They wrote to and visited with their friend Howard Smith of Virginia, the leader of the segregationist bloc, and other Southern Democrats, reminding them that the Civil Rights Act as originally written would mean that black women would have more rights and protections than white women (Brauer 1983). After winning support for the amendment, which was resisted by Northern Democrats and many liberal women because they feared it might derail the legislation, the Southern Democrats then abandoned support for the act in general. However, in a complete reversal, liberal women and their allies now realized that the act could pass with the amendment in it, so they became staunch supporters. From that point forward the success of the amendment prohibiting sex discrimination was the result of "a small but dedicated group of women in and out of Congress, who knew how to take advantage of the momentum generated by a larger social movement to promote their own goals" (Freeman 2008, 185).

Because conservatives north and south were against the bill, the longest Senate filibuster in history only ended when northern corporate leaders and moderate Republicans insisted that Republican conservatives abandon their support for the segregationist Southern Democrats in order to avoid the spread of disruption and unrest to the north. In addition to believing in segregation, the conservatives feared that passage of the Civil Rights Act would require employers to fill quotas, to practice reverse discrimination, and to adopt race-conscious hiring practices. As a result, as historian Jennifer Delton explains: "The final version of the bill specifically prohibited the use of racial quotas to make up for racial imbalances. It also specified that inadvertent, or accidental, discrimination did not violate Title VII. The bill also prohibited the Department of Justice from filing lawsuits against entities that discriminated, including local governments, a significant setback for civil rights proponents that was insisted upon by the southern white Democrats who still had great power in Congress at the time. However, the bill did allow individuals to sue their employers for discrimination in hiring or employment, a far weaker and slower remedy. Signed into law in July 1964, the bill set up the Equal Employment Opportunity Commission (EEOC) to receive and investigate complaints" (Delton 2009, 35–36; see also Skrentny 2002, 85–142).

These executive orders, and the 1964 legislation, were both weak and ambiguous. As Kelly and Dobbin note: "Executive Orders 10925 and 11246 required federal contractors to take 'affirmative action' without defining the term or establishing compliance guidelines. . . . The Civil Rights Act outlawed discrimination without defining the term or establishing criteria for compliance" (Kelly and Dobbin 2001, 91). Moreover, the two agencies charged with monitoring compliance, the OFCC and the EEOC, had small budgets and small staffs, and were totally underequipped to handle the many complaints that began to pour in. As John Skrentny explains, "A backlog of unexamined cases quickly developed that soon reached more than ten thousand, and the average time of investigation far exceeded the legally defined limit of two months" (Skrentny 2002, 88).

In the absence of clear guidelines, but with the increasing fear of lawsuits, at first many companies did nothing. Kelly and Dobbin (2001, 91) write that "between 1961 and 1969, the ambiguity of these laws in the context of weak enforcement produced little change in employment practices." According to Delton, however, a few companies, like DuPont and Lukens Steel, "enthusiastically" reached out to organizations like the Urban League and to black colleges and community organizations. "Even the conservative National Association of Manufacturers," she writes, "suggested that its members seek out black applicants and make connections to local black organizations" (Delton 2009, 38).

At the same time that the federal government sought to address discrimination through affirmative action, albeit in a way that was unclear, bureaucratic, slow, and ineffectual, the sit-ins and boycotts that characterized the early civil rights movement gave way to serious and often violent urban unrest by those who were marginal to the original movement. Philadelphia and Rochester experienced such unrest in 1964, Watts in 1965, another 38 cities in 1966, and, in 1967, in what was the peak of urban unrest in that era, more than 125 cities erupted, including major riots in Detroit and in Newark (Zeitz 2007; McAdam 1982). Between 1964 and 1968, there were 329 major disturbances in 257 cities, which resulted in 220 deaths, 8,371 injuries, and 52,629 arrests (Downes 1970). As sociologist Douglas McAdam writes about the years 1966–1968: "It would not seem an overstatement to argue that the level of open defiance of the established economic and political order was as great during this period as during any other in this country's history, save the Civil War" (McAdam 1982, 182).

But it was not simply African Americans who were growing impatient with the pace of change. So, too, were women, who found themselves at the bottom of the list when it came to enforcement of the new civil rights law by the EEOC. Reacting to the increasing militancy of the young women who were involved in the civil rights and antiwar movements, as well as to their own sense of frustration with the EEOC, some highly visible and accomplished women, led by Betty Friedan, met in 1966 to discuss the formation of a feminist civil rights organization. At this initial meeting, Betty Friedan wrote down on a paper napkin a possible name for the organization —the National Organization for Women—and she also wrote what was to become its "statement of purpose": "The purpose," she wrote, "is to take the actions needed to bring women into the mainstream of American society, now" (Rosen 2000, 75). At about the same time, what Rosen (79–80) refers to as the "sexier young women's liberation movement . . . sprung to life" (Rosen 2000, 79–80) and in their sometimes overlapping but often very different ways both NOW and the emerging women's liberation movement challenged male-centered exclusionary rules at colleges, in government offices, and in corporations. In effect, the ferment generated by the civil rights movement had led to the establishment of an agency, the EEOC, which made it possible for women to organize an effective movement against gender discrimination by using the government as well as universities as their power base.

In the face of defiance in the streets, some of which took place very close to corporate headquarters, along with court challenges and nonviolent but disruptive demonstrations by women in a variety of settings, various companies took actions on their own. For example, after riots in Rochester, New York, in 1967, Joseph Wilson, the CEO of Xerox at the time, concluded that the company should be much more proactive about integrating its workforce, and he made clear to the managers at Xerox that he wanted "a very aggressive program to recruit and hire African-Americans" (Ferrin 2010). After a group of black workers at Xerox brought a class action suit that was settled in 1971, the company instituted sensitivity seminars for management and affirmative action became "an official business priority" (Lynch 2002, 41). By the mid-1980s Xerox implemented a plan to achieve equitable representation of all employee groups throughout the company, and managers were rewarded for meeting such goals. In 1989 Xerox won a congressionally authorized National Quality Award, designed to recognize companies that demonstrated "quality management," primarily for its active experimentation with workforce diversity strategies (Lynch 2002, 42 and 64; see also Thomas 1994, 45–46; and Anand and Winters 2008, 357). As we noted in chapter 3, one of the programs that emerged at Xerox was a summer internship program for minorities and one of those who participated in the program in the late 1970s was Ursula Burns.

DuPont also responded to racial upheaval in ways that opened the company up to diversity. Following Martin Luther King Jr.'s assassination on April 4, 1968, the city of Wilmington experienced a two-day riot that was small compared to those in other cities, but the governor of Delaware exacerbated the existing racial divisions by sending the entire state National Guard to Wilmington, and then refusing to remove it, even after control had been reestablished. Although the mayor, black leaders, and many other civic leaders (black and white, Republican and Democrat) called for sending the troops home, the guardsmen continued to patrol the streets of Wilmington for more than nine months. Because many local residents, and especially African

American residents, believed that DuPont controlled the state of Delaware, the company, which had a very poor record in terms of the hiring and promotion of minorities and women, was heavily criticized for the governor's overreaction. In response, DuPont's leadership implemented various programs over the next few years to increase the number of minority employees and to advance white women and minorities upward through the management ranks. Delton, who devotes an entire chapter to DuPont's "affirmative action efforts," shows that endorsing diversity also allowed DuPont to augment its long-standing, and highly successful, efforts to combat unions. The company realized that it could use the many "human relations" programs that were already in place to fight unions as part of a program to promote "diversity." As she explains:

> Du Pont is a useful case study because it illustrates this transformation. A conservative company, Du Pont was slow to change. But then it did. Its many human relations programs, developed to fight unions, were easily refitted to the project of recruiting, advancing, and retaining minorities and women. Adopting affirmative action in no way impeded its longstanding antiunionism; indeed, in some ways the new affirmative action programs complemented Du Pont's fight against unions. Racial integration did not require that businesses give up their fundamentally conservative goals. (Delton 2009, 279)

Perhaps not coincidentally, DuPont was one of the first major corporations to appoint a Jewish CEO. When the company named Irving Shapiro as its CEO in December 1973, the *Wall Street Journal* announced this appointment with a headline that read "Boss-to-be at DuPont Is an Immigrant's Son Who Climbed the Hard Way." Rare as it was for an immigrant's son to climb the hard way to the CEO office, the more surprising news was that Shapiro was Jewish, definitely a first at DuPont and at that time quite unusual (probably the first) in the *Fortune* 500 except for the few companies that had been founded by Jews (Zweigenhaft and Domhoff 1982, 57). In January 2009, DuPont again surprised its critics when it named a woman, Ellen Kullman, as its CEO. This suggests that the company's commitment to inclusion following the Wilmington riots may have had long-term effects.

The responses by individual companies like Xerox and DuPont were accompanied by a broader attempt to bring the corporate world on board, not only to quell violence and avoid lawsuits, but also to avoid New Deal type interventions along the lines of public work programs. In 1968, Lyndon Johnson responded to the intense ghetto uprisings in 1967 by asking corporate executives to create a National Alliance of Businessmen (NAB) that would quickly hire and train the "hard-core unemployed" for entry level private-sector jobs using government money (within two years, the program had offered jobs to more than 430,000 people and provided summer employment for 300,000 young people). Even though it was subsidized by government money, the fifteen businessmen on the board (from Ford Motor Company, Coca-Cola, ITT, Aluminum Can, McDonnell Douglas, Levi Strauss, and Mobil Oil) saw it not primarily as a government program but, rather, as Delton puts it, "a chance to show what the private sector could do" (Delton 2009, 229, 231–39.). This program was the real-life, on-the-ground origins of an "affirmative action" program that preferentially hired African Americans. It was a clear attempt to restore public order, although this fact was soon denied or ignored by conservative critics of government programs. The program also aided some of the well-educated African Americans who previously had been excluded from middle-level corporate positions (see Collins 1997, for a fine account of the first "black corporate executives").

By the late 1970s, the corporations had taken control of affirmative action. In the view of Dobbin and Sutton (1998), there was a vacuum that the corporations were glad to fill due to the fact that the legislation was ambiguous and had been enforced inconsistently. As they write: "The ambiguity of compliance standards, expanding scope of the law, and fragmentation of administration led organizations to establish specialty departments to signal a commitment to compliance, to import and invent compliance strategies, and to handle federal regulators. Organizations created new offices not because the law dictated that they do so but because the law did not tell them *what* to do" (Dobbin and Sutton 1998, 470). In other words, the corporations took advantage of the vagueness of the law to create departments that could take the initiative in implementing it in a way that would best fit with their overall interests, including the weakening of the union movement. In the process they developed a large cadre of corporate officers who had an important and lucrative turf to defend.

Moreover, the personnel officers whose new responsibilities included trying to figure out how to implement compliance standards, and how to sensitize employees to issues related to affirmative action, realized that they needed help from outside experts. They knew they needed to be educated and trained on these difficult issues, and many companies brought outside specialists to run programs for employees. Matters became even murkier in 1978 when in the Bakke decision the Supreme Court struck down the University of California at Davis's quota system for admission to its medical school, but it left open the possibility that the admissions process could take into account factors that would allow for a "diverse student body." With what Delton (2009, 280) calls its "rhetorical debut" in the Bakke decision, *diversity* became the term of choice for those who were fighting to save as much as they could of the goals that affirmative action sought to achieve: a more open hiring process that would recruit more members of previously underrepresented groups and a workplace free of discrimination (see also Skrentny 2002, 173–78).

In the years following the Bakke decision, one figure emerged as the person best able to help large corporations with the tricky negotiations of "managing diversity": R. Roosevelt Thomas. After graduating in 1966 from Morehouse College as a math major, Thomas received an MBA in finance from the University of Chicago in 1968. He returned to Atlanta and taught at Morehouse from 1968 to 1970, and then he went to the Harvard Business School where he received his doctorate in business administration with a concentration in organizational behavior and stayed on to teach from 1973 through 1978. During his years at Harvard, he was influenced by two Harvard faculty members, Paul Lawrence and Jay Lorsch, and a book they had coauthored in 1967, *Organization and Environment: Managing Differentiation and Integration*. The book, he told us, sparked some ideas about race in large organizations, though he did not put these ideas into action for a number of years. When he left Harvard in 1978, he spent a year working for Harbridge House, an international management consulting firm founded in 1950 by three Harvard Business School professors. Thomas worked mostly in the area of human relations—he had yet to focus on diversity.[2]

He returned to Atlanta to be a dean at Clark Atlanta University, and, while at Clark Atlanta, he taught an executive workshop called "Managing People" that was intended to give African Americans an opportunity to explore managerial issues. He taught the workshop three times, to favorable responses from the participants, but the enrollments were not huge. At this point, a graduate of Spelman College, who worked at Avon, approached him. Apparently Simmons College had been running a course for Avon women employees identified as having high managerial potential, and she asked Thomas if he might teach a course at Clark Atlanta for high-potential African American employees. Thomas created a three-week workshop that included a day or two on multicultural issues, which he ultimately taught at least a dozen times over several years. Avon sent employees to Atlanta for these courses and indications were that the company was clearly quite pleased.

Thomas left Clark Atlanta University in 1983, consulted for about a year, and then, encouraged by his work with Avon, in 1984 he founded and became the president of the nonprofit American Institute for Managing Diversity, Inc. (AIMD). The president of Morehouse College agreed to house the institute there if it could pay its way. Starting with Avon, and then, initially through word of mouth, the institute found many corporate sponsors, including companies Thomas referred to as "significant players" (in our interview with him, he chose not to identify them). A few years later, when Thomas wrote a widely read article in the *Harvard Business Review*, more and more companies learned about AIMD. Thomas also subsequently founded Diversity Consultants, Inc. as a subsidiary of AIMD, which eventually sold this entity for the purpose of funding a small endowment for the institute (Williams 1992). In 1996 he founded Roosevelt Thomas Consulting and Training ("a full service diversity strategy consulting and training organization"), where he serves as CEO.[3]

Thomas has become lionized in the diversity literature. Frederick R. Lynch, the author of *The Diversity Machine* (2002, 326), refers to Thomas as a "star author-consultant." Frank Dobbin (2009), in his book *Inventing Equal Opportunity*, refers to Thomas as "uber-consultant R. Roosevelt Thomas" (16), as "the celebrity diversity consultant R. Roosevelt Thomas" (148), and as "star diversity consultant R. Roosevelt Thomas" (157). Whatever terms are used to describe him, as of the early 1990s he was earning as much as $10,000 per lecture (Lynch 2002, 59), and as of June 2010 he was asking $20,000 for a keynote address.[4]

During the Reagan years, hard-core conservatives fought hard to dismantle affirmative action (by whatever name it was called). But in a battle between what C. Wright Mills (1956, 122) called "sophisticated conservatives" and "old guard conservatives," the sophisticated conservatives prevailed by broadening the meaning of diversity and providing new rationales for it. By then, as Dobbin and Sutton (1998, 471) put it, the "new human resources management movement was championing diversity as the key to expanding markets and improving innovation," and, for the most part, the corporate world was on board. Even such conservative organizations as the National Association of Manufacturers resisted the Reaganites' efforts to do away with affirmative action: "In 1985, the NAM's EEO Committee voted against Reagan's proposals to weaken the OFCC affirmative action requirements. As the Monsanto Company's EEO director put it, 'We're accustomed to setting goals.' Editors at both *Business Week* and *Fortune* favored preserving affirmative action, noting that government regulators and business leaders had worked out affirmative action guidelines, which had resulted in significant progress in workplace integration" (Delton 2009, 278–79).

By the late 1980s, Roosevelt Thomas and the other early diversity consultants had plenty of competition, as dozens of diversity firms emerged performing hundreds, perhaps thousands, of diversity training sessions, but he remained a central figure in the diversity movement. In 1990, Thomas wrote an article for the *Harvard Business Review* titled "Affirmative Action to Affirming Diversity" (reprinted in Thomas 1994) that summarized the new corporate definition of diversity. He began the article by asserting that "Sooner or later, affirmative action will die a natural death. Its achievements have been stupendous but if we look at the premises that underlie it, we find assumptions and priorities that look increasingly shopworn" (Thomas 1994, 27). The shift Thomas advocated was to diversity, and it was Thomas who coined the term "managing diversity." Companies, he argued, might put money and effort into managing diversity out of social and moral responsibility, or, more likely, to avoid legal challenges, but ultimately for them the motivating force is the bottom line. "I believe," he wrote in the *Harvard Business Review* article, "only business reasons will supply the necessary long-term motivation. . . . Learning to manage that diversity will make you more competitive" (Thomas 1994, 34). As Anand and Winters (2008, 359) assert, with that 1990 *Harvard Business Review* article, "Roosevelt Thomas shifted the paradigm of diversity from compliance to a matter of business survival."

At that point, many corporations had endorsed the shift from affirmative action to diversity, hired diversity officers, put diversity plans into effect, and budgeted for training sessions by one or more of the diversity consultants. By 1990 three out of four *Fortune* 500 firms reported that they had diversity programs and more were planning to implement them within the next year (Hays-Thomas 2004, 4), and about that same time one corporate diversity director reported that she heard from about twenty consultants per week (Kelly and Dobbin 2001, 108). The diversity business was booming (according to a 1992 article in the *New York Times*, "diversity, one of the most popular management concepts of the '90s, is becoming a booming multimillion-dollar business"; Williams 1992). In the process, it had shifted the emphasis from the early commitments to equal opportunity and affirmative action to the more diffuse and encompassing concept of "diversity." As Kelly and Dobbin (2001, 108) write, there were by then a wide range of organizations that provided "ample guidance, in the forms of articles, books, videos, conferences, newsletters, and a growing cadre of consultants, in transforming their EEO [equal employment opportunity] and AA [affirmative action] activities into diversity programs."

In 1994, six Texaco employees brought an antidiscrimination lawsuit against that company on behalf of fifteen hundred other employees. The suit languished for two years until a tape recording was released on which various senior executives spoke of African American employees as "black jelly beans" (as in, "That's funny. All of the black jelly beans seem glued to the bottom"). It turned out that their use of the term "black jelly beans" was inspired (if that is the right term) by an analogy Thomas used in a 1993 speech he gave at an oil industry conference in which different colored jelly beans were used to refer to employees of different races (Eichenwald 1996). The release of the tape was followed by front page stories, which, in turn, were followed by a quick settlement, the largest amount ever issued in a class action suit ($115 million, plus an 11 percent pay raise for all black employees).

In addition, the settlement included the agreement by Texaco to institute an "equality and tolerance task force" and to implement "company-wide diversity and sensitivity programs." As one diversity trainer put it, "What Anita Hill did for sexual harassment, Texaco did for diversity training" (Rosin 1998). Anand and Winters (2008, 356) write that as of 2003 "the diversity business was estimated to be an 8 billion dollar industry."

In 1996, Roosevelt Thomas asserted in a book titled *Redefining Diversity* (like his previous book, published by the American Management Association) that what is meant by the word "diversity . . . has changed and is still changing." As he explained: "At one time *diversity* simply meant variety, the existence of multiple versions of the thing in question," but then, he continued, it became a more delicate way of saying "minorities," and even a "sort of code word for 'African American'; when certain organizations and certain individuals say 'diversity,' they really mean 'black.'" The time had come, Thomas explained, for it to be redefined as "appreciating everyone."

Thomas introduced the phrase "managing diversity" to describe the need for creating an environment that enabled all employees to reach their full potential, and he concluded that he found himself "coming back full circle, semantically speaking," because a word that had once meant "multiple versions of the thing in question" and then narrowed itself to just "different kinds of people," now had widened out again (Thomas 1996, xi–xii).

Thus, the argument for diversity, which had replaced affirmative action, was that it was good for business.[5] And since diversity meant "appreciating everyone," it was only good business for corporations to maintain diversity officers and to budget for extensive diversity programs that drew on the expertise of the many consultants who had now carved out a small industry for themselves. But does diversity improve the situation for African Americans, the people who had forced the issue of fairness after centuries of enslavement and Jim Crow exclusion, or make them less visible? This is a question we discuss later in the chapter.

By 2003, when the administration of George W. Bush sought to undermine affirmative action by challenging the admissions policies at the University of Michigan Law School, the sophisticated conservatives in the corporate community again rose to defend the importance of maintaining diversity in admissions. *Fortune* 500 corporations filed briefs, as did the military and organizations representing higher education, which supported the University of Michigan in its policies. The majority decision, written by Sandra Day O'Connor, made explicit mention of these briefs from *Fortune* corporations:

Major American businesses have made clear that the skills needed in today's increasingly global marketplace can only be developed through exposure to

widely diverse people, culture, ideas, and viewpoints. High-ranking retired officers and civilian military leaders assert that a highly qualified, racially diverse
officer corps is essential to national security. Moreover, because universities,
and in particular, law schools, represent the training ground for a large number
of the Nation's leaders (Sweatt v. Painter), the path to leadership must be visibly
open to talented and qualified individuals of every race and ethnicity. Thus, the
Law School has a compelling interest in attaining a diverse student body (cited
in Zweigenhaft and Domhoff 2006, 137).

The Supreme Court, therefore, endorsed the very "path to leadership" that
had assisted many of the African Americans who had risen to positions of
importance in the power elite, including not only Ursula Burns, but one of
the dissenting members of the Supreme Court, Clarence Thomas, who had
been accepted at Yale Law School due to the pressures of affirmative action.
Well, maybe it was the same path. Ursula Burns and Clarence Thomas had
benefited from the early days of affirmative action. The Supreme Court was
endorsing the more watered down, corporatized concept of diversity. Still, the
endorsement of diversity might keep the pipelines flowing for entry into the
corporate world, and perhaps ascendance to the highest positions of power in
the corporation.

Before we turn to the question of whether the pipelines are flowing for all
previously excluded groups, it is important to acknowledge that the sophisticated conservatives once again had beaten back the old guard conservatives,
and the corporate world had become key advocates of diversity, in part because they had played such a central role in defining what diversity was and
what it was not. As Delton explains: "Diversity is almost wholly a corporate
creation, the product of human resources departments. After decades of
'voluntarism' and compliance, corporations had finally succeeded in gaining
control and leadership over the social and demographic changes of the twentieth century. Corporations linked 'diversity goals' to business objectives—the
global marketplace, immigration, manpower—and wove them into personnel
management" (Delton 2009, 281). But are the pipelines still flowing in an age
when there is little or no pressure from social movements or the government
to maintain diversity?

ARE THE PIPELINES FLOWING?

The incorporation of diversity into the corporate structure and the corporate
culture implies that there will be women, African Americans, Latinos, and
Asian Americans in the pipeline, moving upward through the educational
system and the corporations to fill positions in upper management. The evi-

dence is that there are women in the pipeline. As we demonstrated in the first chapter, the increase in the number of women CEOs over the past decade has been much more dramatic than for the other groups we have studied. Moreover, according to the American Council on Education, for the last ten years about 57 percent of the college undergraduates have been women, and women earned higher grades than men (Williams 2010). There has also been an increase in the number of women attending business and law schools. The *Digest of Education Statistics* reports that in 2007–2008 women earned 44.6 percent of the MBAs and 47 percent of the law degrees (tables 289 and 295).[6]

Despite the encouraging educational data, women continue to face obstacles once they enter the corporate world, where the stakes—money and power—are much higher. The most recent report by Catalyst, part of a longitudinal project based on the responses of more than four thousand women who received MBA degrees from twenty-six leading business schools, was not encouraging. Focusing on women who worked full time at companies at the time of the survey, the authors called their study "Pipeline's Broken Promise" and concluded that

> The pipeline is in peril. . . . Women lag men in advancement and compensation from their very first professional jobs and are less satisfied with their careers overall. . . . It's not a matter of different aspirations. The findings hold even when considering only men and women who aspired to CEO/senior executive level. It's not a matter of parenthood. The findings hold even when considering only men and women who did not have children. (Carter and Silva 2010a; see also Carter and Silva 2010b)

Ilene Lang, the president and CEO of Catalyst, expressed her frustration by asserting that "the 'give it time' excuse is just that—an excuse" (Lang 2010).

The percentage of women in the uppermost management positions has leveled off. In a report titled "Women in Management in the United States: 1950–Present," Catalyst found that after steady increases between 1995 and 2002, this trend did not continue: the percentage was 15.7 in 2002, and still 15.7 in 2008 (*Women* 2010). Moreover, women still face genuine obstacles in some sectors of the economy, such as in the world of technology (Miller 2010) and Wall Street (Fabrikant 2010). Our conclusion is that there are, and will continue to be, women in the pipeline, but the percentage of likely candidates for promotion decreases the closer one gets to the top. There will continue to be a small number of women CEOs, and the number might increase somewhat, but it is likely to be a very long time before the percentage of women *Fortune* 500 CEOs is even close to the percentage of women in the larger population. They will remain a highly visible but small group of *Fortune* 500 CEOs.

This grim assessment corresponds to the conclusion we drew in 2006 when we noted that many factors seemed to combine to drive women off the pathway to the top, including an often coarse and male-centered culture that stereotypes women, the still rather closed clubby environment in which white men are more comfortable playing golf, having dinner, and simply hanging out with one another than with women or people of color, and the still unbending work schedule and travel necessities that force many women to choose between their careers and a manageable family life. Some women do stay the course, but others spin off into human relations or public relations positions within the company, start their own small businesses, or work as diversity consultants in their own firms, helping to train the next generation of aspiring women executives (Zweigenhaft and Domhoff 2006, 78–79). We therefore continue to believe that for the most part senior male executives have found ways to incorporate women into the corporate world without ceding any power to them. Even after a decade in which many "new CEOs" have been appointed, as of 2010 about 475 of the *Fortune* 500 CEOs (that is, 95 percent) are men.

If education is the first step toward the CEO office, a prerequisite if you will, then a sufficient number of Asian Americans satisfy this prerequisite to allow for a regular flow into the management pipeline. According to a 2009 report by the U.S. Census, more than 53 percent of all Asian Americans over the age of twenty-five have bachelor's degrees (the corresponding figure for other Americans was 33 percent for non-Hispanic whites, 19 percent for African Americans, and 13 percent for Hispanics). Asian Americans are also more likely than other Americans to have advanced degrees—29 percent have master's degrees, professional degrees (e.g., law degrees, MDs) or doctoral degrees, compared to 9 percent in the general population ("Current Population Survey," U.S. Census, 2009). Asian Americans make up only 4 percent of the population, but in the 2007–2008 academic year, they earned 8.7 percent of the MBAs, 8.8 percent of the law degrees, and 9.8 percent of the master's degrees in engineering. They earned an even higher percentage (11.2) of the master's degrees in computer and information sciences (*Digest of Education Statistics*, tables 289 and 295), as can be seen in their highly visible presence in high-technology firms in Silicon Valley (at one point, estimates indicated that three hundred of the nine hundred high-technology firms in Silicon Valley were headed by Asian Americans; Park 1996).

As is the case with women in the corporate world, once Asian Americans are in management positions there seem to be barriers to advancement (Thompson and DiTomaso 1988; Woo 1994; Hing and Lee 1996; Takamine 2000, 2002; Iwata 2004). They have been stereotyped as not sufficiently assertive, and many have been shunted into highly technical jobs. A few have emerged as CEOs through an entrepreneurial route that has allowed them to completely sidestep such stereotyping, by founding their own companies (Jerry Yang, the cofounder and former CEO of Yahoo comes immediately to mind). Moreover, as we showed in chapter 4, many of the Asian American *Fortune* 500 CEOs were born outside of America, have economically privileged socioeconomic backgrounds, and are highly educated. This is the case for the current CEO of Coca-Cola (Muhtar Kent, from a prominent Turkish family) and the CEO of PepsiCo (Indra Nooyi, from a Brahmin Indian family). In addition, it turns out that the highly visible Asian American immigrant CEOs are only the tip of the corporate and professional iceberg. According to a study by the nonpartisan Fiscal Policy Institute for the *New York Times*, more Asian American immigrants held white-collar jobs than lower-wage jobs in fourteen of the twenty-five largest metropolitan areas. Many of the twenty-five million immigrants who live in the country's largest cities arrive with high levels of education, and many prove to be valuable to corporations in just the ways that we would expect based on the careers of the immigrant CEOs (Preston 2010).

Latinos, the largest and fastest growing ethnic minority group in the United States, are now about 15 percent of the population, surpassing African Americans at about 13 percent. In striking contrast to Asian Americans, they are the least likely of the four underrepresented groups to complete high school and the least likely to attend or graduate from college, which is not unexpected because they more often come from low-income backgrounds and arrive as young adults. As we noted earlier, census data indicate that in 2008 only 13 percent of the Latinos older than twenty-five had completed college degrees.[7] Moreover, in an annual evaluation of the twenty-five best MBA programs for Hispanics, Elsie Morales writes that "Hispanics may account for 14 percent of the U.S. population, but they remain grossly underrepresented in MBA programs" and especially at the top thirty programs (Morales 2010, 1). Figures from the *Digest of Education Statistics* support this claim: Latinos earned only 5.5 percent of all the MBAs given at the end of the 2007–2008 academic year. Similarly, they earned only 6.4 percent of the law degrees conferred that year (*Digest of Education Statistics*, tables 289 and 295).

As is the case for the Asian American CEOs, many of the Latino CEOs were born outside the United States, though some of the most prominent, like Roberto Goizueta of Coca-Cola, come from upper class families in Cuba and left that country shortly before or after its 1959 revolution. Still, there are many other Latin American countries, and many of their residents come to work in corporate America. For example, Amparo ("Ampy") Kollman-Moore, was born in Cartagena, Colombia, and earned a bachelor's degree from the Colombo-American Cultural Institute. She moved to St. Louis in

1970 and rose through the corporate ranks at Mallinckrodt, a $2.8 billion dollar medical supply company. In 1996 she became the president of the company's Latin American division, a $100 million business, and in that capacity she led a staff of two hundred employees. Along the way, she received a master's degree in international business from St. Louis University, where she now teaches as an adjunct faculty member. She understands quite well how her knowledge of more than one culture, and more than one language, helped her professionally: "I made a wonderful career out of understanding the cultures of Latin America and the culture of the United States and how to do business in both." As one reporter portrayed her upscale lifestyle, she lives "on a posh suburban cul-de-sac" (Preston 2010). Though she is not one of the *Fortune* 500 CEOs identified in chapter 4, her successful corporate career reminds us that there is a healthy stream of well-educated immigrants who work in the management ranks of many of the country's largest corporations.

Latinos face the least daunting barriers in terms of stereotypes, especially when they are lighter skinned and phenotypically white. We therefore think the Latino pipeline will continue to flow at a fairly high level, but always below the Latino percentage of the population because of the continuing influx of new low-income adults, especially from Mexico and Central America. This strong flow is especially likely when we take into account that a small but increasing number of men and women from the upper classes in a wide range of Latin American countries are likely to work as managers in American corporations, whether they start in some other country the way Carlos Gutierrez did with Kellogg in Mexico or Alain Belda did with Alcoa in Brazil, or start in this country and then go abroad to begin their move up the corporate ladder.

WILL BLACK PROGRESS CONTINUE?

Although we think the pool of women, Asian American, and Latino corporate executives will continue to expand at the entry and middle levels, we are not so sure in the case of African Americans even though they provided 20 percent of the seventy-four new CEOs and are about 13 percent of the country's population. This is because African Americans face the historically unique "confluence of race, slavery, and segregation" (Pettigrew 1988, 24). They are not in the same situation as immigrants, as seen in comparisons with West Indians and other immigrants of African descent, who are more likely to be successful in the business world and politics for a number of reasons discussed by Mary Waters (1999) and Philip Kasinitz (1992). Therefore, in this section we provide a detailed analysis of the pipeline for black executives.

Although overt racism has declined, more subtle forms of rejection and exclusion persist, which lead to discouragement and withdrawal for many black children by the time they reach their high school years (e.g., Jones 1997; Dovidio 2001; Hodson, Dovidio, and Gaertner 2010). Even for those African Americans who persist in their pursuit of education and have the same credentials as whites, there are invisible forms of job discrimination, as shown in detail for black graduates of a trade school who fare less well than white counterparts in obtaining a job even when they have better school records (Royster 2003). The same pattern occurs at the very top of the corporate system; retired white generals are far more likely to receive lucrative corporate positions, and be invited to join corporate boards, than their equally qualified black counterparts (Moskos and Butler 1996, 50). Based on these systematic findings, it should come as no surprise that African Americans have more difficulty in accumulating the "transformative" wealth assets that make it possible for a family to send its children to college or maintain its socioeconomic standing in the face of long-term illnesses or temporary job losses (Shapiro 2004; Oliver and Shapiro 2006).

Critics of affirmative action argue that market-based incentives are now enough to ensure fairness to African Americans in hiring and promotion, but those who study African Americans in the labor force, such as Sharon Collins (1997), are not so sure. They adduce evidence to suggest that opportunities for African Americans are created by politically mediated means, such as the civil rights movement, riots and property destruction near downtown office buildings, and government programs. If they are right, there is likely to be a decline in the rate of progress, or even a fallback overall, unless the disappearance of government-mediated pressures can be replaced by other sources of support.

We begin our independent assessment of these issues with the finding that 19.6 percent of African Americans over the age of twenty-five have completed undergraduate work, which is slightly higher than the figure for Latinos, but much lower than that for non-Hispanic whites and Asian Americans. Nevertheless, African Americans earned 13.3 percent of the master's degrees in business in 2007–2008, according to the *Digest of Education Statistics*, 65 percent of which were awarded to women. As for law degrees, African Americans earned only 6.8 percent in 2007–2008 and, as was true for the MBAs, far more women than men earned these degrees (63 percent of the African Americans who completed law school were women).

These findings on business and legal education for African Americans would be less impressive if it were not for the emergence over the past five decades of a special corporate-mediated pipeline focused primarily on increasing the number of African Americans in important positions in elite

American institutions, whether business, universities, nonprofit groups, or government. This pipeline begins with programs created to give a boost to elementary school youngsters, some as young as kindergarten age, and it includes programs for middle school students, secondary school students, undergraduates, and graduate students.

To begin with an example of efforts on behalf of very young children, a program called Early Steps was created in 1986 by a group of New York independent schools to increase diversity in that city's elite private elementary schools. As the current executive director explains on the organization's website, the program's mission is to guide "the parents of children of color through the process of applying to independent schools for kindergarten and first grade." By 2009 more than twenty-three hundred children had gone through the program, some of whom have now completed secondary school and gone on to college and to graduate programs.[8] Half of Early Steps's funding comes from its forty-seven independent school partners, and the other half comes from foundations (the organization's board includes headmasters and deans of admissions from various independent schools, and senior executives of corporations).

Turning to the elementary school level, an heir of the Block Drug Company fortune, Michael P. Danziger, created the Steppingstone Foundation in 1990 to provide a program for elementary school children in Boston that since has expanded to two other cities. Although it is primarily an after-school tutoring program for children in the fourth and fifth grades who might qualify for elite educations, its students also participate in a six-week summer session. According to its website: "The goal of the Steppingstone Academy in Boston is to prepare the Scholars to get into, and succeed at, top independent and public exam schools. Success at these schools opens doors previously unimagined to the Scholars." In 1998 the program expanded to Philadelphia, and in 2006 to Hartford. By 2009, Steppingstone was serving 950 students, its alumni had gone on to attend many elite colleges and universities (for example, 14 had gone to Harvard and 5 to Yale), and some had gone on to do postgraduate work at graduate schools, medical schools, and law schools. Among the members of the board of the Steppingstone Foundation are, or have been, John S. Weinberg (Goldman Sachs), Brent E. Shay (Wells Fargo) and Luis A. Ubinas (the president of the Ford Foundation and a childhood friend of Danziger's at the elite Collegiate School in New York; Strom 2007).[9]

Between 2003 and early 2009 the Steppingstone Foundation received 261 grants totaling $8.6 million according to the *Foundation Grants Index Online*, most of which was provided in yearly amounts of $5,000 to $40,000 by the dozens of family foundations created by wealthy corporate families in Boston, Philadelphia, and Hartford. However, it also received $949,000 from the Richard and Susan Smith Family Foundation, based on the billions Richard Smith made through General Cinema; $400,000 from the Block Family Foundation controlled by Danziger's family; and $234,000 from the Boston Foundation, one of many community foundations across the country that supports local nonprofits. (The Boston Foundation, in turn, received its money in large measure from some of the same family foundations that give directly to Steppingstone, such as the Barr Foundation, the largest foundation in Massachusetts with $1 billion in assets, founded by Amos Hostetter, Jr., born into wealth and the founder of Continental Cablevision.)

The oldest and most successful corporate-mediated program designed to help students attend elite boarding schools is A Better Chance (ABC), about which we have written previously (Zweigenhaft and Domhoff 1991, 2003). The brainchild of three New England prep school headmasters, one of whom was Charles Merrill (an heir to the Merrill Lynch fortune), the program began operations in 1963, financed in part by a grant from the Rockefeller Foundation, and a year later fifty-five teenage boys (most of whom were African Americans, but some of whom were Latinos and other students of color) were given scholarships to attend the country's most elite boarding schools. Within a few years ABC was sending more than five hundred students per year to boarding schools and to a small number of very good public schools (mostly in college towns like Amherst, Massachusetts; Hanover, New Hampshire; and Clinton, New York). Sandra Timmons, the program's president since 2003, reports that there are currently nineteen hundred ABC students—65 percent black, 20 percent Latino, 6 percent Asian American, 4 percent multiracial, and 4 percent "other"—in more than three hundred member schools, and that there now are more than twelve thousand alumni of the program.[10]

For many years the main source of funding for ABC was corporate foundations, and every year the annual reports include such familiar names as American Express, Coca-Cola, Goldman Sachs, the Limited, PepsiCo, International Paper, Bristol-Myers Squibb, J. P. Morgan Chase, and Texaco. According to the 2009 annual report, the two largest grants ABC received between September 1, 2008, and August 31, 2009, were from GE and the Morgan Stanley Foundation (both "$100,000+"). More generally, the program received its largest donations between 2003 and early 2009 from the investment banking firm Morgan Stanley ($425,000) and the New York Community Trust ($375,000), which like the Boston Foundation receives its funds from family and corporate foundations, such as $3 million from the Revson Foundation (cosmetics) and $1.2 million from financier George Soros's Open Society Institute. ABC also received $224,000 from the Bialkin Family Foundation (corporate law on Wall Street).

The program continues to receive key leadership from those in the corporate world. The four officers on the current board are Ronald R. Pressman, president and CEO of GE Capital Real Estate; Timothy C. McChristian, a vice president at IBM (and an ABC alum—Andover, 1973); Louise M. Parent, executive vice president and general counsel at American Express; and A. Richard Janiak, managing director at Citigroup. It also has an advisory board that includes ABC alumni who work as executives for American Express, Bank of America, Bloomberg LP, Credit Suisse, MetLife, and UBS, and as lawyers for corporate law firms in Atlanta and New York.

ABC now has been around for so long that some of its most successful early alumni have made enough money to make substantial contributions to the program (for example, the 2009 annual report notes that Tracy Chapman, the well-known singer songwriter, a 1982 ABC graduate of the Wooster School, gave between $25,000 and $50,000, and other ABC alums gave between $10,000 and $25,000). In addition, ABC has established relationships with some highly visible African Americans in the entertainment world, none more visible than Oprah Winfrey who by 2000 had contributed more than $12 million to the organization, and who since then has been ABC's national spokesperson.

So far, none of the ABC graduates has become the CEO of a *Fortune* 500 company, but some of the earliest graduates have attained senior positions in *Fortune* 500 companies and some have become directors of *Fortune* 500 corporations and various nonprofit organizations. For example, William M. Lewis, Jr. (Andover, 1974; Harvard, 1978; MBA Harvard, 1982) worked for Morgan Stanley for twenty-four years until he left in 2004 to become managing director and cochairman of investment banking at another global investment firm, Lazard Frères and Company. It was against company policy at Morgan Stanley to sit on corporate boards, but once he moved to Lazard Frères Lewis went on the board at the Federal Home Loan Mortgage Corporation, known as Freddie Mac, and on the board of Darden Restaurants. Lewis also has been on many nonprofit boards, including both ABC and Andover, the American Museum of Natural History, the Cancer Research Institute, the Carnegie Endowment for International Peace, the Urban League, and the United States Golf Association.

The ABC graduate who thus far has become the highest-ranking executive at a major corporation, Deval Patrick, now the governor of Massachusetts, did so thanks to a major boost from the controversial Texaco "black jelly beans" case we discussed earlier in the chapter. Raised in a large Chicago ghetto by a single mother, Patrick graduated from Milton Academy in 1974 and earned BA and LLB degrees from Harvard in 1978 and 1983. After nearly a decade with a prestigious Boston corporate law firm, he first received national attention in 1994 when Bill Clinton appointed him to be the head of the Civil Rights Division of the Department of Justice. He left the Clinton administration in 1997 and was soon asked to oversee the implementation of the settlement in the race discrimination case against Texaco. Two years later he became a vice president and general counsel at Texaco, and after four years with Texaco he became executive vice president, general counsel and corporate secretary at Coca-Cola. Along the way, he has served on the board of directors at Texaco, Coca-Cola, United Airlines (UAL), and Ameriquest.

As seen by Patrick's career as a lawyer, corporate executive, and elected official, the ABC program has been an important source of African American leaders in many areas of American life. Not only do 96 percent of all ABC students go straight to college, but many attend the very best colleges in the country (the ten colleges most frequently attended by ABC graduates are the University of Pennsylvania, Harvard, Columbia, Brown, Wesleyan, Yale, Tufts, Cornell, Dartmouth, and Stanford; see Zweigenhaft and Domhoff 2003, 65). A 2005 survey of ABC alumni indicated that 53 percent had earned graduate or professional degrees, and, of those, 22 percent had earned MBAs. Almost half of the respondents (47 percent) indicated that they have had careers in business, finance, or law. A 2010 survey of ABC alumni showed similar results, along with the more specific finding that 36 percent of the respondents worked for corporations.[11]

A similar picture emerges from our analysis of the self-reported information that is provided by many—but by no means all—of the thousands of ABC graduates in the *2005 Alumni Directory*. We recorded the names of each alumnus who completed the ABC program by 1995, and who also had received an MBA degree, a law degree, or both: 207 earned MBA degrees (116 men and 91 women) and 250 earned law degrees (152 men and 98 women). Those with an MBA received their degrees from many different schools, though the most frequently attended were Harvard (21), Columbia (19), Stanford (10), UCLA (8), New York University (7), Northwestern (7), and the University of Pennsylvania (7). Some are now working for *Fortune* 500 corporations like Avon, Bank of America, Citigroup, Continental Airlines, IBM, and Merrill Lynch, and some of those are at the vice presidential or senior manager level. Similarly, the law school students went to a wide range of schools, with NYU (14), Georgetown (13), Harvard (12), the University of Pennsylvania (8), the University of Virginia (8), Columbia (7), and Rutgers (7) at the top of the list. Most are working as attorneys in various capacities (in large firms, in small firms; for local, state, or federal government; or other nonprofit organizations), some teach law, some are judges, and some are in the corporate world working for large firms like

Bank of America, BP, Bristol-Myers, Coca-Cola, Exxon, Goldman Sachs, UnitedHealth Group, and Wachovia.

Because of the nature of their experiences at predominantly white boarding schools, graduates of the ABC program are especially well prepared to become diversity specialists if they choose to do so. For example, both La-Pearl Winfrey, a professor and associate dean at the School of Professional Psychology at Wright State University in Dayton, and Greg Pennington, a clinical psychologist who is now the vice president for Human Resources and Senior Leadership Development at Johnson Controls in Milwaukee (#83 on the *Fortune* 500 list in 2010), have directed many diversity-training programs for managers in corporate settings. Similarly, William H. Foster, III, a professor of English at Naugatuck Valley Community College in Connecticut, has conducted diversity programs in schools, corporations, and community agencies. Having spent years at boarding schools like The Masters School (Winfrey) and Western Reserve Academy (Pennington), or excellent public schools like the Amherst Regional High School in Amherst, Massachusetts (Foster), they learned early on how to interact with white people from privileged backgrounds, and how to help them understand and appreciate people of color (Zweigenhaft and Domhoff 2003, 105–6).

This pattern is supported by a recent study of an unidentified program that prepares gifted students of color for placement at elite boarding schools. In his study of a program pseudonymously called RISE, Kramer (2008) found that many of the student participants developed what he calls a "diversifier mindset" when they subsequently attended predominantly white secondary schools. After concluding that their white classmates were hopelessly naive, they decided early on that part of their mission, and increasingly a part of their identity, was to help their white classmates understand an increasingly multicultural world. As Kramer (2008, 288) writes: "The students of color enrolled in the program consider themselves 'diversifiers' of their new prep schools and find a sense of worth and pride in their position as the Other." Kramer's findings suggest that many ABC students, and many students in more recently created programs, might become candidates for positions in the diversity management industry.

Although ABC continues to guide several hundred students of color to elite secondary schools each year, it is no longer the only game in town at the middle and high school levels. Over the years, many other programs, some of them city-based, some regional, and some national, have emerged with the goal of increasing diversity in the educational settings that are especially likely to lead to high-level corporate positions and, for a few, a shot at the CEO office. To take the most prominent example, Gary Simons, a South Bronx school teacher, who was doing graduate work at Columbia University's Teachers College, created Prep for Prep in 1978 to identify promising students of color in New York City and prepare them for independent schools in the city and boarding schools throughout New England. In its first year, the program included three teachers and twenty-five students. Thirty years later, in 2008, when it celebrated its thirtieth anniversary, the mayor of New York City declared the day of the celebration "Prep for Prep" Day. As is the case for Steppingstone and ABC, many Prep for Prep alums have attended elite colleges, and now many have gone on to do postgraduate work (including one Rhodes scholar). According to its website, 92 percent of the program's 1,828 college graduates have graduated from "competitive colleges" and approximately 40 percent have graduated from Ivy League schools (the five most frequently attended colleges have been Harvard, with 171; Wesleyan, with 168; Yale, with 148; Penn, with 147; and Columbia, with 122).[12]

Although the program's founder began his career as a public school teacher, for the last few decades Prep for Prep has been directed by Wall Street lawyers and financiers. The former chair of the board is Martin Lipton, a name partner in the Wall Street firm of Wachtell, Lipton, Rosen and Katz. He was succeeded as chairman of the board by John L. Vogelstein, a senior advisor at the investment bank E. M. Warburg, Pincus & Co. and the managing director of New Providence Asset Management. The president is Scott L. Bok, formerly a managing director at Morgan Stanley and now the CEO of Greenhill and Co., Inc., an investment banking firm. Over the years, Prep for Prep has received tens of millions of dollars from corporate and family foundations. Aileen C. Hefferren, the CEO of Prep for Prep, reports that in the 2009 fiscal year the organization raised $8.8 million from "individual, corporate, foundation and alumni funders," with more than half coming from the members of the board.

The donors to whom the Prep for Prep CEO is referring were led between 2003 and early 2009 by the New York Community Trust ($2.4 million) and Prep for Prep board chair John Vogelstein's Family Foundation ($2.2 million), followed by the Sol Goldman Family Foundation based in a real estate fortune ($1.4 million), and the Third Point Foundation financed by a Wall Street financier ($1.3 million). (For those who want more detail on how this educational support system is funded, the family, community, and corporate foundations that gave large donations to one or more of the four preparatory programs we have discussed—Early Steps, Steppingstone, ABC, and Prep for Prep—are listed in table A3.1 of appendix 3, along with the amounts they gave to each program).

There are also several programs that provide economic and other support for talented students of color with an interest in business careers once they have become undergraduates. For example, for more than twenty-five years the Harvard Business School has sponsored the Summer Venture in Management Program (SVMP), a one-week-long summer program for rising college seniors designed to increase diversity in business schools and in corporate America. As explained on the website, the students "spend evenings analyzing real business cases, and use morning study groups and classes to examine and debate their ideas through lively interaction with peers and faculty." In short, the website goes on to explain, "This is the life of an MBA student at HBS." There is no guarantee that participants will subsequently be admitted to the Harvard Business School, but it helps the school identify promising candidates. All expenses are covered including tuition, room, and board, thanks to the many corporate sponsors that constitute a who's who of *Fortune* 500 companies (in 2009, the sponsors included American Express, Bank of America, Citigroup, Duke Energy, and Exxon Mobil, just to pick five from the top of the alphabet).

In 1970, Frank C. Carr, a white Catholic corporate executive with strong religious convictions, quit his job and founded INROADS, a Chicago-based program dedicated "to develop and place talented minority youth in business and industry and prepare them for corporate and community leadership." That first year found INROADS paying internships for twenty-five college students at seventeen participating corporations. Now, according to the organization's website, INROADS has gone international, with forty offices serving more than twenty-three hundred interns at more than two hundred corporations. The program is supported by fees from corporate clients and foundation grants. Over the past two years, upon graduating from college, 85 percent of the interns were offered full-time positions by the companies that sponsored their internships. The INROADS website includes profiles of a number of "alumni success stories" from among its total alumni population of more than twenty-three thousand over almost three decades, including Pamela Parker, a senior vice president at the Bank of America, William B. Jones, a vice president at Anheuser-Busch, Teri P. McClure, a senior vice president at United Parcel Services (UPS), and Lisa Hamilton, who heads the UPS Corporate Public Relations Group. It appears that many INROADS alumni hold managerial positions in the corporate world and are part of a pipeline that could potentially lead to the CEO office.

In addition, some companies sponsor their own programs. For more than thirty years, Xerox has run a summer internship program called the Xerox College Experiential Learning program (XCEL). More than three thousand students from all over the country have participated. The internships are paid positions, with opportunities to work full time (and in some cases receive academic credit). The program recruits at highly regarded universities, and seeks interns through the National Society for Hispanic Professionals and the

National Society of Black Engineers. For example, Terrance Hamilton, a doctoral student in computer science at the University of California, Riverside, first learned about the Xerox program, the same one in which Ursula Burns participated in 1980, while attending a meeting of the National Society of Black Engineers. Three years in a row, from 2003 through 2005, he left California to spend his summers participating in the XCEL program.[13] He now is a software engineer for Xerox, living in Rochester, New York.

As this brief overview of the corporate-mediated educational network demonstrates, it seeks out promising students of color as early as kindergarten and continues through programs that target graduate students. Without these programs, the statistics for African Americans completing postgraduate business degrees, law degrees, and masters and doctorates in fields such as engineering and computer science would be even lower than they are now, although how much lower we cannot estimate with certainty. However, we can be sure that the numbers of African Americans at elite colleges and universities almost certainly would be lower. According to the statistics provided by the federal government's National Center for Educational Statistics, 7.5 percent of the students enrolled at Ivy League schools in 2008 were black.[14]

Although the corporate-mediated system augments the number of African Americans who graduate from college, and thus become legitimate candidates for management jobs in the corporate world, they are underrepresented among college graduates, among those who graduate from Ivy League schools, and among those who earn higher degrees (though not among those who earn MBAs). In fact, over 40 percent of the students who define themselves as black at prestigious universities such as Princeton and Duke are the children of black immigrants or have one nonblack parent, and some have estimated that they are a majority at Harvard (see Rimer and Arenson 2004).

The general presence of African Americans in the corporate world can be gauged in part through our study of the National Black MBA Association, which was founded in 1970 to provide support and networking opportunities for black executives in general, whatever their academic background or type of employment, as seen by the fact that not all members have an MBA and a significant minority of members work in the nonprofit sector for charitable and fundraising groups, hospitals and medical clinics, elected officials, and government agencies. The group holds annual meetings that are heavily attended by recruiters from major corporations as well as black executives who are not part of the organization (there were between nine thousand and twelve thousand attendees at their meetings in the years between 2008 and 2010). There are also forty-four chapters in major cities across the United States that hold local events throughout the year, often in conjunction with well-known corporations, as well as student chapters on fifteen college campuses, including Bethune-Cookman University, Hampton University, the University of Maryland, North Carolina State University, Ohio State University, and Winston-Salem State University.[15]

The association received financial support from thirty major corporate foundations from 2003 through 2008, starting with $1 million from the Chrysler Foundation, followed by $700,000 from Duke Energy, $245,000 from General Motors, and $208,000 from PNC (a bank that became a "financial services company" in Pittsburgh). Other highly visible donors include Aetna, AT&T, Coca-Cola, General Electric, Kellogg Corporation, Eli Lilly and Company, Procter & Gamble, and Verizon.

Although the association does not release statistics on college backgrounds and corporate affiliations, it does report that 65 percent of its eight thousand members have MBAs, that 76 percent of its members are forty years of age or under, and that there is an even gender balance. In addition, 14 percent of the members earn between $100,000 and $200,000 per year, and 2 percent earn more than $200,000.

If the board of directors is to any degree a cross-section of the more successful senior members, then most of the association's members have bachelor degrees from small non-elite liberal arts colleges and large state universities. Those who have MBAs also tend to earn them from non-elite universities (e.g., Baldwin-Wallace, Long Island University, Marquette, and Pepperdine), although one board member who is a senior manager at a major accounting firm has a Harvard MBA and another is a real estate lawyer who has both an MBA and a law degree from Harvard.

The highest-ranking executive on the board is John Peoples, a former diversity consultant who is now president and general manager for Canadian operations at S. C. Johnson and Son (often called Johnson's Wax), one of the largest privately owned companies in the country (and thus not ranked by *Fortune*), which specializes in home cleaning products such as Drano, Pledge, Shout, and Windex. Peoples is closely rivaled in stature by Keith R. Wyche, the president of Cub Foods, a retail grocery chain with seventy-eight stores in four Midwestern states, which is a subsidiary of Supervalu (#47 on the 2010 *Fortune* 500 list).

Two other directors have high-level jobs as well, one as the chief procurement officer at Bristol-Myers Squibb, the other as the director of strategic planning and manufacturing at Ford Motor. Three have their own consulting firms, which include an emphasis on diversity, and two have management positions in large firms, American Express and Exxon, that focus on diversity. Rounding out the board are the general counsel for the Public Broadcasting System and an urban affairs expert who works closely with Bill and Hillary Clinton.

Based on these findings, we conclude that the National Black MBA Association is a major interface between aspiring black executives, black-owned companies, and the middle levels of the white corporate world, especially at the time of its national meetings. However, it does not seem to be an escalator to the top for the overwhelming majority of its members. It seems more likely that they will continue to work at the middle levels for corporations, nonprofits, and government agencies, usually specializing in personnel management, marketing, and sales.

There is, however, an organization that provides a way for us to estimate the likelihood that blacks will make it to the top in corporate America. The exclusive Executive Leadership Council (ELC), founded in 1986 with just nineteen members, is limited to African Americans who are within three steps of the CEO office in *Fortune* 500 companies, and who also oversee substantial corporate budgets.

Reflecting the rise of black executives in the 1990s, there were 275 members in the ELC by 2001, three-fourths of whom were men (Daniels 2002). As of 2008, the number had increased to 400, two-thirds of whom were men (Carlton and Klassen, 2008).[16] Those within three steps of the top include black men who hold the job titles of president of McDonald's USA, president of Xerox Canada, and a vice president for supply and procurement at Coca-Cola. The black women include the managing director for global philanthropy at J. P. Morgan Chase, a vice president for Kelly Services, and a senior vice president for human resources at Kraft Foods.

In addition to providing a place for top black executives to network with each other and discuss the opportunities for the younger black executives they mentor in their respective companies, the ELC carries out numerous programs for executives at all rungs of the corporate ladder through its Executive Leadership Foundation. The process begins with a three-day program for new executives, "Bright Futures," which features guest speakers, the analysis of business case studies, and group discussions. There is also a five-day "Strengthening the Pipeline" project, described on the ELC's website as the "flagship leadership developmental program" offered by its Institute for Leadership Development & Research. It is meant for "mid-career managers, senior project leaders, directors, and new vice-presidents." There is also a two-day program specifically tailored for black women executives and a black women's leadership group that spends a day or two meeting with government officials in Washington for background briefings. All of these programs cost several thousand dollars to attend.

The many programs carried out by the ELC are made possible by the funding that its foundation receives from large corporations, even more than is received by the National Black MBA Association. This funding begins with the $2,075,000 it received between 2003 and 2008 from BP (now famous for the oil spill in the Gulf of Mexico in 2010), along with $375,000 from General Electric, $375,000 from PepsiCo, and $300,000 from UPS. When smaller grants from other corporate foundations are added to the picture, it suggests to us that corporate America now sees the ELC as playing the same role for the incorporation of black executives that Catalyst plays for women executives. Table 6.1 presents a list of the top ten funders for the ELC and the National Black MBA Association, showing that they shared two major funding sources in common (Coca-Cola and Duke Energy).

Despite the corporate-mediated pipeline and the training institutes and opportunities for networking provided by the National Black MBA Association and the Executive Leadership Council, we nonetheless believe that the percentage of African Americans continues to decline at each step of the corporate ladder even more rapidly than it does for women, Latinos, and Asian Americans. We first of all base this conclusion on a racial, ethnic, and gender analysis of executives at various salary levels that was provided to us by Roderick J. Harrison, a sociologist at Howard University who also has done important work for the Joint Center for Political and Economic Studies on its DataBank, a roster of black elected officials. As can be seen in table 6.2, which includes the number of executives who earned $50,000 or more, $100,000 or more, or $250,000 or more between 2005 and 2008 while working for corporations, partnerships, or wealthy entrepreneurs, the percentage of white men increased at the higher income levels (from 74.4 percent, to 77.6 percent, and to 79.6 percent) while, correspondingly, the percentages for white women, African Americans, and Latinos decreased (the figures stayed

Table 6.1. Largest Ten Corporate Donors to the National Black MBA Association and the Executive Leadership Council, 2003–2008

National Black MBA Association		Executive Leadership Council	
Donor	*Amount*	*Donor*	*Amount*
Chrysler	$1,000,000	BP	$2,075,000
Duke Energy*	$700,000	General Electric	$375,000
General Motors	$245,000	PepsiCo	$370,000
PNC (finance)	$208,000	UPS	$300,000
Citigroup	$135,000	Coca-Cola*	$225,000
Coca-Cola*	$105,000	Moody's	$100,000
Cardinal Health	$100,000	Duke Energy*	$76,000
Eli Lilly and Co.	$95,000	AT&T	$30,000
Delphi	$90,000	Williams Companies	$26,500
Verizon	$75,000	MBIA	$25,000
Total =	$2,753,000		$3,602,500

Note: The source for the information in this table is the *Foundation Grants Index.*

*These companies gave to both the NBMBAA and the ELC.

Table 6.2. Percentages of Executives Earning $50,000+,
$100,000+, and $250,000+ in 2005–2008 Who Were White Men,
White Women, African Americans, Latinos, and Asian Americans

	$50,000+	$100,000+	$250,000+
Total *n* =	566,492	415,265	12,973
White men	74.4	77.6	79.6
White women	15.3	12.9	12.4
Asian American males	3.2	3.7	3.4
Latinos (males)	2.6	2.3	2.2
African American males	1.4	1.3	1.0
Asian American females	0.7	0.6	0.6
Latinas (females)	0.7	0.5	0.5
African American females	0.5	0.3	0.3
Other	.8	.8	

steady for Asian Americans, at about 4 percent, the percentage they represent in the larger population). More to the point, the percentages for white women dropped from 15.3 to 12.4 percent at the highest level, from 3.4 to 2.7 percent for Latinos, and from 2 to 1.3 percent for African Americans. These same general patterns also hold when the sample is subdivided on the basis of who earned master's degrees, professional degrees, or doctoral degrees.[17] We would also note that the findings for women are similar to what was reported in the Catalyst study summarized earlier in the chapter.

It is also noteworthy that the gender ratios for African Americans gradually reversed themselves after college graduation. Although African American women receive more bachelor's and master's degrees, including MBAs, the men outnumber the women by a ratio of 2.7 to 1 at the $50,000+ level, 3.6 to 1 at the $100,000+ level, and 3.2 to 1 at the $250,000+ level, thereby mirroring the gender differences that existed for Latinos and Asian Americans from graduate training onward. (White men were slightly more likely than women to earn MBA and law degrees in 2008—white men earned 59 percent of the MBAs earned by whites, and 56 percent of the law degrees—but for those who earned at least $50,000, the ratio of white men to white women was 4.8 to 1, for those who earned at least $100,000 it was 6.0 to 1, and for those who earned at least $250,000 it was 6.3 to 1).

But to what extent are those who make over $250,000 a year part of the *Fortune* 500 community? This question is not easily answered because there are no available lists of the highest-paid black executives. However, the size of the Executive Leadership Council is the first of two starting points that we use to provide new estimates. Recalling that the ELC had four hundred members in 2008, at first glance this number appears to be a straightforward approximation of the pool of potential African American CEOs. Unfortunately, there are two complicating problems.

First, one-fourth of the current members are not candidates for a CEO position because they have retired, become entrepreneurs, manage black-owned businesses, or left their *Fortune* company job for other reasons, according to an estimate provided to us by one ELC researcher. On the other hand, there's reason to believe that about a quarter of the African Americans who hold positions within three steps of the CEO office do not join the ELC, so it may be that the two problems in making a precise estimate balance each other out.

We base this claim that the two balance each other out on the fact that three of the fourteen African American CEOs (Richard Parsons, former CEO of Time Warner, Aylwin Lewis, former CEO of Kmart, and James Bell, former interim CEO of Boeing) did not join the ELC prior to becoming *Fortune* 500 CEOs.[18] If we therefore assume that only about three-fourths of those who are eligible to do so actually join the organization, and further assume that there are about three hundred ELC members who are currently employed by *Fortune* 500 companies, then we can estimate that there are about four hundred African Americans within three steps of *Fortune* 500 CEO offices.

To turn that raw number into a percentage we relied on estimates (based on interviews with corporate executives) that most *Fortune* 500 companies have anywhere from 20 to 150 people in jobs at those three levels, depending on the size of the company.[19] Using the same conservative estimate of 20 people per *Fortune* 500 company that we used in 2003, we conclude that there is a relevant cohort of about 10,000 people. We therefore can estimate that African Americans constitute about 4 percent (400 divided by 10,000) of those within three steps of the CEO position, about the same as the 3–5 percent estimate we made in 2003 based on ELC membership at the time (Zweigenhaft and Domhoff 2003, 137). If we were to double the estimate of the number of people within three steps of the CEO office from 20 to 40, enlarging the cohort pool to 20,000, this would reduce the estimate for the number of African Americans from 4 percent to 2 percent. Either way, African Americans are more underrepresented at the steps below the CEO level than are other underrepresented groups.

We are able to cross-check this estimate and narrow our focus from three steps from the CEO office to just one step thanks to a second approach made possible by the increasing corporate use of the Internet to introduce potential investors and customers to what is variously called its "management team," "executive team," "corporate leadership," or "senior leadership committee," all of whom typically report directly to the CEO. Starting with #1 on the 2010 *Fortune* 500 list, we selected the first five corporations whose websites included both photographs and information about educational degrees earned for their senior executive officers. If the corporation's website did not include either photographs or the degrees earned and the schools attended for the majority of the senior executives, we simply skipped that company and went on to the next one on the *Fortune* list; we then did the same thing four more times, starting with #101 on the list, #201 on the list, #301, and #401. The final sample of twenty-five companies included such well-known names as Bank of America, General Electric, MasterCard, Staples, Verizon, and Western Union.[20] We entered each executive's name into a file, coding for gender and ethnicity, degrees obtained, and the schools from which they received these degrees. We also coded for whether or not the senior manager was the CEO of the company (which allowed us to exclude those who are CEOs from the others on the management team).[21]

This process produced a sample of 307 senior executives. As might be expected from our earlier results on education background, almost all of these men and women had gone to college and many had earned postgraduate degrees: 29.7 percent had MBA degrees, 16 percent law degrees, and another 17 percent either an MA, a medical degree, or a doctoral degree. Since we also know that most future CEOs are inside candidates or are senior officers at other *Fortune* 500 firms, this sample can be seen as a representative snapshot of the candidate pool when it comes to the actual appointment of a *Fortune* 500 CEO, although this statement needs to be qualified somewhat due to the fact that those in staff positions, such as legal officers (usually called "general counsel"), public relations officers, and human resources officials are far less likely to be chosen for the top spot compared to the "line" executives who have responsibility for the units that make and sell the company's product, thereby contributing to revenues and profits. Table 6.3 shows that the majority of these senior corporate officers were white males (66.0 percent), a finding that should surprise no one at this point in the book. Not quite one in five (18.8 percent) were white women, 7.8 percent were Asians (mostly men), and 4.2 percent were Hispanic (mostly men). For African Americans, the flow through the pipeline was indeed down to a trickle, with only 2.6 percent (seven males, one female).

This finding that there are only 8 African Americans in the top circle at 25 companies implies that there are only about 160 African Americans one step from the CEO's office in the entire *Fortune* 500. We were able to check this estimate further by finding the black executives in the remaining *Fortune* 500 companies that provided pictures on the Internet for their leadership group. We found photographs for 3,072 executives at 262 companies, 91 of whom were African Americans (69 men, and 22 women, a ratio of 3.1 to 1 that is consistent with our findings on executives making $250,000 and over). This finding on black executives at the additional 262 companies (3.0 percent) is almost exactly what we expected based on our original sample of 25 corporations. Either using the first 25 companies we looked at, or the subsequent

Table 6.3. Senior Executives at Twenty-five *Fortune* 500 Corporations

	Number	Percentage	High School or BA Only	Master's Degree	MBA	Law Degree	PhD or MD	Ivy League
White men	204	66.0	70	20	61	30	10	37
White women	58	18.8	14	7	15	12	4	9
African American men	7	2.3	0	1	3	5	0	3
African American women	1	0.3	1	0	0	0	0	0
Latinos	11	3.6	2	2	4	1	1	2
Latinas	2	0.6	1	0	1	0	0	2
Asian American men	20	6.5	3	3	7	1	4	4
Asian American women	4	1.3	1	0	3	0	0	0
Totals	307	99+	92	33	94	49	19	57

262 companies, we conclude that there are only between 150 and 160 black executives currently on senior leadership teams. Moreover, if we examine the positions held by the 99 black executives in the full sample of 287 corporations, we find that 45 percent of them have staff appointments such as general counsels, public relations officers, and human resources officers, which as we noted, are less likely to lead to CEO appointments. This is especially the case for the 23 women in the full sample, 18 of whom have such positions.

When our findings are analyzed in terms of the number of companies with at least one African American in the top management group, there are only 76 in the total sample of 287 corporations, just over one in every four, because 16 companies have two or more black leaders, with General Mills (5), Merck (4), Eastman Kodak (3), and PepsiCo (3) heading the list. (After we did this general analysis in the summer of 2010, one of the four black executives at Merck, Kenneth C. Frazier, was named CEO as of January 2011.) There are no obvious similarities among these 76 companies except for the fact that 11 of them are public utilities companies, including 6 (CMS Energy, Entergy, Exelon, Pacific Gas & Electric, Progress Energy, and Scana) with two African American leaders, 70 percent of whom have operational bottom-line responsibilities.

Furthermore, just as we found five years ago that the larger corporations were more likely than smaller ones to have African Americans on their boards of directors (Zweigenhaft and Domhoff 2006, 100–101), so too in this study are the largest companies more likely to have black managers or executives within the corporation's inner circle. For companies in the top 100 and for companies ranked between 101 and 200, 4 percent of the executives on the leadership teams were black; for the companies ranked 201 to 300, the percentage dropped to 2.1 percent; for the companies ranked 301 to 400, the percentage dropped to 1.9 percent, and for the companies ranked 401 to 500 it dropped to 1.1 percent.[22]

So whether we look at salaries over $250,000 a year, the number of members in the elite Executive Leadership Council, or the number of African Americans known to be part of the top leadership teams at 287 *Fortune* 500 firms, we conclude that they are very few in number and a smaller percentage of the pool of potential CEOs than is the case for white women, Latinos, or Asian Americans.

WILL THE PROGRESS CONTINUE?

The findings on the proportions of various groups at high salary levels and on senior management teams confirm our previous conclusion that we will continue to see women appointed as CEOs with some regularity (though nowhere near to the degree we might expect now that women earn almost half of all the MBA and law degrees). It is also likely that there will be more Latino and Asian American CEOs, most of whom will be males, and many of whom will have been born and educated outside the United States (among the thirty-seven Latino and Asians in our sample from the leadership teams of the twenty-five corporations, slightly more than half were born and educated outside the United States, many of whom currently head global operations for their companies in other parts of the world). However, as our detailed analysis in the previous section concluded, we do not expect any increase in the percentage of African Americans who become CEOs, even though some of the African Americans in this sample appear likely to be serious contenders for the CEO office in their own company or some other *Fortune* 500 company (e.g., Raymond J. McGuire, the head of global investment banking at Citigroup, a graduate of Hotchkiss, with undergraduate, law, and MBA degrees from Harvard).

Based on information compiled in 1980, Nancy DiTomaso, a professor of management and global business at Rutgers, concluded that African Americans held only 4.7 percent of the executive, administrative, and managerial positions even though they were 11.7 percent of the population at the time. Nor did she see the prospects for the future as any better because African Americans were receiving only 4 percent of the master's degrees in business and management (Latinos were at 1.5 percent, and Asians Americans at approximately 3 percent).

Moreover, she predicted that the situation for Latinos and Asian Americans was more likely to improve than for African Americans because their enrollments in higher education had increased from 1976 to 1985 by 20.5 percent for Latinos and 54.5 percent for Asian Americans at a time when the numbers for African Americans had declined by 19.2 percent (DiTomaso and Thompson 1988, 5). She and a coauthor came to similar conclusions in 2004 drawing on then-current information (Post and DiTomaso 2004, 2). Our findings, based on statistics gathered between 2005 and 2010, suggest that DiTomaso's conclusions are still accurate.

We also conclude from our findings in this chapter that the "market-is-enough" theory of occupational advancement is very likely wrong. The small percentage of women and people of color who make it to senior leadership teams despite their excellent educations and career experience is solid evidence that politically mediated remedies are needed to increase diversity at the very top. In the case of African Americans, the failure of the market-mediation theory is masked in part by the injection of a relative handful of elite-trained African American students from the corporate-financed educational and support network, although it is also clear that some African Americans have made their way in the white corporate world after graduating from HBCUs and state universities.

THE CONTINUING IRONY OF DIVERSITY

Diversity, as we have made clear throughout this book, has many meanings and dimensions. It helped save the little that remained of earlier affirmative action programs from the full ravages of old guard conservatives. Then it became a useful part of the corporate community's desire to create and dominate a globalized corporate economy. But its most important dimensions are ironic ones that struck us very early in our work on diversity in the American power structure (Zweigenhaft and Domhoff 1998, 2006).

Based on the research that we have presented in this book, by us and others, we continue to see the rise of diversity as an irony. It was generated as a response to social movements that called for greater equality, fairness, and social justice, but it ended up in good part as a way to stabilize the social system by providing opportunities for women from high-income families, young adults of color who have gained the educational skills and social capital provided by a prep school education, and well-to-do immigrants who earn highly visible corporate and political positions. These changes did bring about somewhat greater diversity within the corporate elite, but those who earn more than $250,000 a year in executive positions are still overwhelmingly white (92 percent) and overwhelming male (86.2 percent). In fact (and here is another irony), if the diversity programs served to undercut labor unions, as Delton (2009) suggests, then the new diversity may have contributed to the increased gaps in wealth and income between those at the top and other workers. At the least, diversity did nothing to prevent greater inequality even though it brought some individuals into the corporate power structure.

Our analysis of the stabilizing dimension of diversity has its roots in social psychological studies of tokenism, which show that putting a very few members of the excluded group into the privileged in-group decreases the likelihood of the deprived group taking any collective action to change the social structure. Instead, most members of the out-group turn to individual striving rather than providing leadership for social movements. They may even develop a degree of self-blame because they are not among the few in their group who have risen to the top. Others may come to be more accepting of their situation out of knowing and liking a few members of the in-group (Wright and Taylor 1998, 1999; Wright and Lubensky 2009; Pettigrew 2010). These small-group experimental findings fit with the more general real-world sociological argument that the emphasis on individual striving in America's deeply rooted liberal ideology invariably leads to an analysis of social problems that ends up by blaming the victim for what is in fact a product of the social structure (Ryan 1976; Sennett and Cobb 1972).

Our argument, however, has to be tempered by the fact that interactions between the dominant group and the excluded group can lead to a decrease in prejudice by the dominators, thereby making social change more likely. It also is complicated by the fact that increased group contact can heighten the awareness on the part of the newcomers of the relative deprivation between the haves and the have-nots, making them more, not less, likely to call for change. Clearly, the context of the interactions must be taken into account, for, as Pettigrew (2010, 426) points out, there is a "complex relationship between intergroup contact and the mobilization of the disadvantaged for social change." In the case of the context we have focused on—mostly dominant white male CEOs and the relative handful of new CEOs from previously unrepresented groups—we do not see either of these tempering factors playing a key role, and we therefore conclude that the increased contact has decreased the likelihood of mobilization for major social change.

Drawing on the more positive outcomes that can take place when there are close interactions between the dominators and the dominated, various events in American racial history have been seen as turning points, starting with the Supreme Court decision in 1954 outlawing the legislatively mandated segregated schools in Delaware, Kentucky, Maryland, Missouri, Oklahoma, and West Virginia as well as the eleven states that seceded from the Union in 1860. The early years of the civil rights movement reinforced the sense for many observers that the racial situation was about to change, and there have in fact been considerable declines in various antiblack beliefs and actions.

The appointment of Colin Powell as chairman of the Joint Chiefs of Staff in 1989 by President George H. W. Bush was seen as a major turning point by two sociologists, one black, one white, who spent their careers studying race relations. They concluded that his appointment was "an epic event in American race relations, whose significance has yet to be fully realized" (Moskos and Butler 1996, 114). More recently, the election of Barack Obama to the presidency in 2008 is sometimes hailed as another turning point.

However, the careers of Colin Powell and Barack Obama also can be seen as exceptions that reinforce traditional values and maintain the status quo. That is, each was able to avoid or overcome racial barriers for well-known reasons that have been documented in many studies, including ours—lighter skin color, parents who immigrated to the United States, an upbringing in a military family or a career in the military, attendance at an elite private school or a Catholic high school (where discipline is strict), or a biracial heritage.

Powell, as a case in point, is a light-skinned son of West Indian immigrants who pursued a career in the least discriminatory institution in American society, the military, so he is an exception on not one but three factors. As for Obama, he is a light-skinned biracial person raised in predominantly white environments by his white mother and maternal grandparents, and he also had the advantage of seven years at an elite and overwhelmingly white private school for the wealthy in Honolulu, an undergraduate degree from Columbia, and a law degree from Harvard, along with a summer internship at a prestigious corporate law firm in Chicago and a year working for a corporation in New York. And yet, the focus of his story as he tells it, and as his vociferous critics exaggerate and distort it, is on his four years with his mother in Indonesia, where he attended a Muslim-oriented elementary school, his internal musings about his African father, who he saw for a few days at a time only once or twice in his life, his three years as a community organizer after college, and his self-chosen adult identification as an African American.

The ironies of diversity were no better on display than in the Republican Party in the years between 2000 and 2008. With only one black elected official in Congress, J. C. Watts, a former Democrat from the House district encompassing the University of Oklahoma, where he starred as the Sooners' quarterback; with a small percentage of black delegates to the presidential conventions in 2000, 2004, and 2008; and with an even smaller percentage of black supporters in the electorate, the Republicans nonetheless flooded those conventions with black speakers and celebrities at every possible opportunity. They thereby sought to demonstrate to African Americans and whites alike that their extreme conservatism did not include racism. Even more ironically, Bush appointed more African Americans to his cabinet (four), including Powell as secretary of state, than any other president except Clinton (who appointed five), and he appointed the same number of Latinos as Clinton did (three; see Zweigenhaft and Domhoff 2006, 115–18, 156–60 for details).

Several studies of the social backgrounds of CEOs show, as does ours, that most of them do not come from the top 1 or 2 percent of the social ladder. Instead, they come from the top one-third, which leads many political scientists and commentators to breathe a sigh of relief. The United States, they conclude, is a pluralistic and open society after all. As for the very few who do rise from the bottom two-thirds to the top few percent, they rarely do so without help of some kind, such as a scholarship or assistance from a relative.

Even most stories about millionaires who rise from rags to riches, or who became millionaires despite dropping out of college, usually do not survive careful scrutiny. For example, Sam Walton, the founder of Wal-Mart, was indeed from a low-income family and, after graduating from college, he did work as a management trainee at J. C. Penney, but he also had a father-in-law who was a well-to-do small-town banker and rancher who could loan him $20,000 in 1945 (the equivalent of $242,420 in 2010 dollars), a sum of money that less than 10 percent of present-day Americans have in their savings accounts or stock portfolios. Or, to cite another popular example, William Gates, the Microsoft multibillionaire, is not your usual college dropout but the son of a corporate lawyer in Seattle and a graduate of the elite Lakeside School in that city. He left Harvard after a year and a half to pursue what he realized was a once in a lifetime opportunity that he was able to capitalize on thanks to the skills and contacts that he had developed in prep school and at Harvard.

Sociologists have documented the rigidity of the class system in articles with titles like "Law and Inequality: Race, Gender . . . and, of course, Class" (Seron and Munger 1996) and "Class in the United States: Not Only Alive, But Reproducing" (Kendall 2006). But upper class novelist Louis Auchincloss, a graduate of Groton and Yale, and a Wall Street lawyer for most of his life, put it more bluntly in an interview with the *Financial Times* in 2007, three years before his death at age ninety-two: "I grew up in the 1920s and 1930s in a nouveau riche world, where money was spent wildly, and I'm still living in one! The private schools are all jammed with long waiting lists; the clubs—all the old clubs—are jammed with long waiting lists today; the harbors are clogged with yachts; there has never been a more material society than the one we live in today. . . . Where is this 'vanished world' they talk about?" he asked. "I don't think the critics have looked out the window!" (Noble and McGrath 2010). Like Auchincloss, we can only shake our heads in puzzlement at those who claim that America in recent years has been characterized by Horatio Alger rags to riches stories and upward mobility.

The problems of climbing up from the bottom are greatly magnified for the vast majority of African Americans who are not from the small (and usually lighter skinned) black middle class that developed during the century of segregation, are not descendants of West Indians (such as Colin Powell, former congresswoman Shirley Chisholm, and Obama's attorney general, Eric Holder), or do not have a biracial heritage and a white upbringing (such as Harvard law professor Lani Guinier, *New Yorker* author Malcolm Gladwell, and, of course, Barack Obama). Attitudes toward African Americans are more positive, and they are accorded courtesy and respect in public settings by most white Americans, but neighborhoods are almost as segregated as in the past and schools are more segregated in the North and in the South than they were thirty years ago (Pettigrew 2008). Even before the great recession caused by the bursting of the housing bubble and Wall Street financial gambling, African Americans had far fewer wealth assets than white Americans: the wealth gap between whites and blacks more than quadrupled over the course of a generation, increasing from $20,000 in 1984 to $95,000 in 2007 (Shapiro, Meschede, and Sullivan 2010).

That gap has grown even larger because housing in African American neighborhoods has lost even more value than housing in white neighborhoods, along with a greater number of foreclosures, destroying much of the wealth that the black middle class had accumulated (Shapiro, Meschede, and Sullivan 2010). For example, a study in 2010 by the Pew Research Center demonstrated that the percentage of blacks who said that their homes are now worth less than they owe was almost twice as high as it was for whites (35 percent as opposed to 18 percent), as are the percentages for unemployment or reductions in hours of work per week (Austin 2010).

There are some black millionaires, especially in the worlds of entertainment and sports, but there are not very many, far fewer than in the white population (Oliver and Shapiro 2006, Shapiro 2004, Shapiro, Meschede, and Sullivan 2010). As for high black incomes outside the worlds of entertainment and sports, if we look again at the government statistics on all those executives and professionals who made over $50,000 a year between 2005 and 2008, and focus strictly on whites and African Americans, there were 521,995 whites compared to only 11,271 African Americans; therefore, although whites outnumber blacks by 6 to 1, the ratio of those earning more than $50,000 is just over 46 to 1.

Thus, the small amount of diversity we have documented in this book by focusing on seventy-four CEOs does not translate into an open and equality-oriented social structure in terms of opportunity, education, and income. No matter how many individual exceptions seem to exist, and there may even be several million in a society of 300 million people, the lives of most Americans are severely circumscribed far more than most people realize by class, color, and gender.

Appendix 1

The New CEOs: A List

This appendix provides the names and basic biographical information on the seventy-four new CEOs that we discuss in the main text of the book—date of birth, educational background, the company for which they serve (or have served) as CEO, their directorships outside their home corporation (if any), and their membership (if any) on any of five major policy discussion groups that are thought by some political sociologists to have an important role in formulating general corporate policies on key issues and in preparing corporate leaders for appointments to top-level government positions (Burris 2008; Useem 1984; Domhoff 2010, chap. 4)

Fifty-two of the seventy-four CEOs are—or once were—members of the boards of ninety-six companies other than their own. Eighteen of the companies have had two or more of the seventy-four on their boards at one time or another in recent years. PepsiCo's board has included four of the new CEOs in addition to its own CEO, Indra Nooyi, as has Citigroup, where Vikram Pandit is CEO. Cisco, Coca-Cola, General Motors, Procter & Gamble, and Staples have hosted three of the diverse CEOs as outside directors.

Thirteen of the CEOs in this appendix are or have been members of the Business Council, whose role as an informal advisor to the executive branch of the federal government goes back to the 1930s (McQuaid 1982). The Business Roundtable, founded in 1972, and known through network analysis to be at the heart of the corporate policy network since that time, includes or has included eight people listed in this appendix, all of whom also have been or are members of the Business Council (Burris 2008). The much larger Council on Foreign Relations, which has over two thousand members, many of them foreign policy experts and journalists, has extended membership to eight of the diverse seventy-four. The Conference Board, with three, and the

Committee for Economic Development, with one, trail far behind the other three policy groups.

As might be expected from earlier research, it is the CEOs with the most outside corporate directorships who tend to be in policy groups, and especially the Business Council/Business Roundtable nexus. It therefore can be concluded that the following eight CEOs who serve or have served on both the Business Council and the Business Roundtable are or have been central figures in the corporate community above and beyond their home corporations: Brenda Barnes, CEO of Sara Lee from 2005 to 2010, with five outside directorships; Kenneth Chenault, CEO of American Express, with three outside directorships; Fred Hassan, CEO of Schering-Plough, with one outside directorship; Anne Mulcahy, CEO of Xerox from 2001 to 2009, with two outside directorships; Antonio Perez, CEO of Eastman Kodak, with one outside directorship; Patricia Russo, CEO of Lucent Technologies from 2002 to 2008, with three outside directorships; Ronald Williams, CEO of Aetna, with two outside directorships; and Patricia Woertz, CEO of Archer Daniels Midland, with one outside directorship.

Perhaps readers will find other patterns and links in the information that follows.

1. **Aguirre, Fernando** (1958–)
   CEO: Chiquita Brands (2004–)
   College: BS, 1980 (Business Administration), Southern Illinois University
   Fortune 1000 directorships held: Coca-Cola Enterprises, Univision Communications

2. **Alapont, Jose** (1951–)
   CEO: Federal Mogul (2005–)
   College: BS (Industrial Engineering), Universidad Politecnica De Valencia
   Postgraduate: PhD (Philology), Universitat de València

3. **Ayer, Ramani** (1947–)
   CEO: Hartford Financial Services (1997–)
   College: BA, 1969 (Chemical Engineering), Indian Institute of Technology
   Postgraduate: MS, PhD, 1973, Drexel University

4. **Babrowski, Claire** (1957–)
   CEO: Acting CEO, RadioShack (2007)
   High school: Ottawa Township High School, 1975 (Ottawa, IL)
   Postgraduate: MBA, 1995, University of North Carolina
   Fortune 1000 directorships held: McDonald's, Toys "R" Us

5. **Banga, Ajay** (1960–)
   CEO: MasterCard (2010–)
   College: BA (Economics), Delhi University
   Postgraduate: MBA, 1981, Indian Institute of Management
   Fortune 1000 directorships held: Citigroup, Kraft Foods
   Policy groups: Council on Foreign Relations
6. **Barad, Jill** (1951–)
   CEO: Mattel (1997–2000)
   High school: Whitestone Academy (Whitestone, NY)
   College: BA, 1973 (English and Psychology), Queens College
7. **Barnes, Brenda** (1953–)
   CEO: Sara Lee (2005–2010)
   High school: East Leyden High School (Franklin Park, IL)
   College: BA, 1975 (Economics), Augustana College
   Postgraduate: MBA, 1978, Loyola University Chicago
   Fortune 1000 directorships held: Avon Products, New York Times, PepsiAmericas (subsidiary of PepsiCo), Sears, Roebuck & Co., Staples
   Policy groups: Business Council, Business Roundtable
8. **Bartz, Carol** (1948–)
   CEO: Yahoo (2009–)
   High school: Elma High School (Elma, WI)
   College: BA, 1971 (Computer Science), University of Wisconsin.
   Fortune 1000 directorships held: Autodesk, Cisco Systems, Intel, Network Appliance
9. **Belda, Alain** (1943–)
   CEO: Alcoa (1999–2008)
   College: BA, 1965 (Economics), Mackenzie University, Brazil
   Fortune 1000 directorships held: Citigroup, DuPont, IBM
   Policy groups: The Conference Board
10. **Bell, James A.** (1948–)
    CEO: Interim CEO, Boeing (2005)
    College: BA, 1971 (Accounting), Cal State
    Fortune 1000 directorships held: Dow Chemical
11. **Braly, Angela** (1961–)
    CEO: WellPoint (2007–)
    High school: Richardson High School, 1979 (Richardson, TX)
    College: BA, 1982 (Finance), Texas Tech
    Postgraduate: JD, Southern Methodist University
    Fortune 1000 directorships held: Procter & Gamble
    Policy groups: Business Council

12. **Burns, Ursula** (1948–)
    CEO: Xerox (2009–)
    High school: Cathedral High School (New York, NY)
    College: BS, 1980 (Engineering), New York University
    Postgraduate: MS, 1981 (Mechanical Engineering), Columbia University
    Fortune 1000 directorships held: American Express, Banta, Boston Scientific

13. **Cantu, Carlos** (1993–2003)
    CEO: ServiceMaster (1994–1999)
    College: BA (Agricultural Economics), Texas A&M
    Fortune 1000 directorships held: Exelon, Unicom

14. **Chenault, Kenneth** (1951–)
    CEO: American Express (2001–)
    High school: Waldorf School (Garden City, NY)
    College: BA, 1973 (History), Bowdoin
    Postgraduate: JD, 1976, Harvard
    Fortune 1000 directorships held: IBM, Procter & Gamble, Quaker Oats
    Policy groups: Business Council, Business Roundtable, Council on Foreign Relations

15. **Conde, Cristobal** (1959–)
    CEO: SunGard Data (2002–)
    High school: Nido de Aguilas (the American School in Santiago)
    College: BS, 1981 (Astronomy and Physics), Yale

16. **de Molina, Alvaro** (1957–)
    CEO: GMAC Financial Services (2008–2009)
    High school: Bergen Catholic High School, 1975 (Oradell, NJ)
    College: BA (Accounting), Fairleigh Dickinson University
    Postgraduate: MBA, Duke University; MBA, 1988, Rutgers
    Fortune 1000 directorships held: Bank of America

17. **Diaz, Paul** (1961–)
    CEO: Kindred Healthcare (2004–)
    College: BA, 1984 (Finance), American University
    Postgraduate: JD, 1988, Georgetown University

18. **Elsenhans, Lynn** (1956–)
    CEO: Sunoco (2008–)
    College: BA, 1978 (Math), Rice
    Postgraduate: MBA, 1980, Harvard
    Fortune 1000 directorships held: International Paper

19. **Ferguson, Roger W. Jr.** (1951–)
    CEO: TIAA-CREF (2008–)
    High school: Sidwell Friends (Washington, DC)
    College: BA, 1973 (Economics), Harvard
    Postgraduate: JD, 1979; PhD, 1981 (Economics), Harvard
    Policy groups: Committee for Economic Development, Council on Foreign Relations
20. **Fiorina, Carly** (1954–)
    CEO: Hewlett-Packard (1999–2005)
    High school: Charles E. Jordan High School (Durham, NC)
    College: BA, 1976 (Medieval History and Philosophy), Stanford
    Postgraduate: MBA, 1980 (Marketing), University of Maryland; MS, 1989 (Management), MIT
    Fortune 1000 directorships held: Cisco Systems
21. **Frazier, Kenneth C.** (1954–)
    CEO: Merck (2011–)
    College: BA, Pennsylvania State University
    Postgraduate: JD, Harvard Law School
    Fortune 1000 directorships held: Exxon Mobil
    Policy groups: Council on Foreign Relations
22. **Fuller, Marce** (1960–)
    CEO: Mirant (2001–2005)
    College: BS, 1983 (Electrical Engineering), University of Alabama
    Postgraduate: MS, 1984 (Engineering), Union College
23. **Gangwal, Rakesh** (1953–)
    CEO: US Airways (1998–2001)
    High school: Don Bosco School, Park Circus (Kolkata, India)
    College: BTech, 1975 (Mechanical Engineering), Indian Institute of Technology
    Postgraduate: MBA, 1979, University of Pennsylvania
    Fortune 1000 directorships held: Boise Cascade, OfficeMax, PetSmart
24. **Goizueta, Roberto** (1931–1997)
    CEO: Coca-Cola (1981–1997)
    High school: Cheshire Academy (Cheshire, CT)
    College: BS, 1948 (Chemical Engineering), Yale University
    Fortune 1000 directorships held: Ford Motors, Eastman Kodak, SunTrust Banks
    Policy groups: Council on Foreign Relations

25. Gold, Christina (1947–)
   CEO: Western Union (2006–)
   High school: Beaconsfield High School, 1965 (Beaconsfield, Quebec)
   College: BA, 1969, Carleton University
   Fortune 1000 directorships held: First Data, ITT Industries, New
      York Life Insurance
   Policy groups: The Conference Board
26. Graham, Katharine (1917–2001)
   CEO: Washington Post (1977–1991)
   High school: The Madeira School (McLean, VA)
   College: BA, 1938 (American History), University of Chicago
   Policy groups: Council on Foreign Relations
27. Gupta, Rajiv (1945–)
   CEO: Rohm and Haas (1999–2009)
   College: BA (Mechanical Engineering), Indian Institute of Technology
   Postgraduate: MS (Operations Research); MBA (Finance), Drexel
      University
   Fortune 1000 directorships held: Consol Energy
28. Gutierrez, Carlos (1953–)
   CEO: Kellogg (1999–2004)
   Fortune 1000 directorships held: Colgate-Palmolive
29. Hallman, Cinda (1945–2008)
   CEO: Spherion (2001–2004)
   High school: Ashdown High School (Ashdown, Arkansas)
   College: BA (Math), University of Arkansas
30. Hassan, Fred (1945–)
   CEO: Schering-Plough (previously Pharmacia, 1997–2009)
   College: BA (Chemical Engineering), University of London
   Postgraduate: MBA, Harvard University
   Fortune 1000 directorships held: Avon Products
   Policy groups: Business Council, Business Roundtable
31. Inouye, Wayne (1953–)
   CEO: Gateway (2004–2006)
   High school: Yuba City High School (Yuba City, CA)
   College: University of California, Berkeley, no degree
32. Ivey, Susan (1958–)
   CEO: Reynolds American (2004–2011)
   High school: Fort Lauderdale High School (Fort Lauderdale, FL)
   College: BS, University of Florida
   Postgraduate: MBA, Bellarmine College

33. **Jha, Sanjay K.** (1963–)
    CEO: Co-CEO, Motorola (2008–)
    College: BA (Engineering), University of Liverpool
    Postgraduate: PhD (Electronic and Electrical Engineering), University of Strathclyde
    Fortune 1000 directorships held: Qualcomm
34. **Jung, Andrea** (1959–)
    CEO: Avon Products (1999–)
    College: BA (English Literature), Princeton University
    Policy groups: Business Council
35. **Kent, Muhtar** (1952–)
    CEO: Coca-Cola (2008–)
    High school: Tarsus American College High School (Turkey)
    College: BS (Economics), University of Hull
    Postgraduate: MA (Administrative Sciences), City University of London
36. **Kullman, Ellen** (1956–)
    CEO: DuPont (2009–)
    High school: Tower Hill School (Wilmington, DE)
    College: BA (Mechanical Engineering), Tufts
    Postgraduate: MBA, Northwestern
    Fortune 1000 directorships held: General Motors
37. **Kumar, Sanjay** (1962–)
    CEO: Computer Associates (2000–2004)
    College: Furman University (no degree)
38. **Lewis, Aylwin B**. (1954–)
    CEO: Kmart/Sears (2004–2008)
    High school: Jesse Jones High School (Houston, TX)
    College: BBA (Management) and BA (English Literature), University of Houston
    Postgraduate: MBA, University of Houston; MA (Human Resource Management), Houston Baptist University
    Fortune 1000 directorships held: Disney, Halliburton, Sears Holdings, Yum Brands
39. **Meyrowitz, Carol** (1954–)
    CEO: TJX (2007–)
    Fortune 1000 directorships held: Staples
40. **Mohapatra, Surya N.** (1950–)
    CEO: Quest Diagnostics (2004–)
    College: BS (Electrical Engineering), Sambalpur University (India)

Postgraduate: MS (Medical Electronics), University of Salford; PhD (Medical Physics), University of London
Fortune 1000 directorships held: ITT

41. **Mulcahy, Anne** (1952–)
    CEO: Xerox (2001–2009)
    College: BA, 1974 (English/Journalism), Marymount
    Fortune 1000 directorships held: Citigroup, Target
    Policy groups: Business Council, Business Roundtable

42. **Nakasone, Robert C.** (1947–)
    CEO: Toys "R" Us (1998–1999)
    High school: Verdugo Hills High School (Los Angeles, CA)
    College: BA (Economics), Claremont McKenna College
    Postgraduate: MBA, University of Chicago
    Fortune 1000 directorships held: Hormel Foods, Staples, Tenet Healthcare

43. **Nishimura, Koichi** (1938–)
    CEO: Solectron (1992–2003)
    High school: John Muir High School (Pasadena, CA)
    College: BA, 1963 (Engineering), San Jose State University
    Postgraduate: MS, 1968 (Engineering), San Jose State University; PhD, (Engineering) Stanford University

44. **Nooyi, Indra** (1955–)
    CEO: PepsiCo (2006–)
    High school: Banasthali High School (Kathmandu)
    College: BS, 1976 (Chemistry, Math, and Physics), Madras Christian College
    Postgraduate: MBA, 1978, Indian Institute of Management, Calcutta; MA, 1980 (Public and Private Management), Yale University
    Fortune 1000 directorships held: Motorola

45. **O'Neal, E. Stanley** (1951–)
    CEO: Merrill Lynch (2002–2007)
    High school: West Fulton High School (Atlanta, GA)
    College: BS, 1974 (Industrial Administration), Kettering University
    Postgraduate: MBA, 1978, Harvard University
    Fortune 1000 directorships held: Alcoa, General Motors
    Policy groups: Council on Foreign Relations

46. **O'Neal, Rodney** (1954–)
    CEO: Delphi (2007–)
    College: BS, 1976, Kettering University
    Postgraduate: MA, Stanford University
    Fortune 1000 directorships held: Goodyear, Sprint Nextel

47. **Osorio, Claudio** (1959–)
    CEO: CHS Electronics (1993–)
    Postgraduate: Law degree, 1980, Universidad Catolica Andres Bello (UCAB), Venezuela; MBA, 1982, Instituto de Estudios Superiores, Venezuela
48. **Otis, Clarence Jr.** (1956–)
    CEO: Darden Restaurants (2005–)
    High school: Jordan High School (Los Angeles, CA)
    College: BA, 1977 (Economics and Political Science), Williams College
    Postgraduate: JD, 1980, Stanford University
    Fortune 1000 directorships held: Travelers Companies, Verizon, VF Corporation
    Policy groups: Business Council
49. **Pandit, Vikram** (1957–)
    CEO: Citigroup (2007–)
    High school: Dadar Parsee Youths Assembly High School (Mumbai)
    College: BS, 1976 (Electrical Engineering), Columbia University
    Postgraduate: MS, 1977 (Electrical Engineering), Columbia University; MBA, 1980, Columbia University; PhD, 1986 (Finance), Columbia University
    Fortune 1000 directorships held: Morgan Stanley
50. **Park, Chong S.** (1948–)
    CEO: Maxtor (2004–2006)
    College: BA (Management), Yonsei University
    Postgraduate: MA (Management), Seoul National University; MBA, University of Chicago; PhD (Business Administration), Nova Southeastern University
    Fortune 1000 directorships held: Computer Sciences, Seagate
51. **Parsons, Richard D.** (1948–)
    CEO: Time Warner (2001–2007)
    High school: John Adams High School (Queens, NY)
    College: BA, 1968 (History), University of Hawaii
    Postgraduate: JD, 1971, Albany Law School
    Fortune 1000 directorships held: Citigroup, Estee Lauder
52. **Perez, Antonio** (1945–)
    CEO: Eastman Kodak (2005–)
    College: BS (Electrical Engineering), Madrid University
    Fortune 1000 directorships held: Schering-Plough
    Policy groups: Business Council, Business Roundtable

53. **Perez, William** (1947–)
    CEO: Wrigley (2006–2008)
    High school: Western Reserve Academy, 1965 (Hudson, Ohio)
    College: BA, 1969 (Government), Cornell University
    Postgraduate: MBA, 1970, Thunderbird School of Global Management
    Fortune 1000 directorships held: Hallmark, Johnson & Johnson, Kellogg, May Department Stores, Nike

54. **Raines, Franklin D.** (1949–)
    CEO: Fannie Mae (1999–2004)
    High school: Franklin High School (Seattle, WA)
    College: BA, 1971 (Political Science), Harvard University
    Postgraduate: Rhodes scholar, Oxford University; JD, 1976, Harvard University
    Fortune 1000 directorships held: AOL, Boeing, PepsiCo, Pfizer, TIAA-CREF, Time Warner
    Policy groups: Business Council, Council on Foreign Relations

55. **Rand, A. Barry** (1944–)
    CEO: Avis (1999–2001)
    High school: Archbishop Carroll High School (Washington, DC)
    College: BA (Marketing), American University
    Postgraduate: MBA, 1973, Stanford University
    Fortune 1000 directorships held: Abbott Laboratories, Agilent Technologies, Ameritech, AT&T, Campbell Soup, Honeywell

56. **Rosenfeld, Irene** (1953–)
    CEO: Kraft (2006–)
    High school: West Tresper Clarke High School, 1971 (Long Island, NY)
    College: BA, 1975 (Psychology), Cornell University
    Postgraduate: MS, 1977 (Business Administration), Cornell University; PhD 1980 (Marketing and Statistics), Cornell University
    Fortune 1000 directorships held: AutoNation, PepsiCo

57. **Rosput Reynolds, Paula** (1956–)
    CEO: Safeco (2006–2008)
    College: BA, 1978 (Economics), Wellesley College
    Fortune 1000 directorships held: AGL Resources, Air Products and Chemicals, Coca-Cola, Delta Airlines

58. **Ruiz, Hector** (1945–)
    CEO: Advanced Micro Devices (2002–2008)
    High school: Eagle Pass High School (Eagle Pass, TX)
    College: BA, 1968 (Electrical Engineering), University of Texas

Postgraduate: MS, 1970 (Electrical Engineering), University of Texas; PhD, 1973 (Quantum Electronics), Rice University

Fortune 1000 directorships held: Eastman Kodak

59. **Russo, Patricia** (1953–)

    CEO: Lucent (2002–2008)

    High school: Lawrence High School (Lawrence Township, NJ)

    College: BA (Political Science and History), Georgetown University

    Fortune 1000 directorships held: Avaya, Schering-Plough, Xerox

    Policy groups: Business Council, Business Roundtable

60. **Sammons, Mary** (1946–)

    CEO: Rite Aid (2003–2010)

    College: BA (French), Marylhurst University

    Fortune 1000 directorships held: First Horizon

61. **Sandler, Marion** (1931–)

    CEO: Co-CEO, Golden West Financial (1973–2006)

    College: BA, 1952 (Business), Wellesley College

    Postgraduate: MBA, 1958, New York University

62. **Scott, Eileen** (1953–)

    CEO: Pathmark Stores (2002–2005)

    College: BA, 1976 (Business), William Paterson University

    Postgraduate: MBA, 2009, New York University

    Fortune 1000 directorships held: Dollar Tree Stores

63. **Sen, Laura** (1956–)

    CEO: BJ's Wholesale Club (2009–)

    High school: Wakefield High School (Wakefield, MA)

    College: BA, 1978 (French), Boston College

64. **Thompson, John W.** (1949–)

    CEO: Symantec (1999–2009)

    High school: John F. Kennedy High School (Riviera Beach, FL)

    College: BA, 1971 (Business Administration), Florida A&M

    Postgraduate: MBA, 1983, MIT

    Fortune 1000 directorships held: La-Z-Boy, NiSource, Seagate, United Parcel Service

    Policy groups: Business Council

65. **Trujillo, Solomon** (1951–)

    CEO: US West (1995–2000)

    College: BA, 1973 (Business), University of Wyoming

    Postgraduate: MBA, 1974, University of Wyoming

    Fortune 1000 directorships held: Bank of America, Electronic Data Systems, Gannett, PepsiCo, Target

66. **Tsai, Gerald** (1921–2008)
    CEO: American Can (then Primerica) (1986–1987)
    High school: St. John's Middle School (China)
    College: BA (Economics), Boston University
    Postgraduate: MA (Economics), Boston University
    Fortune 1000 directorships held: Saks, Sequa, Triarc
67. **Wachner, Linda** (1946–)
    CEO: Warnaco (1986–2001)
    College: BA, 1966 (Business Administration), SUNY, Buffalo
    Fortune 1000 directorships held: Travelers Companies
68. **Wang, Charles B.** (1944–)
    CEO: Computer Associates (1976–2000)
    High school: Brooklyn Technical High School
    College: BS, 1966 (Math), Queens College
69. **Ward, Lloyd D.** (1949–)
    CEO: Maytag (1999–2000)
    College: BS, 1970 (Engineering), Michigan State
    Postgraduate: MBA, 1984, Xavier
    Fortune 1000 directorships held: General Motors, J. P. Morgan Chase
70. **White, Tony** (1946–)
    CEO: Perkin-Elmer (1995–2008)
    College: BA, 1969, Western Carolina University
    Fortune 1000 directorships held: Applera, AT&T, C. R. Bard, Ingersoll Rand
71. **Whitman, Meg** (1956–)
    CEO: eBay (1998–2007)
    High school: Cold Spring Harbor High School
    College: BS, 1977 (Economics), Princeton University
    Postgraduate: MBA, 1979, Harvard University
    Fortune 1000 directorships held: Gap, Goldman Sachs, Procter & Gamble
72. **Williams, Ronald A.** (1950–)
    CEO: Aetna (2006–)
    College: BA (Psychology), Roosevelt University
    Postgraduate: MS, 1984 (Management), MIT
    Fortune 1000 directorships held: American Express, Lucent Technologies
    Policy groups: Business Council, Business Roundtable, Conference Board

73. **Woertz, Patricia** (1953–)
     CEO: Archer Daniels Midland (2006–)
     College: BS, 1974 (Accounting), Pennsylvania State University
     Fortune 1000 directorships held: Chevron
     Policy groups: Business Council, Business Roundtable
74. **Yang, Jerry** (1968–)
     CEO: Yahoo (1994–2008)
     High school: Piedmont Hills High School (San Jose, CA)
     College: BS, 1990 (Electrical Engineering), Stanford University
     Postgraduate: MS, 1990 (Electrical Engineering), Stanford University
     sity
     Fortune 1000 directorships held: Cisco Systems, Inc.

Appendix 2

Baby-Faced and More: CEOs and Skin Color

Richard L. Zweigenhaft and Kyle Riplinger

This appendix provides more detail about the research on skin color and CEOs that we have summarized in chapters 3 and 4. Here we include more information concerning the methods we used and more detailed statistical analyses. We do so to provide the interested reader with a clearer sense of the type of basic work that goes into developing the findings that we have chosen to summarize more briefly in the text. The main study described here was performed during the 2009–2010 academic year by Zweigenhaft and Kyle Riplinger (at the time, a senior psychology major at Guilford College in Greensboro, North Carolina).

In the past few decades, a number of African American males have made it to the highest levels of power in America, including more than a dozen members of presidential cabinets and three members of the United States Senate, as well as the fifteen CEOs of *Fortune* 500 corporations we profiled in chapter 3, and, as of January 20, 2009, the president of the United States.

They are the most recent success stories in a long history of accomplishments by African Americans, but we wondered if they are atypical among African Americans in that they might have a somewhat lighter skin color, a possibility we entertained based on the fact that many researchers have found in the past that highly successful African Americans tended to be light skinned. For example, Horace Mann Bond found that many "early Negro scholars" were "light-complexioned" individuals from families that had been part of the antebellum "free colored population" or born to "favored slaves." He explained their success in the following way: "The phenomenon was not due, as many believed, to the 'superiority' of the white blood; it was a social and economic, rather than a natural selection. Concubinage remained an openly sustained relationship between white men and Negro women in the South for fifty years after the Civil War; the children of such unions were more likely to have parents with the money, and the tradition, to send a child to school, than the former field hand slaves who were now sharecroppers and day laborers" (Bond 1966, 559).

Even after the civil rights movement of the 1960s, and the emphasis within that movement that "black is beautiful," researchers continued to find that lighter-skinned African Americans were advantaged in many ways, and that darker-skinned African Americans were more likely to experience discrimination than lighter-skinned African Americans. Decades of research has demonstrated that lighter-skinned African Americans complete more years of higher education and earn more money than darker-skinned African Americans (e.g., Ransford 1970; Hughes and Hertel 1990; Keith and Herring 1991; Herring, Keith, and Horton 2004; and Keith 2009).

These educational advantages are part of a much larger constellation of differences. Hochschild and Weaver (2007, 643) summarize many of the findings in this literature in the following way: "Dark-skinned blacks in the United States have lower socio-economic status, more punitive relationships with the criminal system, diminished prestige, and less likelihood of holding elective office compared with their lighter counterparts." They go on to note that "some evidence suggests, in fact, that intra-racial disparities are as detrimental to a person's life chances as are disparities traditionally associated with racial divisions" (2007, 644). Similarly, lighter-skinned Mexican Americans have better life chances than darker-skinned Mexican Americans on a variety of measures (Arce, Murguia and Frisbie 1987; Telles and Murguia 1990; Allen, Telles, and Hunter 2000; Hunter 2002), as do lighter-skinned Puerto Ricans (Rodriguez 1989). Asian Americans with dark skin tones are more likely to report that they have experienced job discrimination (Herring, Thomas, Durr, and Horton 1998).

Not surprisingly, then, many of the African Americans who have entered the higher circles of power in the corporate, political, and military worlds in recent years have tended to have lighter skin tones than other African Americans. As part of their research on diversity in the power elite, Zweigenhaft and Domhoff (1998, 110–13) showed ninety magazine-quality photographs drawn from *Current Biography*, from various articles in *Ebony*'s November 1995 fiftieth-anniversary issue, and from the October 1994 issue of *Ebony* on black interlocking directors, to two undergraduates who rated the photos using the Skin Color Assessment Procedure (see Bond and Cash 1992). Some of the ninety photos were of individuals who had served on *Fortune*-level corporate boards, had been in presidential cabinets, or were senior officers in the military, but most were of prominent African American men and women who had not held such positions of institutional power. Those who were in positions of power were rated significantly lighter skinned than the control group of prominent African Americans who were not in power positions.

More recently, Livingston and Pearce (2009a) used photos of CEOs to look at something psychologists have called "babyfaceness." A body of research in social psychology has revealed that some adults are seen as "baby-faced," as opposed to most adults who are seen to have "mature" faces. Those seen as "baby-faced" tend to be perceived as more warm, trustworthy, and innocent than "mature-faced" adults, and they tend to be treated with greater patience, compassion, and sensitivity (see Zebrowitz 1997, 83–116). Whereas previous studies have shown that having a baby face works against white males in positions of leadership, Livingston and Pearce (2009a) hypothesized that having a baby face might be advantageous to African Americans in leadership positions because they would be perceived as less threatening.

They asked 120 students to rate forty photos of CEOs (ten current and former African American male *Fortune* 500 CEOs, ten white males who have been CEOs at the same companies as the black CEOs, ten white female CEOs of *Fortune* 500 companies, and ten more white male CEOs randomly sampled from the remaining *Fortune* 500 companies). They found that raters perceived the ten black CEOs as significantly more baby-faced than the thirty white CEOs. They drew the following conclusion about babyfaceness, one quite similar to the one Zweigenhaft and Domhoff (1998) drew about skin color: "Babyfaceness is a disarming mechanism that facilitates the success of Black leaders by attenuating stereotypical perceptions that Blacks are threatening" (Livingston and Pearce 2009a, 1229).

Livingston and Pearce (2009a, 1234) also asked their student raters to assess skin color, using a four-point scale with 1 as the lightest and 4 as the darkest. They found no significant relationship between babyfaceness and skin color. Not surprisingly, the black CEOs did receive higher ratings on skin color (M = 3.12) than the white CEOs (M = 1.79; Livingston and Pearce 2009b). However, Livingston and Pearce (2009a) did not include a control group of other prominent and successful African Americans, so it is not possible to conclude based on their study that the African American CEOs were especially light skinned as well as baby-faced.

Therefore, in a study done specifically for this book, we sought to extend the previous work reported in Zweigenhaft and Domhoff (1998) on the skin color of African American corporate directors and Livingston and Pearce's (2009a) research on the babyfaceness of African American CEOs by comparing the skin color of African American CEOs to another group of prominent, well-educated, and successful African American males, the presidents of historically black colleges and universities (HBCUs). Our reasoning for this choice is that African American men who have become college or university presidents are well educated and highly successful, but, unlike the CEOs of *Fortune* 500 companies, they have not had to rise through the ranks of pre-dominantly white institutions (and thus are not as likely to need to be light skinned). At the same time, we know that blacks favor light-skinned blacks (e.g., Herring 2004; Craig 2009; Glenn 2009; Keith 2009), so we expected that the differences could be small.

Although it was not our primary focus, we also report on and discuss the skin color ratings of white women, Latino, and Asian American CEOs of *Fortune* 500 corporations.

METHODS

We presented photographs to two sets of student raters. The first group, con-sisting of ten undergraduates at Guilford College, a small liberal arts college in North Carolina, looked at 65 photographs drawn from Google Images. We chose formal, head and shoulders, publicity-type photos, many of which were the official photos from the corporate sites of the companies for which the CEOs worked, though some of the photos had appeared in various business magazines (such as *Business Week*, *Forbes*, or *Fortune*). The CEO photos were of the 13 African American men who as of January 2010 had been CEOs of *Fortune* 500 corporations (Ursula Burns became the first African American woman CEO of a *Fortune* 500 company, Xerox, in January 2010, and Kenneth Frazier became CEO of Merck in January 2011; neither was included in this study); 12 of the 15 Latinos who had been CEOs of *Fortune* 500 corporations by January 2010 (all had been male); and a sample of 20 white male CEOs from similar-sized *Fortune* 500 companies as those that had appointed the African American males and Latinos. In addition to these 45 photos, we randomly selected photographs of 20 male college presidents whose schools were included on "The White House Initiative on Historically Black Colleges and Universities." These 20 male HBCU presidents, as we have indicated, served as the "control group" for the African American CEOs.

We presented these same 65 photographs, along with another 42 photo-graphs, to a second set of twenty undergraduates enrolled at Guilford College. This larger set of photos, also presented in a random order, included two additional sets of photographs, obtained in the same manner from Google Images: 18 photographs of Asian Americans who had been CEOs of *Fortune* 500 companies by January 2010 (there had been 19 Asian American CEOs, 16 men and 3 women, but we were unable to obtain an acceptable photograph for one of the men), and photographs of the 24 white women who had become CEOs of *Fortune* 500 companies by January 2010.

We seated each student in front of a computer screen. After filling out an informed consent form, each student was given $5 for his or her participation (our hope was that students would take their participation a bit more seriously if paid than if not paid).[1] The students were given a scoring sheet on which to record their ratings (using a pen or a pencil). Using Windows Picture Viewer, each student briefly saw a screen that included all of the photos, and then was shown a larger image of each individual photo, one at a time, and asked to rate each photo in two ways. First, students were asked to rate the photo on a 1–10 skin color scale, with 1 being the lightest and 10 being the darkest. Second, if they were among the first ten student raters, who saw only 65 photos, they were asked to identify the person in the photo as African American, Latino, or White; if they were among the next twenty student raters, who saw 107 photos, they were asked to identify the person in the photo as African American, Asian American, Latino, or White.

In addition, as a way to compare the ratings of the photos we obtained via Google Images, almost all of which were color photos, and the grayscale photos used in the Livingston and Pearce (2009a) study, we also showed our raters 20 black and white photos of CEOs, 10 of which were the grayscale photos used by Livingston and Pearce, and 10 of which were drawn from the photographs of the white CEOs in our sample. Finally, participants were debriefed about the purpose of the study, and thanked for their participation.

RESULTS AND DISCUSSION

The thirty undergraduate raters ranged in age from 18 to 50, with a mean of 24.3 and a median of 21. Seventeen were women, and thirteen were men. Eighteen were white, ten were African American, one described herself of mixed race (one white parent and one African American parent), and one was from the Middle East. There were no meaningful differences in the skin color ratings based on the age or gender of the raters, nor were there meaningful differences between the ratings of those in the 65-photo condition and those in the 107-photo condition, so when possible we have combined the data from the thirty student raters in the analyses that follow.

As a check to ensure that the photos used in this study were comparable to those used in Livingston and Pearce's study of babyfaceness (2009a), we compared the ratings of the photographs that we used and the photographs that they used for ten of the African American CEOs. When the scores for all ten CEOs were combined, the two sets of ratings were highly correlated ($r = .60$, $n = 300$, p < .001). When we looked at the correlations separately for the ten CEOs, each was statistically significant, and they ranged from as low as $r = .41$ ($n = 30$, $p < .02$) for Richard Parsons, former CEO of Time Warner

Appendix 2

and current chair of Citigroup) to $r = .59$ ($n = 30$, $p < .001$) for Aylwin Lewis, former acting CEO of Kmart. In sum, although some of the color photographs that we used were less similar than others to the grayscale photographs used by Livingston and Pearce (2009a) in terms of the ratings of skin color, collectively and individually they correlated significantly.

Mean Skin Color Ratings

Table A2.1 shows the mean skin color ratings for the photos of the 13 African American CEOs combined, those of the 12 Latino CEOs combined, those of the 20 white male CEOs combined, and those of the 20 presidents of historically black colleges and universities combined (because all thirty raters viewed these photos, the sample size for this analysis is $n = 30$). The white male CEOs received the lowest (that is, lightest) skin color ratings, M = 2.27, followed by the Latino CEOs, M = 2.86, the African American CEOs, M = 6.33, and, finally, the African American presidents of HBCUs, M = 7.04. A repeated measures analysis of variance reveals that the differences are highly significant, and post hoc analyses reveal that the differences between the ratings for each group and each of the other three groups were also highly significant. That is, and most relevant for our primary hypothesis, the African American CEOs, though rated as significantly *darker* than white and Latino CEOs, also were rated as significantly *lighter* skinned than the presidents of the HBCUs.

When we did the same analysis for the twenty raters who saw photos of white women CEOs and Asian American CEOs as well as the same photos of white male, Latino, African American CEOs, and the photos of presidents

Table A2.1. Skin Color Ratings of White Male, Latino, and African American CEOs of *Fortune* 500 Companies, and Presidents of Historically Black Colleges and Universities (HBCUs)

	Photos of White Male CEOs (n = 20)	Photos of Latino CEOs (n = 12)	Photos of African American CEOs (n = 13)	Photos of Presidents of HBCUs (n = 20)
Mean rating =	2.27[a,b,c]	2.86 [b,c,d]	6.33 [a,c,d]	7.04 [a,b,d]
St. dev. =	(.653)	(.698)	(.862)	(.778)
Number of raters	30	30	30	30
F =	419.88			
df =	3			
p <	.001			

a = significantly different ($p < .05$) from the ratings for the Latino CEOs
b = significantly different ($p < .05$) from the ratings for the African American CEOs
c = significantly different ($p < .05$) from the ratings for the presidents of HBCUs
d = significantly different ($p < .05$) from the ratings for the white male CEOs

of HBCUs, the white women were rated as the lightest (M = 1.97), followed by the white men (M = 2.12), the Latinos (M = 2.68), the Asian Americans (M = 3.47), the African Americans (M = 6.27) and, finally, the presidents of the historically black colleges and universities (M = 7.06). As can be seen in table A2.2, repeated measures analysis of variance again showed that the differences were highly significant, and the post hoc analyses revealed that the differences between the ratings for each group and each of the other groups were also significant (even the difference between the white women and the white men). Notably, the Latinos and the Asian Americans were seen as much closer to the skin color of the whites than that of the two groups of African Americans. To use Bonilla-Silva's term, they might be seen to have been given "honorary white status" (Bonilla-Silva 2004; Bonilla-Silva and Dietrich 2009; Forman, Goar, and Lewis 2002).

Identifying Ethnicity

More than 90 percent of the time, respondents accurately identified the ethnicity of the African American CEOs, the white CEOs, and the presidents of HBCUs. Moreover, within the group of African American CEOs, raters were accurate 90 percent of the time or more for twelve of the thirteen CEOs. Although for the African American CEOs and African American presidents of HBCUs there was a statistically significant correlation between the skin color ratings and accuracy of identification ($r = .18$, $df = 989$, $p < .001$; one respondent left one of these ratings blank, and thus $n = 989$ instead of 990), it was far from a perfect relationship, and clearly skin color was not the only factor that contributed to the 10 percent of ethnicity misidentifications for the African American CEOs and college presidents. As various researchers have noted (e.g., Thompson and Keith 2004), many other phenotypic features, including hair texture, broadness of nose, and fullness of lips, are relevant to the identification of ethnicity, and thus skin color was a significant but not perfect predictor of accurate ethnic identification for the African Americans.

The raters were much less accurate when it came to the Latino CEOs. The overall accuracy rate was only 31 percent. Two of the Latinos were misidentified by all thirty of the raters (Fernando Aguirre, CEO of Chiquita Brands since 2004, and William Perez, former CEO of both Nike and Wrigley). All thirty of the student raters categorized Aguirre and Perez as "white." Another five Latino CEOs were misidentified by 75 percent or more of the raters (Jose Alapont, Cristobal Conde, Paul Diaz, Roberto Goizueta, and Tony White); when they were not identified as Latinos, these five Latino CEOs were almost always categorized by the raters as white, though in a few cases some were thought to be Asian American or African American. Only four of the Latino

Table A2.2. Skin Color Ratings of White Women, White Male, Latino, Asian American, and African American CEOs, and Presidents of Historically Black Colleges and Universities (HBCUs)

	Photos of White Women CEOs (n = 24)	Photos of White Male CEOs (n = 20)	Photos of Latino CEOs (n = 12)	Photos of Asian American CEOs (n = 18)	Photos of African American CEOs (n = 13)	Photos of Presidents of HBCUs (n = 20)
Mean rating =	1.97 [b,c,d,e,f]	2.12 [a,c,d,e,f]	2.68 [a,b,d,e,f]	3.47 [a,b,c,e,f]	6.27 [a,b,c,d,f]	7.06 [a,b,c,d,e]
St. dev. =	(.551)	(.661)	(.755)	(.724)	(.960)	(.850)
Number of raters	20	20	20	20	20	20

F = 281.50
df = 5
p < .001

a = significantly different (p < .05) from the ratings for the white women CEOs
b = significantly different (p < .05) from the ratings for the white male CEOs
c = significantly different (p < .05) from the ratings for the Latino CEOs
d = significantly different (p < .05) from the ratings for the Asian CEOs
e = significantly different (p < .05) from the ratings for the African American CEOs
f = significantly different (p < .05) from the ratings for the presidents of HBCUs

CEOs were identified as Latinos by 50 percent or more of the raters (Alain Belda, Carlos Gutierrez, Solomon Trujillo, and Hector Ruiz). Skin color was a significant predictor of whether or not the raters identified the Latino CEOs as Latino: the correlation between skin color and accuracy of identification was $r = .36$, $p < .001$). Table A2.3 presents a summary of the identification patterns for each of the twelve Latino CEOs. (Many Latinos identify themselves as white. It therefore is more accurate to say that the raters did or did not identify them as Latinos than to say that they correctly or incorrectly identified them as Latinos; see Skrentny 2002, 263).

The raters were more likely to identify the Asian American CEOs as Asian Americans than they were to identify the Latino CEOs as Latinos, but they were less accurate than they were in identifying the ethnicities of the white CEOs, the African American CEOs, or the African American presidents of HBCUs: only 55 percent of the photographs of the Asian American CEOs were accurately identified. One (Rakesh Gangwal) was misidentified by all twenty raters (the photographs that the first ten raters looked at did not include the Asian American or the women CEOs), and four (Fred Hassan, Muhtar Kent, Indra Nooyi, and Laura Sen) were misidentified by 75 percent or more of the raters.

A more careful examination of accuracy rates for the eighteen photographs of Asian American CEOs reveals a distinctive split: the accuracy rate was quite high (91 percent) for the eight Chinese and Japanese American CEOs (Wayne Inouye, Andrea Jung, Robert Nakasone, Koichi Nishimura, Laura Sen, Gerald Tsai, Charles Wang, and Jerry Yang), but it was much lower (31 percent) for the remaining ten Asian CEOs, seven of whom were Indians (Ramani Ayer, Rakesh Gangwal, Rajiv Gupta, Surya Mohapatra, Indra Nooyi, Vikram Pandit, Sanjay Jha), one of whom was from Sri Lanka (Sanjay Kumar), one from Pakistan (Fred Hassan), and one from Turkey (Muhtar Kent).

Table A2.3. Identification of Ethnicity for the Latino CEOs

	Latino	*White*	*Asian*	*Black*	*Total*
Aguirre, Fernando	0	30	0	0	30
Alapont, Jose	6	23	0	1	30
Belda, Alain	20	2	7	1	30
Conde, Cristobal	2	26	1	1	30
Diaz, Paul	5	25	0	0	30
Goizueta, Roberto	5	25	0	0	30
Gutierrez, Carlos	22	5	3	0	30
Perez, Antonio	9	20	1	0	30
Perez, William	0	30	0	0	30
Ruiz, Hector	15	7	6	2	30
Trujillo, Solomon	21	7	1	1	30
White, Tony	5	25	0	0	30

Table A2.4. Identification of Ethnicity for the Asian American CEOs

	Asian	White	Latino	Black	Total
Ayer, Ramani	7	0	9	4	20
Gangwal, Rakesh	6	3	11	0	20
Gupta, Rajiv	0	20	0	0	20
Hassan, Fred	3	10	7	0	20
Inouye, Wayne	20	0	0	0	20
Jha, Sanjay	11	0	9	0	20
Jung, Andrea	17	0	2	1	20
Kent, Muhtar	1	9	10	0	20
Kumar, Sanjay	13	0	6	1	20
Mohapatra, Surya	11	0	8	1	20
Nakasone, Robert	19	0	1	0	20
Nishimura, Koichi	12	4	2	2	20
Nooyi, Indra	2	2	6	10	20
Pandit, Vikram	14	3	3	0	20
Sen, Laura	1	9	0	0	20
Tsai, Gerald	20	0	0	0	20
Wang, Charles	20	0	0	0	20
Yang, Jerry	20	0	0	0	20

This highly significant pattern ($x^2 = 124.58$, $df = 1$, $p < .001$) demonstrates once again that those within the artificial category of "Asian American" that we are using are diverse, not only in terms of the countries they come from, but in terms of how easily identifiable they are as Asian Americans.

Moreover, as can be seen in table A2.4, there was tremendous variability in the kinds of errors that the raters made when they did not identify the Asian American CEOs as Asian Americans. Slightly more than one-third of the misidentifications indicated that they thought the person was white (38 percent), about half the time they were thought to be Latinos (52 percent), and about 11 percent of the time they were thought to be African Americans (and most of these errors were based on the photograph of Indra Nooyi, the CEO of PepsiCo—ten of the twenty raters thought she was African American). Revealingly, there was absolutely no correlation between skin color and the ability to identify Asian American CEOs as Asian Americans ($r = .01$), indicating that the ability to identify the Asian American CEOs was based on facial features and hair color, not skin color.

Ethnicity of Rater

The twelve students of color were neither more nor less accurate in identifying ethnicity than the eighteen white student raters. The students of color, however, did rate the CEOs as having lighter skin. As can be seen in table A2.5, their skin color ratings for the photographs of those in each of the

Table A2.5. White and Nonwhite Raters, Skin Color Ratings

	White raters (n = 18)	Nonwhite raters (n = 12)	t	df	p <
Mean ratings, white women CEOs (st. dev.)	2.15 (.501)	1.71 (.545)	1.85	18	.08
Mean ratings, white male CEOs (st. dev.)	2.44 (.598)	2.01 (.673)	1.81	28	.08
Mean ratings, Latino CEOs (st. dev.)	3.10 (.619)	2.51 (.678)	**2.48**	**28**	**.02**
Mean ratings, Asian American CEOs (st. dev.)	3.86 (.504)	2.90 (.634)	**3.74**	**18**	**.001**
Mean ratings, African American CEOs (st. dev.)	6.51 (.660)	6.05 (1.07)	1.46	28	.15
Mean ratings, presidents of HBCUs (st. dev.)	7.29 (.552)	6.67 (.938)	**2.25**	**28**	**.03**
Mean ratings, all photos (st. dev.)	4.43 (.441)	3.91 (.750)	**2.38**	**28**	**.02**

groups were lower than the ratings made by the white raters (though only three of these six comparisons reached conventional levels of statistical significance). When all of the skin color ratings are combined, the average rating for the students of color was significantly lower (that is, lighter) than the average rating for the white students ($t = 2.38$, $df = 28$, $p < .02$).

CONCLUSION

People perceive and judge skin color amidst an array of other cues, and these perceptions and judgments are influenced by these other factors. As Charis Thompson observes: "People learning to see socially relevant skin tone differences perceive the shade of skin embedded in other ethnoracial marking systems such as hair, language, dress, age, gender, season, type of work, posture, and so on. Perceiving skin tone always involves its intersection with these other attributes and their wider meanings and horizons" (Thompson 2009, 132). It is not surprising, therefore, that Maxine Thompson and Verna Keith (2004) report the following: "Skin color is highly correlated with other phenotypic features—eye color, hair texture, broadness of nose, and fullness of lips. Along with light skin, blue and green eyes, European shaped noses, and straight as opposed to 'kinky' hair are all accorded higher status, both within and beyond the African American community" (2004, 47; see also Blair, Judd, and Chapleau 2004). Therefore, both babyfaceness and light skin function in complex ways, as part of a larger constellation of factors that affect how one is perceived by others and how one feels about oneself.

For many years, social scientists have studied the presentation of self in everyday life (Goffman 1959). People have control over some aspects of how they present themselves, but not others. Skin color is not easily changed, nor is the appearance of being baby-faced. People do, however, have control over other aspects of their appearance, such as the clothes they wear and the way they cut their hair, and they have some control over how they are perceived (do they make eye contact? do they have a firm handshake?). Luo (2009) reports that in difficult economic times, when jobs are scarce, some highly qualified African Americans have taken to "whitening" their resumes—they have deleted affiliations with African American organizations, or even have left off African-sounding names that identify them as African Americans.

The lighter skin color of African American CEOs of *Fortune* 500 companies, therefore, can be seen as one of many factors that contributes to others (especially whites) perceiving them as capable but nonthreatening and as able to work effectively as leaders of predominantly white institutions. Some of the things that factor into this impression may be under their control, and others may not be. They may or may not be conscious of the extent to which they present themselves as nonthreatening, and those with whom they work, especially their corporate boards and CEOs of other *Fortune* 500 companies, may not be conscious of the extent to which their relatively lighter skin contributes to their acceptability.

Appendix 3

Corporate, Family, and Community Foundations: How the Corporate Pipeline Supports Low-Income Students of Color

This appendix is based on the invaluable accumulation of information provided by the Foundation Center (headquartered in New York City) through its *Foundation Grants Index*, which lists all foundation donations as well as the recipients of those grants. The *Index*, designed primarily for those who seek grants, provides additional information, such as the location of the donors and recipients, but it is the names of foundations and their recipients, along with the size of the grants, that is relevant for our purposes. The information in the *Index* is based on the tax forms that all foundations must file each year with the Internal Revenue Service in order to maintain their tax-free status. They are required, therefore, to reveal a great deal of information that is useful to researchers as well as government officials, including their sources of income, the recipients of their grants, and how much they paid their top officers.

This online resource is available in the Foundation Center's offices in Atlanta, Cleveland, New York, San Francisco, and Washington, as well as in many local community foundations and some public libraries. In our case, we accessed the index in July 2010, at the Community Foundation of Santa Cruz County. At that time, the regularly updated information included grants for 2003 to early 2009, although there had as yet been very few grants for 2009.

Several hundred foundations provided nearly seventeen hundred grants of $1,000 or more for the four preparatory educational programs we described in chapter 6: Early Steps, Steppingstone, A Better Chance, and Prep for Prep. Table A3.1 includes a list of those family, corporate, and community foundations that met one of two criteria for cumulative donations between 2003 and early 2009. First, foundations are listed if they gave $50,000 or more to any one of the four prep programs. Second, they are listed if they gave $10,000

Table A3.1. Family, Community, and Corporate Foundations That Gave $50,000 or More to One of the Four Educational Programs or $10,000 or More to Two or More of the Programs, 2003–2009

Donors	State	Financial Source	Early Steps	Steppingstone	A Better Chance (ABC)	Prep for Prep
Family Foundations						
Achelis Foundation	NY	American Hard Rubber Company/early 20th century (foundation now controlled by venture capitalist John Irwin III of Hillside Capital)	$30,000			$50,000
Ahmanson Foundation	CA	Insurance/savings & loan			$60,000	
Alg Family Foundation (Anne L. Gilchrist)	NY	Anne Gilchrist Hall is an officer of Prep for Prep and her husband John H. Hall is a corporate lawyer who has served on the Prep for Prep board since 1986				$902,000*
Herbert Allen Foundation	NY	Finance (Allen & Co.)	$210,000*			$270,000*
Altman Foundation	NY	Dry goods store, early 20th century			$100,000	$480,000
Elizabeth Raymond Ambler Trust	CT	Donor, Elizabeth Raymond Ambler (controlled by trust lawyer Thomas T. Adams)			$56,750	
Fred and Katherine Andersen Foundation	MN	Privately owned window and door mgt. company			$72,000	
Douglas A. Hirsch & Holly S. Anderson Family Foundation	NY	Finance (Seneca Capital Management)				$50,000

Foundation	State	Industry				
Annenberg Foundation (CA)	CA	Publishing (e.g., TV Guide)				$100,000
Lloyd G. Balfour Foundation	MA	Balfour Company (class rings and graduation products)		$250,000		
Barr Foundation	MA	Communications (donor, Amos Hostetter, Jr., cofounder of Continental Cable)		$300,000		
Arthur Belfer Foundation	NY	Belco Corporation (oil and gas)	$15,000			$100,000
Biaklin Family Foundation	NY	Corporate law			$224,430	
Leon D. Black Family Foundation	NY	Finance (Apollo Global Management)				$102,000*
Lloyd & Laura Blankfein Foundation	NY	Finance (partner in Goldman Sachs)				$312,500
Adele & Leonard Block Foundation	MA	Drug stores		$400,000*		
Booth Ferris Foundation	NY	Banking (J.P. Morgan Chase controls it)				$100,000
Daniel & Estrellita Brodsky Family Foundation	NY	Real estate (The Brodsky Organization)				$53,500
Carolyn & Kenneth D. Brody Foundation	DC	Finance (Goldman Sachs and then Winslow Partners)				$100,000
Burke Family Foundation	PA	Communications (donor Stephen B. Burke is chief operating officer for Comcast)		$246,000		
Chartwell Charitable Foundation	CA	Media (Univision)				$150,000

(continued)

Table A3.1. (Continued)

Donors	State	Financial Source	Early Steps	Steppingstone	A Better Chance (ABC)	Prep for Prep
Claneil Foundation	PA	Office equipment and supplies (Claneil Enterprises)		$60,000		
Steven A. & Alexandra M. Cohen Foundation	CT	Finance (SAC Capital Advisors)				$52,000
Concordia Foundation	MD	Insurance (John D. Roberts, former AIG executive)				$80,235
Geraldine Dodge Foundation	NJ	Rockefeller inheritance/ Remington Arms			$115,000	
Dyson Foundation	NY	Private investment firm (Dyson-Kissner-Moran)				$60,000
Educational Foundation of America	CT	Publishing (donors, founders of Prentice-Hall, Inc)				$60,000
Emwiga Foundation	NY	Finance (Willard J. Overlock, a partner in Goldman Sachs)				$773,500
Sherman Fairchild Foundation	MD	Aviation and semiconductors (Fairchild Semiconductors)				$200,000
Paul & Phyllis Fireman Charitable Foundation	MA	Apparel/shoes (Fireman was a founder and CEO of Reebok International)		$125,000		
Daniel Neidich and Brooke Garber Foundation	NY	Finance (partner in Goldman Sachs and Dune Capital Management)	$5,000			$215,000*

Foundation	State	Description/Industry				
Genesis Foundation	NY	Colombian and American entrepreneurs, industrialists, and financial investors				$55,000
Georgescu Family Foundation	CT	Advertising (former CEO of Young & Rubicam)			$56,700	
Sol Goldman Charitable Trust	NY	NY real estate				$1,400,000*
Niki & Joe Gregory Charitable Foundation	NY	Finance (Joe Gregory, a partner at Lehman Brothers before its bankruptcy in 2008)				$50,000
Grousbeck Family Foundation	CA	Communications/sports (Harold Grousbeck cofounded Continental Cablevision and an owner of Boston Celtics)		$430,000		
Charles Hayden Foundation	NY	Finance (Hayden Stone)		$270,000		
Heckscher Foundation for Children	NY	Mining (New Jersey Zinc Company)	$75,000	$60,000		
Hettinger Foundation	NY	Real estate/horse racing (John A. and William R. Hettinger)		$50,000		
Highland Street Connection	MA	Temporary staffing (TAD Resources)		$155,000		
Jacobson Family Trust Foundation	MA	Finance (Highfields Capital Mgt.)		$322,250		
Esther & Joseph Klingenstein Fund	NY	Financial advisers (Klingenstein, Fields, & Co.)	$56,000	$79,600		

(continued)

Table A3.1. (*Continued*)

Donors	State	Financial Source	Early Steps	Steppingstone	A Better Chance (ABC)	Prep for Prep
Henry Kravis Foundation	NY	Finance (Kohlberg Kravis Roberts Holding Company)				$250,000
Lambert Family Foundation	NY	Drug stores (donor, Harry W. Lambert, former president of Eckerd Drugs)	$62,500			
Larson Family Foundation	MA	Finance (Sowood Capital Mgt., Jeffrey B. Larson, dissolved in 2007 due to losses)		$75,000		
Brook J. Lenfest Foundation	PA	Cable services/investments (Suburban Cable, NetCarrier, Brook Capital Group)		$10,000	$35,000	
Liu Foundation	NY	Arthur Liu owns Chinese language radio stations in the US through Multicultural Radio Broadcasting, Inc.				$140,000
Loeb Family Foundation (aka Third Point Foundation)	NY	Finance (Loeb, Rhodes)				$1,275,129*
Lone Pine Foundation	CT	Finance (Lone Pine Capital)				$250,000
Lumina Foundation for Education	IN	Has $770 million endowment from USA Group's sale of its student loan business to Sallie Mae in 2000				$75,000

Organization	State	Description				
Maher Family Foundation	NY	Finance (donor, James R. Maher, CEO, BlackRock Kelso Capital Corporation)				$320,000*
Ambrose Monell Foundation	NY	Mining (Monell was an early leader of the International Nickel Corporation)				$75,000
Robert Niehaus Foundation	NY	Finance (Greenhill Capital Partners)	$5,000			$150,000
Amelia Peabody Foundation	MA	Merchandising/finance (family inheritance)		$100,000		
Perelman Family Foundation	NY	Finance (MacAndrews & Forbes Holdings)				$50,000
Pincus Family Foundation	NY	Finance (Warburg Pincus)			$80,000	$125,000
Pinkerton Foundation	NY	Detective and security work for corporations (Pinkerton National Detective Agency/Pinkerton, Inc.)				
Reeder Foundation	MA	Finance (donor, Paul A. Reeder III, Par Capital Management)		$70,000		
Regals Foundation	NY	Finance (Timothy R. Barakett, Atticus Capital)				$60,000
Smith Richardson Foundation	CT	Cough drops/VapoRub remedies (Vicks Chemical Company)			$57,500	
Thomas A. Rodgers, Jr., Family Foundation	MA	Suits for firefighters (Globe Manufacturing Company)		$50,000		
Rothfield Family Foundation	NY	REI Capital & Jones Apparel Group				$205,000*

(continued)

Table A3.1. (Continued)

Donors	State	Financial Source	Early Steps	Steppingstone	A Better Chance (ABC)	Prep for Prep
Robin Brown & Charles Seelig Family Foundation	NY	Finance (Goldman Sachs & Dune Capital Mgt.)				$73,000*
Peter Jay Sharp Foundation	NY	Hotels and real estate in NYC				$165,000
Shippy Foundation	NY	Heirs to the Singer Sewing Machine fortune		$50,000		
Marty & Dorothy Silverman Foundation	NY	Leasing (National Equipment Rental)				$96,300
Richard & Susan Smith Family Foundation	MA	Movie theaters (General Cinema)		$1,216,000*		
Starr Foundation	NY	Insurance (donor C. V. Starr founded a forerunner of AIG)			$40,000	$1,440,000
Teagle Foundation	NY	Oil (Standard Oil of New Jersey, 1930s)				$80,000
Tsunami Foundation	FL	Finance (donor Anson M. Beard Jr. is a retired partner of Morgan Stanley)				$55,000
Tudor Foundation	CT	Tudor Investment Corp. (real estate fortunes of the Malloy and Rabinowitz families)	$140,000	$150,000*	$60,000	
John & Barbara Vogelstein Foundation	NY	Finance (Warburg Pincus)				
John S. Weinberg Foundation	NY	Finance (partner in Goldman Sachs)		$282,249*		$1,586,000*

Name	State	Description			
John F. Welch, Jr. Foundation	FL	CEO of General Electric, 1981–2001	$30,000	$20,000	
Whispering Bells	NY	Publishing (donor Peter Workman owns Workman Publishing Co.)			$312,000*
Wille Family Foundation	CT	Financial data (donor Howard Wille is cofounder of FactSet Research Systems)			$55,000
Corporate Foundations					
American Express	NY	Banking/travel	$85,000	$150,000*	$10,000
Bank of America	NC	Banking			$120,000
Citi Foundation	NY	Banking		$20,000*	$425,000*
Coca-Cola	GA	Soft drinks	$75,000	$100,000	
Comcast	PA	Communications			
Credit Suisse Americas	NY	Banking		$15,000	$210,000*
Deutsche Bank Americas	NY	Banking		$50,000	$160,000
Epker-Sinha	MA	Finance (Par Capital Mgt.)	$128,500*		
General Mills	MN	Cereals		$60,000	
Hearst Foundation	NY	Publishing	$110,000		$150,000
Hess Foundation	NJ	Oil (Hess Oil)	$827,500		$10,000
J. P. Morgan Chase	NY	Banking	$10,000	$50,000	$50,000
Lehman Brothers	NY	Finance (bankrupt in 2008)		$50,000*	
Liberty Mutual	MA	Insurance	$200,000	$5,000	
Lincoln Financial	PA	Insurance/retirement plans	$215,000		
Macy's Foundation	NY	Department stores			$97,500
Moody's Foundation	NY	Business publications/bond ratings			$198,000*
Morgan Stanley	NY	Finance		$425,000*	$40,000

(continued)

Table A3.1. (*Continued*)

Donors	State	Financial Source	Early Steps	Steppingstone	A Better Chance (ABC)	Prep for Prep
TD Charitable Foundation	ME	TD Bank (from Maine to Florida)			$52,500	
Timken Foundation	OH	Steel/roller bearings (Timken Company)			$54,000	
Verizon Foundation	NJ	Communications		$10,000	$20,000	
Wachtell, Lipton, Rosen & Katz Foundation	NY	Corporate law firm				$700,000*
Community Foundations						
Boston Foundation	MA	Private donors and other foundations		$234,000	$32,000	
Community Foundation for Greater Atlanta	GA	Private donors and other foundations			$70,715	
New York Community Trust	NY	Private donors and other foundations	$1,000	$1,254,000	$37,250	$2,403,500
San Francisco Foundation	CA	Private donors and other foundations		$58,000	$50,000	
Seattle Foundation	WA	Private donors and other foundations			$10,000	$42,300
Silicon Valley Community Foundation	CA	Private donors and other foundations		$169,450		

*The donations with asterisks were given by foundations with a member of their board also on the board of the program that received the grant.

or more to two or more of the four. If a foundation met either of those criteria, then its donations of less than $10,000 to any of the remaining programs were also listed. For example, the $5,000 that Liberty Mutual's corporate foundation gave to ABC is listed because Liberty Mutual qualified for inclusion based on the two grants totaling $200,000 to Steppingstone in 2007 and 2008. Similarly, the $1,000 that the New York Community Trust gave to Early Steps is listed because it also gave over a million dollars to both Steppingstone and Prep for Prep, along with $37,500 to ABC.

The table is divided into separate sections for family, corporate, and community foundations so readers can see if and how they may play different roles within different organizations. We have identified the source of the wealth for each of the foundations, although the information is not as complete as we would like it to be in two or three instances. We believe that the information provided in this appendix is useful in and of itself because few studies have explored the large network of foundations and nonprofit organizations created by their financial relationship. The important exception to this statement is the work based on information from the 1970s by sociologist Mary Anna Colwell (1980, 1993), which discovered the clusters of moderate and ultraconservative foundations and nonprofits that tended to work together.

Moreover, the patterns of giving revealed in this appendix also raise many questions that could be explored in future studies concerning corporate power. For example, why would one Wall Street firm's foundation (Morgan Stanley) give large donations to A Better Chance and a family foundation funded by a major figure in another Wall Street firm (Warburg Pincus) give even larger amounts to Prep for Prep? Is there an informal parceling out of responsibility or can an explanation be found by studying the membership on boards of trustees? Or are both at play, along with other factors?

Readers may wonder why the New York Community Foundation would give donations to all four programs, or why community foundations in San Francisco and Seattle would be giving to one or more programs based on the East Coast. Part of the answer is to be found in the fact that community foundations sometimes serve as managers for the charitable funds of wealthy individuals who maintain control of where the funds will be donated. In fact, many of the specific donations by the New York Community Trust that we have added together are often for a few thousand dollars (along with a handful of donations for $250,000 to $1,000,000), which fits with the idea that individuals control these funds. Similarly, the donations from community foundations in San Francisco and Seattle may reflect the ties of wealthy individuals to Boston or New York, but future research is needed to provide a more complete answer as to why community foundations are large donors to these programs. As to the source of the very large specific grants from community foundations, our research reveals that much of it comes from family and corporate foundations, and even other community foundations, but it would take us too far afield to present those findings here.

Readers may also notice that the ABC program receives funds from more states than the others, a difference that would be even more apparent if all grants down to $1,000 were included. This pattern is very likely due to the fact that ABC has affiliates and support groups (e.g., Andover Committee for A Better Chance in Massachusetts and A Better Chance in Lower Merion in Pennsylvania) in many different states, including Minnesota and Georgia. In addition, ABC now receives substantial gifts from many alumni who are likely to live all around the country.

In examining this information on how foundation funding primes the corporate pipeline, it may be useful to keep in mind that these findings are typical for nonprofit organizations in general. Virtually all of them, whether working on issues related to the inner cities or supporting the fine arts, receive a varying but significant percentage of their funds from one of the three types of foundations, and often from all three. When corporate profits suffer, most nonprofit organizations suffer too. Future studies might explore the implications of this conclusion in terms of the societal power of CEOs and the wealthy families that own large blocks of stock in corporations. If nonprofits such as these four educational organizations are as dependent on foundations as we suspect they are, then it may not be correct to think of nonprofits in general as a "third" or "independent" sector apart from the private sector on the one side and government on the other, especially when some nonprofits receive government grants as well. Perhaps it might be useful to explore the degree to which many of these organizations are part of a larger corporate community (Domhoff 2009, 2010, chaps. 4 and 5).

Two studies have approached the possibility that nonprofits are therefore a part of the corporate community by looking at membership on boards of directors for corporations, foundations, and various nonprofit organizations. In a study using information on the directors of 201 corporations, 20 New York corporate law firms, 11 foundations, and 25 nonprofit organizations of different types in 1970, it was found that two foundations (the Rockefeller and Sloan foundations) and seven nonprofits (four policy-discussion organizations, two universities, and the Metropolitan Museum of Art) joined sixteen top banks and corporations as the twenty-five most central organizations in a network based on shared trustees and directors (Salzman and Domhoff 1983, 209–11). A study deploying a more refined network methodology and similar information from the late 1990s for 100 corporations and 109 nonprofits found that the most central fifty organizations consisted of thirty-two corporations, four foundations, six charities, and eight policy-discussion organizations (Moore et al. 2002, 737).

Putting aside any possible broader implications of the findings reported in this appendix, we hope the information provided in the tables in chapter 6 and this appendix will lead more social scientists to take advantage of the *Foundation Grants Index* as an excellent starting point for their own research on the role of foundations and nonprofits.

Notes

NOTES TO CHAPTER 1

1. Technically she became president of the company and did not formally become chair of the board until 1979. It is not clear if or when she formally held the title of CEO, but she is generally referred to as having been the CEO from 1963 until her retirement in 1991.

2. Two African American men had been CEOs of companies that were on the *Fortune* 500 list either before or after they were CEO: Clifton Wharton was CEO at TIAA from 1987 to 1992 (it made the *Fortune* 500 list in 1998 and has been on it ever since) and Erroll Davis was CEO of Alliant Energy from 1998 to 2005 (Alliant was on the *Fortune* 500 list in the early 1990s, but during the time Davis was CEO, and since that time, it has been in the *Fortune* 1000 but not in the *Fortune* 500). In addition, two more were named in 1999 to companies that were close to the *Fortune* 500 or were to be on the list within a few years: A. Barry Rand at Avis (Avis was on the *Fortune* 500 in 2000 and 2001) and John W. Thompson at Symantec (Symantec was not on the 500 list in 1999, but it was #461 in 2008).

NOTES TO CHAPTER 2

1. See Domhoff 2010 (chap. 5) for an analysis of the many ways in which corporations attempt to shape public opinion on specific issues and at the same time reinforce a general antigovernment ideology through a wide-ranging network of foundations, think tanks, policy-formation groups, public relations firms, and advertising agencies.

2. In response to a complaint from the Sandlers, the *New York Times* made four corrections in this lengthy article, one of which was to change the title to "Once trusted mortgage pioneers, now scrutinized" (see Moss and Fabrikant 2008).

3. In a series of studies, Catalyst has found that companies with more women senior executives and companies with more women on their boards are more profitable than companies with fewer women. Catalyst CEO Ilene Lang summarized these studies in the following way: "Catalyst's 'Bottom Line' studies have shown that *Fortune* 500 companies with more women in senior management, on average, financially outperform those with fewer women. The same is true for companies with more women board directors—even more so with three or more women board directors" (Lang 2010).

In its October 25, 2010, edition, *Forbes* magazine compared the stock performance of the twenty-six companies headed by women they had deemed the "100 most powerful women" with companies headed by men (this included some women who run companies outside the United States, such as Anne Lauvergon, the CEO of Areva, a French corporation). They found that the companies headed by women on the Power Women list outperformed the overall market by 28 percent, and outperformed their respective industries by 15 percent (Ozanian 2010, 71).

For a look at what some have called "glass cliffs," the precarious circumstances and the increased risk that some women face in leadership positions (including women directors on *Fortune* boards), see Ryan, Haslam, Hersby, Kulich, and Wilson-Kovacs (2009).

4. Ann Livermore, who began working at Hewlett-Packard in 1982, stayed with the company, and as of 2010 she was an executive vice president. In 2009 she was #6 on *Fortune*'s "Highest Paid Women" list, with a total compensation package of $17.3 million (and #13 on *Fortune*'s "Most Powerful Women" list).

5. *The Economist* article did not list an author. Though the article portrays Bartz as "hardened" and "occasionally ruthless," it did not mention that she is widely known for what is generally considered a macho trait, being foulmouthed. In early May 2010, *Esquire* ran an article titled "Hi, I'm Carol Bartz . . . Are You an Asshole?" in which the author cites many examples of Bartz using salty language, and explaining "Cursing is part of the job. Everybody has this funny reaction to it. I don't know what the big deal is" (Fussman 2010). Later that same month, Bartz again made waves in the blogosphere (and in the national press) for telling an interviewer to "fuck off." As the *New York Times* righteously intoned, "Investors should be wary of executives spouting obscenities at critics—even the pesky blogger whom Ms. Bartz cursed out on Monday" ("No expletives, please," *New York Times*, May 26, 2010, B2).

6. In the eighth edition of *The American Class Structure in an Age of Growing Inequality,* Dennis Gilbert (2011, 14) proposes a six-part model that includes the capitalist class, which makes up about 1 percent of the population and consists of investors, heirs, and top executives whose typical annual income is about $2 million; the upper middle class, which includes about 14 percent of the population and consists of upper managers, professionals, and medium-sized business owners whose typical annual income is about $150,000; the middle class, about 30 percent of the population, consisting of lower managers, craftsmen, and semi-professionals, with a typical income of about $70,000; the working class, also about 30 percent, consisting of people who work in low-skill manual labor, clerical work, and retail sales, and earn about $40,000; the working poor, about 13 percent, consisting of the lowest-paid manual,

retail, and service workers, and earning about $25,000; and the underclass, about 12 percent of the population, including unemployed, people on public assistance, and people who work part-time menial jobs. In using this model, we have attempted in this and subsequent chapters to estimate the percentage of the CEOs from the capitalist and upper middle classes, which together make up 15 percent of the population. At times we will use the term *upper class* instead of *capitalist class*.

7. In May 2010, Brenda Barnes went on temporary medical leave after she had a stroke at the age of 56. She resigned and gave up her board seat in August ("Sara Lee Chief Is Leaving after a Stroke," 2010).

8. Perhaps the most impressive higher degree was earned by Eileen Scott, a graduate of William Paterson University in New Jersey, who started as a clerk and part-time bookkeeper and became CEO of Pathmark in 2002. After she retired as CEO at Pathmark in 2005, Scott returned to school and in 2009, at the age of 56, she earned an MBA in finance from New York University.

NOTES TO CHAPTER 3

1. The average board size in 1971 was about 14, so there were 7,000 seats on *Fortune* 500 boards. Some, like Patricia Harris, held seats on more than one board, so she was probably the only African American woman among somewhere between 6,000 and 6,500 men, almost all of whom were white (Vancil 1987, 9). Boards increased in size by 1975, to 16, dropped again to 14 in 1995, and were down to 11.2 in 2004 (see Weidenbaum 1995, and Zweigenhaft and Domhoff 2006, 42, n34).

2. "Ursula M. Burns," Times Topics, *New York Times*, online, updated May 21, 2009.

3. "Ursula M. Burns," *New York Times*. After she was named president of Xerox in 1997, Burns told a reporter, "My perspective comes in part from being a New York black lady, in part from being an engineer. I know I'm smart and have opinions worth being heard" (Usborne 2009).

4. See chapter 2 (note 6), which provides a summary of the model used by Dennis Gilbert (2011, 14) in the eighth edition of *The American Class Structure in an Age of Growing Inequality*.

5. We have not been able to find out Rodney O'Neal's socioeconomic background, but we do know he is the cousin of Stanley O'Neal (and that his family visited Stanley's family every summer) and that he, like Stanley, went to college at Kettering University, a school run by General Motors for its employees. Few who attended Kettering were from economic privilege, so we think it is safe to assume that Rodney O'Neal was not from a family in the top 15 percent of the socioeconomic structure.

6. Stephanie Streeter, who was CEO from 2002 until 2006 of Banta, a *Fortune* 1000 company, was a four-year starter in the late 1970s on the Stanford women's basketball team (Zweigenhaft and Domhoff 2006, 82, n24). In March 2009 she became CEO of the U.S. Olympic Committee, the same job held previously by Lloyd Ward (Hersh 2009). Streeter's athletic background demonstrates that more and more women in senior executive positions have participated in competitive sports. Sharon

Napier, the CEO of an advertising agency, for example, answered a question about her leadership style by explaining that "much of what I learned about leadership I learned playing basketball, whether it was as a player or from my coaches," and went on to note "I use basketball analogies a lot" (Bryant 2010a).

7. These findings were not reported in their article, but Livingston and Pearce were kind enough to send them to us in response to our e-mail request (for which we thank them). The photos they used were drawn from the web (in their case, the *Fortune* website at http://money.cnn.com/magazines/fortune/fortune500) and converted to grayscale. See appendix 2 for a detailed comparison between our respondents' ratings of the photographs they used and the photographs that we used.

8. $r = .60$, $n = 300$, $p < .001$.

9. Though we have no evidence that the other new CEOs are babyfaced, it is likely that they, too, tend to present themselves in ways that are nonthreatening. Consider this description in a *New Yorker* article of Vikram Pandit, the Indian CEO of Citigroup, in which the author compares Pandit with Pandit's white male predecessors at Citigroup: "I spoke with Pandit in a sparsely furnished hotel room. Citi's leaders—from Walter Wriston, in the nineteen-seventies, to John Reed, in the nineteen-eighties, and Sanford Weill, in the nineteen-nineties—have tended to be formidable and forbidding. Pandit affects a down-to-earth demeanor. He offered me a cup of coffee and insisted that I sit on a comfortable upholstered chair while he perched on a cheap plastic one" (Cassidy 2010, 49).

10. This organization was formerly known as the American Association of Retired Persons. It changed its name to AARP in 1999 because it no longer requires its members to be retired and to show that its focus had become broader than issues related to retired persons.

11. On the one-year anniversary of September 15, 2008, the *New York Times* ran vignettes of twelve of the most "famous names on Wall Street," describing, as the title put it, "Where the Players Landed." One of these was E. Stanley O'Neal, about whom the *Times* wrote the following:

THEN. He was ousted as the chief executive of Merrill Lynch in 2007 after the firm built up a big portfolio of troubled mortgages.

NOW. He now serves as a director on several boards, including Alcoa and Memorial Sloan-Kettering Cancer Center. He and his wife are "active supporters" of Bronx Preparatory, a charter school, according to his spokesman.

According to his friends, Mr. O'Neal puts a high priority on his workouts. He plays squash with his son at the New York Athletic Club and golfs in Purchase, N.Y., as well as on Martha's Vineyard, where he owns a waterfront home ("Financial Crisis One Year Later: Where the Players Landed" 2009).

NOTES TO CHAPTER 4

1. More recently, Juan F. Casas and Carey S. Ryan (2010, 2), in their work on Latino immigration, explain that they use the term *Latino* rather than *Hispanic*, for two reasons: "We chose the term *Latino* as opposed to *Hispanic* or some other label for two reasons. First, our focus is on people of Latin American heritage, many of whom prefer

the term *Latino*. Second, the term *Hispanic* refers to people of Spanish origin, that is, people from Spain, thus excluding the indigenous populations of Latin America."

2. Walter Kissling, whose German parents immigrated to Costa Rica but who was born and grew up in Costa Rica, became CEO of H. B. Fuller in 1995. The company had been on the *Fortune* list from 1984 through 1994, but it was not on the list the year he was appointed, or during his four years as CEO, so we have not included him.

3. Many upper class families in the Caribbean sent their children to American boarding schools. In her essay "A White Woman of Color" (1998), the writer Julia Alvarez explains how this worked in the Dominican Republic, where she grew up; see also her novel *How the Garcia Girls Lost Their Accents* (Alvarez, 1992) for a fictional portrayal of the useful connections between the boarding school graduates who grew up to join the CIA and their Caribbean classmates from elite families.

4. Goizueta's father's gift of $8,000 in 1960 is the equivalent of $58,967 in 2010 dollars.

5. The Associated Press obituary (10/18/97) said $20, the *New York Times* obituary said $40 (10/19/97), and Greising writes that it was $200 (1998, 22). In an article in *USA Today*, Jones (1999) claims that Goizueta "often told the story of how he left in 1960 with $200 and 100 shares of Coca-Cola stock." As with many defining stories one tells about oneself, the facts may vary in different renditions. See Zweigenhaft 2004, on the way the media tend to skew the obituaries of tycoons.

6. Although the use of distinctive Hispanic names can be a useful methodology to estimate large populations (Zweigenhaft and Domhoff 2006, 153–54), it is risky to depend on distinctive Hispanic names to identify the ethnic background of an individual. Two former CEOs who sound like they are Latinos are not (at least not without really stretching the boundaries of what is already a pretty broad category). David I. Fuente, CEO of Office Depot from 1987 to 2000, was born and raised in Chicago. He is the descendent of Sephardic Jews, which means that his ancestors were most likely expelled from Spain or Portugal in the fifteenth century. Similarly Arthur C. Martinez, the CEO of Sears from 1995 until 2000, sounds Latino but isn't. The Community Affairs office at Sears informed us that Martinez is mostly of Irish descent, and that "a family member married someone from Spain generations ago and that is where the name came from." *Hispanic Business* has included both Fuente and Martinez on its lists of Hispanic CEOs of *Fortune* 1000 companies (Zate 1998), as has the Hispanic Association on Corporate Responsibility (HACR) in its Corporate Governance Studies. Both *Hispanic Business* and HACR also have included Robert D. Glynn, Jr., the CEO of PG&E from 1997 to 2004, but we have not been able to find any other evidence in print that he is Hispanic and the public relations department at PG&E did not respond to our queries.

7. Perhaps because so many of the Latino and Asian CEOs were born and raised in other countries, for many of them it was harder to find accurate information about their parents' educations and occupations than it was for the American-born men and women who became CEOs. When our usual sources (searches on Lexis-Nexis, Google, etc.) did not lead to the information we sought, we tried to contact the CEOs themselves or the companies they worked for.

In a few cases, what sociologists call "social capital" came in handy. For example, when we could not confirm the class background through the usual sources for

William Perez, the former CEO of Nike and Wrigley Corporation, and when our attempts to contact him through the public relations department at Wrigley were not fruitful (he no longer worked there), we drew on a personal contact. We knew that Perez had attended a prep school in Cleveland, Western Reserve Academy, and one of us has a college friend who was a student at that school at about the same time as Perez. We wrote him and asked for help contacting Perez. Our friend was able to provide us with Perez's personal e-mail, we wrote Perez and within hours he answered our question (in fact, over the next few days we exchanged a series of e-mails with Perez, and he answered a number of questions for us), including the fact that his father had very little formal education at the college level and that he started as a production supervisor at a Goodyear plant in Colombia. His father rose through the ranks and subsequently ran that plant and then he ran all the Goodyear plants in Latin America. In terms of class background, we therefore concluded that Perez was raised in the upper one-third of the class structure in Colombia.

8. We thank Amanda Heins, account executive at Ruder Finn Public Relations, for helping us to obtain this information about Cristobal Conde's family background (Amanda Heins, e-mail message to the first author, November 12, 2009).

9. A chi-square test that looks at whether or not the raters accurately identified the twelve Latinos as Latinos was highly significant ($x^2 = 80.57$, $df = 11$, $p < .001$). As was true for the skin color ratings and the ethnic identification for the photos of the African American CEOs, accurate identification of ethnicity for Latinos was significantly related to skin color ($r = .36$, $n = 240$, $p < .001$), but, obviously, not based solely on it.

10. We have not included Winston Chen, the CEO of Solectron from 1984 to 1987 because the company did not make the *Fortune* 500 until after he left the company. Similarly, we have not included Allen Chao, the founder and CEO of Watson Pharmaceuticals because the company has been on the *Fortune* 1000 list but not the *Fortune* 500 list.

11. An article about Pandit in *New York Magazine* describes his father as "a middle class pharmaceutical executive," once again reminding us of the slippery use of the term *middle class* both by the executives themselves and by the media. Then, as if ignoring his own claim that the family was "middle class," the writer adds: "His family was of the Maharashtrian Brahmin caste, traditionally known as priests and scholars (Pandit, in fact, means 'priest' or 'learned person'), who frequently enter the business class in Indian society" (Hagan 2009).

12. This study was conducted prior to the appointment of Ajay Banga, so his photograph was not included.

13. These differences were statistically significant ($t = 5.25$, $df = 178$, $p < .001$). We did not include Laura Sen, whose mother was Irish and father Chinese, in this comparison.

NOTES TO CHAPTER 5

1. In his research on the 1936 presidential campaign, Mike Webber (2000, 13) found very similar results: 83 percent of 960 donors who were listed in *Standard &*

Poor's Register of directors of the United States and Canada for that year gave to the Republicans. Michael Patrick Allen (1991) reports a very similar figure for the directors of 270 top companies in the same year. These findings are also consistent with findings in later decades (Alexander 1971; Heard 1960; Domhoff 1990, chap. 9).

2. These differences approach statistical significance: $F = 1.70$, $df = 3$, $p < .17$. A comparison between the *Fortune* rankings for the companies headed by African Americans and the *Fortune* rankings for the other three groups combined is statistically significant: $t = 1.97$, $df = 74$, $p < .05$, $r = .22$, as is the difference between the rankings for the African American CEOs and the Latino CEOs: $t = 2.19$, $df = 27$, $p < .03$, $r = .39$. The research described in this chapter was performed prior to the appointments of Ajay Banga as CEO at MasterCard in July 2010 and Kenneth Frazier as CEO of Merck in January 2011, so the sample for the Asian Americans included only nineteen, not twenty, and the sample for the African Americans included only fourteen, not fifteen, CEOs.

Because the control group of white male CEOs was chosen based on a matching system in which their companies were ranked near those in the target groups, the average *Fortune* ranking for the white CEOs (M = 191) did not differ significantly from the rankings of any of the other groups. The average rankings for the other control group, the Jewish CEOs (M = 132) revealed that of the six groups they were most likely to be CEOs of larger companies. A one-way analysis of variance with *Fortune* ranking as the dependent variable is significant ($F = 3.26$, $df = 5$, $p < .01$), and post hoc Tukey tests reveal that the only between-group comparison that was significant was between the Jewish CEOs (whose companies had the lowest rankings) and the Latino CEOs (whose companies had the highest rankings, $p < .01$).

3. $x^2 = 6.99$, $df = 1$, $p < .01$, $r = .30$.

4. The data from the analyses in the following three paragraphs are based on a 2006 data set provided to us by Cliff Staples, professor of sociology at the University of North Dakota, for which we are grateful. Some of the new CEOs have been asked to join additional *Fortune* boards since then, and some have joined policy boards (in some cases, after they had left their positions as CEOs). We have included those newer directorships, and policy memberships, in appendix 1.

5. $x^2 = 17.63$, $df = 5$, $p < .003$, $r = .20$.

6. These comparisons are either statistically significant or close to statistically significant whether a *t*-test is performed comparing the new CEOs versus the Jewish and gentile male CEOs ($t = 1.79$, $df = 168$, $p < .08$, $r = .07$), an analysis of variance comparing the six groups ($F = 2.49$, $df = 5$, $p < .03$), or an analysis of variance among the three groups (the new CEOs, the Jewish CEOs, and the gentile male CEOs; $F = 3.33$, $df = 2$, $p < .04$). When we compare the African American CEOs with all the others on this variable, they score significantly higher ($t = 2.80$, $df = 168$, $p < .006$, $r = .21$); similarly, when we compare the African American and women CEOs with all the others, the difference is statistically significant ($t = 2.45$, $df = 168$, $p < .02$, $r = .19$).

7. Although Khurana indicates that it has become normative, if not universal, for *Fortune*-level corporations to use search firms to seek new CEOs, Charan (2009) cites a study by the public affairs firm Burson-Marsteller that found that only slightly more

than a third (37 percent) of the *Fortune* 1000 companies "are run by external recruits" (Charan 2009, 129).

8. The *New York Times* data and *Business Week* data correlated at $r = .69$, the *New York Times* data and *Forbes* correlated at $r = .72$, and *Business Week* data and *Forbes* data correlated at $r = .61$.

9. Just as Parsons, a Republican, was slow to endorse Obama, so too were many prominent African American Democrats. According to *Washington Post* writer and editor Eugene Robinson (2010), there was a generational divide, in which highly successful older African Americans, like civil rights leader and former congressman Andrew Young, "uberlawyer" Vernon Jordan, and Congressman John Lewis, part of what Robinson labels Transcendent Black America, initially endorsed Hillary Clinton because they thought Obama was so unlikely to win: "In the luxurious but not entirely serene precincts of Transcendent Black America, Hillary Clinton was the smart, conservative play, the best that could be hoped for" (146).

10. For details about the methodology used, see http://www.thecro.com/node/783.

11. For details about their methodology, see http://www.nafe.com/web?service =direct/1/ViewArticlePage/dlinkFullArticle&sp=S2232&sp=245.

NOTES TO CHAPTER 6

1. Eric Holder, the first African American to hold the position of attorney general, correctly made the connection between the activists who worked in the South during the civil rights movement and his appointment. As he said in a moving speech at the fiftieth anniversary celebration of the Student Nonviolent Coordinating Committee (SNCC), there is a direct line between the lunch counters and the doors to the Oval Office: "Let me be very clear: there is a direct line, a direct line, from that lunch counter to the Oval Office and to the fifth floor of the United States Department of Justice where the Attorney General sits. Today, as I stand before leaders who I've admired all my life, I fully understand that I also stand on your shoulders" (Davidson 2010).

2. The information in this and the next two paragraphs about Thomas are based on a phone interview with the first author, July 6, 2010.

3. The website for Roosevelt Thomas Consulting and Training is http://www .rthomasconsulting.com/.

4. Thomas's $20,000 speaking fee for a keynote address is drawn from the website of Premiere Speakers Bureau, www.premierespeakers.com/roosevelt_thomas.

5. As Post and DiTomaso (2004, 3) point out, the business case for diversity includes the cost of not managing diversity well. As they write: "Most important in this regard is the withdrawal of effort that is likely by employees who feel that they are not fully able to participate in an organization. Hence, those organizations that are not effective in managing diversity well are not only likely to face higher costs in production of goods or services, but they are also likely to lose out on attracting a diverse customer base, to have difficulty tapping into a wider pool of talent, and to fail in generating the kind of creativity that is necessary to stay ahead of the competition."

6. We are grateful to sociologist Roderick J. Harrison at Howard University for guiding us to the *Digest of Education Statistics* that we have used in this and subsequent paragraphs. The *Digest of Education Statistics* is an online publication provided by the Institute of Education Sciences (IES) at the National Center for Education Statistics, U.S. Department of Education.

7. "Hispanic Americans by the Numbers," U.S. Census Bureau, www.infoplease .com/spot/hhmcensus1.html.

8. Phone interview by the first author with Jacqueline Y. Pelzer, executive director of Early Steps, May 27, 2010. Because of the challenge of keeping track of students after they have left the first grade, Early Steps, unlike some of the programs discussed below, does not have complete information on the number of its students who go on to attend college or which colleges they attend.

9. The Block Drug Company was controlled by the family until it was sold in 2001 to GlaxoSmithKline for $1.24 billion.

10. This information is in ABC's *2009 Annual Report*. See www.abetterchance .org/FileUploads/A%20Better%20Chance%20Annual%20Report%20FY09.pdf.

11. We wish to thank Sandra E. Timmons, the president of ABC, for sharing the findings of both surveys with us. We also thank her for sharing a copy of the *2005 Alumni Directory* with us.

12. "Measures of Success," www.prepforprep.org/podium/default.aspx?t = 126417.

13. See "Xerox Intern Program Helps Route College Students to Success," from CSRwire, the Corporate Social Responsibility Newswire, www.csrwire.com/press/ press_release/24065-Xerox-Intern-Program-Helps-Route-College-Students-To-Success.

14. This information comes from the Center for Education Statistics, the Institute of Education Sciences, maintained by the U.S. Department of Education. We thank Rory Kramer of the University of Pennsylvania for guiding us to the College Navigator on this useful website (www.nces.ed.gov/collegenavigator/).

15. The information in this and the next few paragraphs is from the Black MBA website: www.nbmbaa.org/home.aspx?PageID = 637&.

16. Pamela G. Carlton and David A. Klassen, who are executives at Springboard, an executive and leadership consulting firm, carried out this 2008 research for the Executive Leadership Council.

17. These compensation figures were drawn from the detailed occupation variable on the Current Population Survey (CPS) and the American Community Survey (ACS) and analyzed for us by Roderick J. Harrison. He used the code for "1110XX MGR-CHIEF EXECUTIVES AND LEGISLATORS." ACS tabulations were run for this category, restricting the sample to "1 Employee of a private for-profit company or business, or of an individual, for wages, salary, or com" (other values include employment by nonprofits, government, and self-employment). We asked Harrison to restrict the tabulation to those who usually worked full time (thirty-five or more hours) in the prior year. We used the combined 2005–2008 ACS information he provided to us because the unweighted N's in the CPS were quite low, even when we pooled the most recent three years (2007–2009) available.

18. We thank Ancella Livers, the executive director of the Institute for Leadership Development & Research at the Executive Leadership Council for providing

this information in an e-mail to the first author on June 17, 2010, and for the broader perspective that she shared in a phone interview with him on June 2, 2010.

19. Jeffrey Palmer, a senior executive at Home Depot in 2001 (when it was #23 on that year's *Fortune* list), estimated that the company had fifty to seventy-five people within three steps of the CEO office (Palmer left Home Depot in December 2001 to work for Pep Boys, a smaller company with fewer people within three steps of the CEO office). More recently, we asked a senior executive at a *Fortune* 500 company that is between #350 and #400 on the 2010 *Fortune* list and who was previously a senior executive at a larger *Fortune* company (one that is between #50 and #100 on the 2010 list) how many employees were within three steps of the CEOs at those two corporations. She estimated that seventy-five to eighty people were within three steps of the CEO office at her current company, and twice that many at her previous employer (for the Palmer estimate, see Zweigenhaft and Domhoff 2003, 139, n1).

20. The twenty-five corporations (and their 2010 *Fortune* rankings) were as follows: General Electric (#4), Bank of America (#5), Hewlett-Packard (#10), Citigroup (#12), Verizon (#13), Staples (#101), Google (#102), Oracle (#105), 3M (#106), Deere (#107), TRW (#201), Navistar (#202), Liberty Global (#210), United States Steel (#211), AutoNation (#212), Quest (#303), Western Digital (#304), Ball Corp. (#307), VF Corp. (#310), Darden (#311), Amerigroup (#404), Avis (#409), Master-Card (#411), Western Union (#413), and Eastman Chemical (#415).

21. Although we know from our skin color studies that it is often difficult to recognize Latinos and Asian Americans, for this study we also had the benefit of having access to the person's name and being able to obtain biographical information on him or her if we had any doubt as to their race or ethnicity. As a reliability check, we had a second rater assess the ethnicity for 103 of the photographs (the executives from the five largest corporations). The interjudge reliability was $r = .94$ for all the photographs, and there was over 90 percent agreement for all groups except for the Latinos, which was 88.9 (8 of 9).

22. These differences are statistically significant: $x^2 = 29.94$, $df = 4$, p < .001, $r = .32$.

APPENDIX 2

1. The first author wishes to thank Guilford College for providing research funds to allay the costs of paying participants in this study.

References

Abelson, Reed. 1999. A push from the top shatters a glass ceiling. *New York Times*, August 22, A1, A23.

———. 2010. A scrappy insurer wrestles with reform. *New York Times*, Business section, 1 and 6.

Adler, Nancy. 2009. Health disparities through a psychological lens. *American Psychologist* 64: 663–73.

Adler, Nancy, Archana Singh-Manoux, Joseph Schwartz, Judith Stewart, Karen Matthews, and Michael Marmot. 2008. Social status and health: A comparison of British civil servants in Whitehall-II with European- and African-Americans in CARDIA. *Social Science & Medicine* 66: 1034–45.

Alba, Richard. 2009. *Blurring the color line: The new chance for a more integrated America*. Cambridge, MA: Harvard University Press.

Alba, Richard, and Dalia Abdel-Hady. 2005. Galileo's children: Italian Americans' difficult entry into the intellectual elite. *Sociological Quarterly* 46: 3–18.

Alexander, Herbert. 1971. *Financing the election, 1968*. Lexington, MA: Heath Lexington Books.

Allen, Michael Patrick. 1991. Capitalist response to state regulation: Theories of the state and political finance in the New Deal. *American Sociological Review* 56: 679–89.

Allen, Walter, Edward Telles, and Margaret Hunter. 2000. Skin color, income and education: A comparison of African Americans and Mexican Americans. *National Journal of Sociology* 12: 129–80.

Alvarez, Julia. 1992. *How the Garcia girls lost their accents*. New York: Plume.

———. 1998. A white woman of color. In *Half and half: Writers on growing up biracial and bicultural*, edited by Claudine Chiawei O'Hearn, 139–49. New York: Pantheon.

Anand, Rohini, and Mary-Frances Winters. 2008. A retrospective review of corporate diversity training from 1964 to the present. *Academy of Management Learning and Education* 7: 356–72.

Anderson, Sarah, Chuck Collins, Sam Pizzigati, and Kevin Shih. 2010. CEO pay and the great recession. *17th Annual Executive Compensation Survey*. Washington, DC: Institute for Policy Studies, September 1.

Andrea Jung. 2007. *Biography Resource Center Online*, January 2. galenet.galegroup .com/servlet/BioRC.

Arango, Tim. 2009. Parsons is named chairman of Citigroup. *New York Times*, January 21.

Arce, Carlos H., Edward Murguia, and W. Parker Frisbie. 1987. Phenotype and life chances among Chicanos. *Hispanic Journal of Behavioral Sciences* 9: 19–32.

Arndt, Michael. 2004. Untitled. *Business Week*, May 17, p. 14.

Austin, Algernon. 2010. Uneven pain: Unemployment by metropolitan area and race. Issue Brief #278. Washington, DC: Economic Policy Institute, June 8.

Bajaj, Vikas, and Andrew Martin. 2010. Who needs cash (or borders)?, *New York Times*, October 16, Business section, 1 and 4.

Baltzell, E. Digby. 1958. *Philadelphia gentlemen: The making of a national upper class*. Glencoe, IL: The Free Press.

———. 1964. *The Protestant establishment: Aristocracy & caste in America*. New York: Vintage.

Barboza, David. 2000. Maytag's chief executive resigns, citing differences. *New York Times*, November 10.

Barry, Dan. 1997. Facing rough times, Charles Wang tries a new style. *New York Times*, February 4, Business section, 1.

Benoit, Denise. 2007. *The best-kept secret: Women corporate lobbyists, policy & power in the United States*. Piscataway, NJ: Rutgers University Press.

Berenson, Alex. 2002. Market place: A gift raises questions on Computer Associates. *New York Times*, December 3, C1.

———. 2007. Ex-executive agrees to pay $800 million in restitution. *New York Times*, April 13.

Berger, Marilyn. 2001. Katharine Graham of *Washington Post* dies at 84. *New York Times*, July 18, A1.

Berle, Adolf A. 1959. *Power without property; A new development in American political economy*. New York: Harcourt Brace.

———. 1964. Economic power and the free society. In *The corporation take-over*, edited by Andrew Hacker, 92–97. New York: Vintage Books.

Berle, Adolf A., and Gardiner C. Means. 1932. *The modern corporation and private property*. New York: Macmillan.

Berman, Phyliss. 2004. The cosmopolitan touch. *Forbes*, June 21.

Birger, Jon. 2006. Patricia Woertz, the outsider: To be its CEO, famously insular ADM picked not only a woman but a newcomer. *Fortune*, October 2.

Blagg, Deborah. 1983. The best of both worlds and other myths. *Harvard Business School Bulletin*, June.

Blair, Irene V., Charles M. Judd, and Kristine M. Chapleau. 2004. The influence of Afrocentric facial features in criminal sentencing. *Psychological Science* 15: 674–79.

Bohan, Caren. 2008. McCain, Obama discuss possible treasury secretary picks. *Reuters*, October 7.

Bond, Horace Mann. 1966. The Negro scholar and professional in America. In *The American Negro reference book*, edited by John P. Davis, 548–89. Englewood Cliffs, NJ: Prentice Hall.

Bond, Selena, and Thomas F. Cash. 1992. Black beauty: Skin color and body images among African American college women. *Journal of Applied Social Psychology* 22: 874–88.

Bonilla-Silva, Eduardo. 2004. From biracial to tri-racial: The emergence of a new racial stratification system in the United States. In *Skin deep: How race and complexion matter in the "color-blind" era*, edited by Cedric Herring, Verna Keith, and Hayward D. Horton, 224–39. Urbana-Champaign: University of Illinois Press.

Bonilla-Silva, Eduardo, and David R. Dietrich. 2009. The Latin Americanization of U.S. race relations: A new pigmentocracy. In *Shades of difference: Why skin color matters*, edited by Evelyn Nakano Glenn, 40–60. Stanford, CA: Stanford University Press.

Brady, Erik. 2010. Education secretary Arne Duncan credits basketball with life assist. *USA Today*, March 17.

Brauer, Carl. 1983. Women activists, southern conservatives, and the prohibition of sex discrimination in Title VII of the 1964 Civil Rights Act. *Journal of Southern History* 49: 37–56.

Brennan, Carol. 2005. Aylwin Lewis. *Contemporary Black Biography*. Gale Research Inc. Retrieved September 13, 2009, from Encyclopedia.com: www.encyclopedia.com/doc/1G2-3449300030.html.

Brooks, John. 1999. *The go-go years: The drama and crashing finale of Wall Street's bullish 60s*. New York: John Wiley and Sons.

Bryant, Adam. 2009. Corner office: Clarence Otis, Jr. *New York Times*, June 7, Business section, 2.

———. 2010a. Corner office: On her team, it's all about bench strength. *New York Times*, May 7.

———. 2010b. We're family, so we can disagree. *New York Times*, February 21, Business section, 1 and 9.

Bumiller, Elisabeth. 2008. Ousted executive provides a feminine face to the McCain campaign. *New York Times*, June 6.

Burris, Val. 2000. White supremacist networks on the Internet. *Sociological Focus* 33: 215–35.

———. 2008. The interlock structure of the policy-planning network and the right turn in U.S. state policy. *Research in Political Sociology* 17: 3–42.

Burrough, Bryan, and John Helyar. 1990. *Barbarians at the gate: The fall of RJR Nabisco*. New York: Harper and Row.

Cameron, Edward. 1960. *Samuel Slater, father of American manufactures*. Freeport, ME: Wheelright Company.

Carlson, Margaret. 2010. Republicans need to quit playing the ugly losers. *Greensboro News & Record*, March 28, H1.

Carlton, Pamela G., and David A. Klassen. 2008. *Black women executives research initiative: Findings*. Alexandria, VA: Executive Leadership Council.

Carter, Nancy M., and Christine Silva. 2010a. *Pipeline's broken promise*. New York: Catalyst (Catalyst Publication Code D96 ISBN# 0–89584–306–4).

———. 2010b. Women in management: Delusions of progress. *Harvard Business Review*, March, online.

Casas, Juan F., and Carey S. Ryan. 2010. How Latinos are transforming the United States: Research, theory, and policy. *Journal of Social Issues* 66: 1–10.

Cassidy, John. 2010. What good is Wall Street? *New Yorker*, November 29, 49–57.

Catalyst census of women board directors: A call to action in a new era of corporate governance. 2003. New York: Catalyst.

Chafe, William. 1980. *Civilities and civil rights: Greensboro, North Carolina and the black struggle for freedom*. New York: Oxford University Press.

Chambers, Marcia. 1995. *The unplayable lie: The untold story of women and discrimination in American golf*. New York: Golf Digest/Pocket.

Charan, Ram. 2009. Ending the CEO succession crisis. In *Harvard Business Review on CEO succession*, 125–51. Boston: Harvard Business School Publishing.

Coke CEO Roberto C. Goizueta Dies at 65. 1997. *Cable News Network*, October 18.

Collins, Sharon M. 1997. *Black corporate executives: The making and breaking of a black middle class*. Philadelphia: Temple University Press.

Colwell, M. 1980. The foundation connection: Links among foundations and recipient organizations. In *Philanthropy and cultural imperialism: The foundations at home and abroad*, edited by R. F. Arnove, 413–52. Boston: G. K. Hall & Co.

Colwell, M. 1993. *Private foundations and public policy: The political role of philanthropy*. New York: Garland.

Cose, Ellis. 2002. Rethinking black leadership. *Newsweek*, January 28, 42–43.

Craig, Maxine Leeds. 2009. The color of an ideal Negro beauty queen: Miss Bronze 1961–1968. In *Shades of difference: Why skin color matters*, edited by Evelyn Glenn, 81–94. Stanford, CA: Stanford University Press.

Craig, Susanne. 2011. Citi gives Pandit a raise. *New York Times*, January 21.

Crenshaw, Kimberle. 1991. Mapping the margins: Intersectionality, identity politics, and violence against women of color. *Stanford Law Review* 43: 1241–99.

Current Population Survey. U.S. Census. 2009.

Daniels, Cora. 2002. 50 most powerful black executives in America. *Fortune*, July 22, 63.

Dash, Eric. 2007. Robert Rubin, the new chairman at Citigroup, hits the ground running. *New York Times*, November 7.

Davidson, Carl. 2010. We'll never turn back: SNCC 50th anniversary celebrates vanguard role in battles for democracy. April 25. www.carldavidson.blogspot.com.

de la Garza, Rodolfo, Louis De Sipio, F. Chris Garcia, John Garcia, and Angelo Falcon. 1992. *Latino voices: Mexican, Puerto Rican, and Cuban perspectives on American politics*. Boulder, CO: Westview.

Delton, Jennifer. 2009. *Racial integration in corporate America, 1940–1990*. New York: Cambridge University Press.

Desai, Sreedhari, Arthur Brief, and Jennifer George. 2010a. When executives rake in millions: Meanness in organizations. Paper presented at the annual meeting for the International Association for Conflict Management, June 24–27, in Boston, MA.

———. 2010b. Meaner managers: A consequence of income inequality. In *Social decision making: Social dilemmas, social values, and ethical judgments*, edited by R. M. Kramer, A. E. Tenbrunsel, and M. H. Bazerman, 315–32. New York: Taylor & Francis.

Deutsch, Claudia H. 2003. Private sector: An apparent heir at Xerox. *New York Times*, section 3, p. 2.

DiTomaso, Nancy, and Donna E. Thompson 1988. Minority success in corporate management. In *Ensuring minority success in corporate management*, edited by Donna E. Thompson and Nancy DiTomaso, 3–24. New York: Plenum.

Dobbin, Frank. 2009. *Inventing equal opportunity*. Princeton, NJ: Princeton University Press.

Dobbin, Frank, and John Sutton. 1998. The strength of the weak state: The rights revolution and the rise of human resources management divisions. *American Journal of Sociology* 104: 441–76.

Dobrzynski, Judith H. 1995. How to succeed? Go to Wellesley. *New York Times*, October 29.

Domhoff, G. William. 1990. *The power elite and the state: How policy is made in America*. Hawthorne, NY: Aldine de Gruyter.

———. 2006. *Who rules America? Power, politics & social change*. 5th ed. New York: McGraw-Hill.

———. 2007. C. Wright Mills, Floyd Hunter, and fifty years of power structure research. *Michigan Sociological Review* 21: 1–54.

———. 2009. The power elite and their challengers: The role of nonprofits in American social conflict. *American Behavioral Scientist* 52: 955–73.

———. 2010. *Who rules America? Challenges to corporate and class dominance*. 6th ed. New York: McGraw-Hill.

Domhoff, G. William, and Hoyt B. Ballard. 1968. *C. Wright Mills and the power elite*. Boston: Beacon Press.

Dovidio, John. 2001. On the nature of contemporary prejudice: The third wave. *Journal of Social Issues* 57: 829–49.

Downes, Brian T. 1970. A critical re-examination of the social and political characteristics of riot cities. *Social Science Quarterly* 51: 349–60.

Dreier, Peter. 2009. Citizens confront WellPoint: Poster child for health insurance reform. *Huffington Post*, September 22, online.

Driscoll, Dawn Marie, and Carol R. Goldberg. 1993. *Members of the club: The coming of age of executive women*. New York: Free Press.

Duhigg, Charles. 2008. Pressured to take more risk, Fannie reached tipping point. *New York Times*, October 4.

Dundes, Alan. 1984. *Life is like a chicken coop ladder: A portrait of German culture through folklore*. New York: Columbia University Press.

Edwards, Harry. 1983. Athletic performance in exchange for an education—A contract unfulfilled. *The Crisis*, May, 10–14.

———. 2000. Crisis of black athletes on the eve of the 21st century. *Society* 37, March/April, 9–13.

Eichenwald, Kurt. 1996. Investigation finds no evidence of slur on Texaco tapes. *New York Times*, November 11.

Fabrikant, Geraldine. 2010. Fewer women betting on Wall Street careers. *New York Times*, January 30, Business section, B3.

Fast, Nathaniel, Deborah Gruenfeld, Niro Sivanathan, and Adam Galinsky. 2009. Illusory control: A generative force behind power's far-reaching effects. *Psychological Science* 20: 502–8.

Ferrin, Lindsay. 2010. Where you are is not necessarily who you are. *Rochester Woman Magazine*, January 15.

Financial crisis one year later: Where the players landed. 2009. *New York Times*, September 13, Business section, 3.

Flynn, Laurie J. 2007. In primary, tech's home is a magnet. *New York Times*, August 24.

Forman, Tyrone A., Carla Goar, and Amanda E. Lewis. 2002. Neither black nor white: An empirical test of the Latin Americanization thesis. *Race & Society* 5: 65–84.

Fost, Dan. 2006. Do they have a good marriage? You can take that to the bank. *San Francisco Chronicle*, June 4.

Francia, Peter L., John C. Green, Paul S. Herrnson, Lynda W. Powell, and Clyde Wilcox. 2005. Limousine liberals and corporate conservatives: The financial constituencies of the Democratic and Republican parties. *Social Science Quarterly* 86: 761–78.

Freeman, Jo. 2008. *We will be heard: Women's struggles for political power in the United States*. Lanham, MD: Rowman & Littlefield.

Fussman, Cal. 2010. Hi, I'm Carol Bartz . . . are you an asshole? *Esquire*, May 3.

Galinsky, Adam, Joe Magee, M. Ena Inesi, and Deborah Gruenfeld. 2006. Power and perspectives not taken. *Psychological Science* 17: 1068–74.

Gates, Henry Louis. 1995. Powell and the black elite. *New Yorker*, September 25, 63–80.

———. 2004. Breaking the silence. *New York Times*, August 1, A11.

George, Amiso M., and Maggie B. Thomas. 2006. Denials, cover-ups, and apologies: How "résumé gate" ended the once rising career of RadioShack's Dave Edmondson, and lessons for the rest of us. Paper presented at the annual meeting of the Association for Business Communication, October 25–28, in San Antonio, TX.

Gilbert, Dennis. 2011. *The American class structure in an age of growing inequality*, 8th ed. Los Angeles: Pine Forge Press.

Glenn, Evelyn Nakano. 2009. *Shades of difference: Why skin color matters*. Stanford, CA: Stanford University Press.

Goffman, Erving. 1959. *The presentation of self in everyday life*. New York: Doubleday.

Graham, Katharine. 1997. *Personal history.* New York: Knopf.

Green, Donna. 1998. Q&A/Richard Parsons: From law to president of Time Warner. *New York Times,* May 17, 3.

Gregory, Frances, and Irene Neu. 1962. The American industrial elite in the 1870s: Their social origins. In *Men in business: Essays on the historical role of the entrepreneur,* edited by William Miller, 193–211. New York: Harper Torchbooks.

Greising, David. 1998. *I'd like the world to buy a Coke: The life and leadership of Roberto Goizueta.* New York: John Wiley and Sons.

Gutierrez, Carlos M. (written with Amy Zipkin). 2001. The boss: My many citizenship quests. *New York Times,* August 22, C6.

Hagan, Joe. 2009. The most powerless powerful man on Wall Street. *New York Magazine,* March 1.

Hansell, Saul. 1997. American Express names apparent successor to chief. *New York Times,* February 28, C2.

Hays-Thomas, Rosemary. 2004. Why now? The contemporary focus on managing diversity. In *The Psychology and Management of Workplace Diversity,* edited by Margaret S. Stockdale and Faye J. Crosby, 3–30. Malden, MA: Blackwell Publishing.

Heard, Alexander. 1960. *The costs of democracy.* Chapel Hill: University of North Carolina Press.

Heenan, David. 2005. *Flight capital: The alarming exodus of America's best and brightest.* Vincennes, IN: Davies-Black Publishing.

Hepp, Christopher K. 2010. New Merck CEO Kenneth C. Frazier has Philadelphia roots. *Philadelphia Inquirer,* December 1.

Herring, Cedric. 2004. Skin deep: Race and complexion in the "color-blind" era. In *Skin deep: How race and complexion matter in the "color blind" era,* edited by Cedric Herring, Verna M. Keith, and Hayward Derrick Horton, 1–21. Urbana and Chicago: University of Illinois Press.

Herring, Cedric, Melvin Thomas, Marlese Durr, and Hayward Derrick Horton. 1998. Does race matter? The determinants and consequences of self-reports of discrimination victimization. *Race & Society* 1: 109–23.

Hersh, Philip. 2009. New USOC chief Stephanie Streeter: "This is not a palace coup." *Los Angeles Times,* March 8.

Hing, Bill Ong, and Ronald Lee. 1996. *Reframing the immigration debate: A public policy report.* Los Angeles: LEAP Asian Pacific American Public Policy Institute and UCLA Asian American Studies Center.

Hochschild, Jennifer L., and Vesla Weaver. 2007. The skin color paradox and the American racial order. *Social Forces* 86: 643–70.

Hodson, Gordon, John Dovidio, and Samuel Gaertner. 2010. The aversive form of racism. In *The psychology of prejudice and discrimination: A revised and condensed edition,* edited by Jean Lau Chin, 1–13. New York: Praeger.

Hughes, Michael, and Bradley Hertel. 1990. The significance of color remains: A study of life chances, mate selection, and ethnic consciousness among black Americans. *Social Forces* 69: 1105–20.

Hunter, Margaret L. 2002. "If you're light, you're alright:" Light skin color as social capital for women of color. *Gender & Society* 16: 175–93.

Iwata, Edward. 2004. Boards seat few Asian-Pacific Americans. *USA Today*, April 14.

Job creators prefer John McCain 4-to-1 over Barack Obama. 2008. *Chief Executive Magazine*, September/October.

Jones, Del. 1999. Cuban Americans thrive. Many started over with nothing but determination. *USA Today*, January 19, Money section, 3B.

———. 2002. Many successful women say sports teaches valuable lessons. *USA Today*, March 26, Money section.

———. 2008. Board diversity expands political spectrum: Directors of color back wider range of candidates. *USA Today*, August 20, B1.

Jones, James M. 1997. *Prejudice and racism*, 2nd ed. New York: McGraw-Hill.

Joy, Lois. 2008. Advancing women leaders: The connection between women board directors and women corporate officers. Research Report, July. New York: Catalyst.

Karabel, Jerome. 2005. *The chosen: The hidden history of admission and exclusion at Harvard, Yale, and Princeton*. Boston: Houghton Mifflin.

Kasinitz, Philip. 1992. *Caribbean New York: Black immigrants and the politics of race*. Ithaca, NY: Cornell University Press.

Kaufman, Leslie. 2001a. Questions of style in Warnaco's fall. *New York Times*, May 6, Business section, 3 and 6.

———. 2001b. After 15 years, Warnaco chief's short goodbye. *New York Times*, November 17, C14.

Keith, Verna M. 2009. A colorstruck world: Skin tone, achievement, and self-esteem among African American women. In *Shades of difference: Why skin color matters*, edited by Evelyn Nakano Glenn, 25–39. Stanford, CA: Stanford University Press.

Keith, Verna M., and Cedric Herring. 1991. Skin tone and stratification in the black community. *American Journal of Sociology* 97: 760–78.

Kelly, Erin L., and Frank Dobbin. 1998. How affirmative action became diversity management: Employer response to antidiscrimination law, 1961–1996. *American Behavioral Scientist* 41: 960–84.

———. 2001. How affirmative action became diversity management: Employer response to antidiscrimination law, 1961–1996, In *Color lines: Affirmative action, immigration and civil rights options for America*, edited by John D. Skrentny, 87–117. Chicago: University of Chicago Press.

Kendall, Diana. 2006. Class in the United States: Not only alive, but reproducing. *Research in Social Stratification and Mobility* 24: 89–104.

———. 2008. *Members only: Elite clubs and the process of exclusion*. Lanham, MD: Rowman & Littlefield.

Khurana, Rakesh. 2002. *Searching for a corporate savior: The irrational quest for charismatic CEOs*. Princeton, NJ: Princeton University Press.

Kramer, Rory. 2008. Diversifiers at elite schools. *Du Bois Review* 5, 287–307.

Labaton, Stephen. 2004a. Control that was maybe too remote. *New York Times*, September 29, C1 and C9.

———. 2004b. Chief says Fannie May did nothing wrong. *New York Times*, October 7, C1 and C10.

————. 2004c. Chief is ousted at Fannie Mae under pressure. *New York Times*, December 22, C4.

Lacey, Robert. 1986. *Ford: The men and the machine*. Boston: Little Brown.

Lammers, Joris, Diederik Stapel, and Adam Galinsky. 2010. Power increases hypocrisy: Moralizing in reasoning, immorality in behavior. *Psychological Science* 21: 737–44.

Lang, Ilene H. 2010. Have women shattered the glass ceiling? *USA Today*, April 14.

Lavelle, Louis. 2002. Executive pay. Special report #3778. *Business Week*, April 15, 80.

Leinster, Colin. 1987. Jerry Tsai listens to his mother. *Fortune*, August 17.

Leonhardt, David. 1999. The saga of Lloyd Ward. *Business Week*, August 9, 59–70.

Lewis, Michael. 2007. Agony, or in the bunker with Stan. www.bloomberg.com, November 6.

Limonic, Laura. 2008. Latinos and the 2008 presidential elections: A visual data base. New York: Center for Latin American, Caribbean & Latino Studies. web.gc.cuny.edu/lastudies/latinodataprojectreports/Latinos%20and%20the%20 2008%20Presidential%20Elections%20A%20Visual%20Data%20Base.pdf.

Livingston, Robert W., and Nicholas A. Pearce. 2009a. The teddy-bear effect: Does having a baby face benefit black chief executive officers? *Psychological Science* 20: 1229–36.

————. 2009b. E-mail message to first author. November 3.

Llorente, Elizabeth. 2004. The breakfast champ. *Hispanic Business*, January.

Lloyd, Fonda Marie, and Mark Lowery. 1994. The man behind the merger. *Black Enterprise*, October, 76.

Luo, Michael. 2009. "Whitening" the resume. *New York Times*, December 6, Week in Review section, 3.

Lynch, Frederick R. 2002. *The diversity machine: The drive to change the "white male workplace."* New Brunswick, NJ: Transaction.

Markoff, John. 1998. Trailblazer in the Silicon jungle. *New York Times*, November 1, section 3, p. 2.

————. 2005. When + adds up to minus. *New York Times*, February 10, C1, C7.

Martin, Andrew. 2009. Give BB&T liberty, but not a bailout. *New York Times*, August 1, B1.

Martin, Andrew, and Eric Dash. 2010. Naming a new chief, MasterCard signals it is open to changes. *New York Times*, April 12, B4.

McAdam, Doug. 1982. *Political process and the development of black insurgency*. Chicago: University of Chicago Press.

McKinley, Jesse. 2011. California runner-up bypasses review of race. *New York Times*, January 23, A18.

McQuaid, Kim. 1982. *Big business and presidential power from FDR to Reagan*. New York: Morrow.

Miller, Claire Cain. 2010. Out of the loop in Silicon Valley: In the wide-open world of tech, why so few women? *New York Times*, April 18, Business section, 1, 8–9.

Miller, William. 1962. American historians and the business elite. In *Men in Business*, edited by William Miller, 309–28. New York: Harper and Row.

Mills, C. Wright. 1956. *The power elite*. New York: Oxford University Press.

Moore, G., S. Sobieraj, J. Whitt, O. Mayorova, and D. Beaulieu. 2002. Elite interlocks in three U.S. sectors: Nonprofit, corporate, and government. *Social Science Quarterly* 83: 726–44.

Morales, Elsie. 2010. Top 25 MBAs for Hispanics. Poder 360°. www.poder360.com/article_detail.php?id_article=2021&pag=1.

Moran, Nancy. 2007. O'Neal ranks no. 5 on payout list. *Bloomberg News*, November 2, online.

Morgenson, Gretchen. 2004. At Fannie, the ties that blind. *New York Times*, December 26, Business section, 1 and 6.

———. 2005. How to slow runaway executive pay. *New York Times*, October 23, section 3, p. 1.

———. 2006. Corporate America's pay pal. *New York Times*, October 15.

———. 2009. They left Fannie Mae, but we got the legal bills. *New York Times*, September 6, Business section, 1 and 6.

Moskos, Charles C., and John Sibley Butler. 1996. *All that we can be: Black leadership and racial integration the army way*. New York: Basic Books.

Moskowitz, Milt. 1982. The 1982 black corporate directors' lineup. *Business Society Review* 1982: 54.

Moss, Michael, and Geraldine Fabrikant. 2008. Once trusted mortgage pioneers, now scrutinized. *New York Times*, December 24, A1.

Murguia, Edward, and Tyrone Forman. 2003. Shades of whiteness: The Mexican-American experience in relation to Anglos and blacks. In *White out: The continuing significance of race*, edited by Ashley Doane and Eduardo Bonilla-Silva, 63–79. New York: Routledge.

Newcomer, Mabel. 1955. *The big business executive: The factors that made him, 1900–1950*. New York: Columbia University Press.

Noble, Holcomb B., and Charles McGrath. 2010. Louis Auchincloss, chronicler of New York's upper crust, dies at 92. *New York Times*, January 27, A31.

Nocera, Joe. 2008a. Self-made philanthropists. *New York Times*, March 9, The Money Issue, pp. MM58ff.

———. 2008b. *Good guys & bad guys: Behind the scenes with the saints and scoundrels of American business (and everything in between)*. New York: Penguin.

Norris, Floyd. 2006. RadioShack chief resigns after lying. *New York Times*, February 21.

Oboler, Suzanne. 1995. *Ethnic labels, Latino lives*. Minneapolis: University of Minnesota Press.

Oliver, Melvin L., and Thomas M. Shapiro. 2006. *Black wealth/white wealth: A new perspective on racial inequality*. New York: Routledge.

One tough Yahoo! Life has tested Carol Bartz far more than even running Yahoo! will. 2009. *Economist*, January 15.

Otterman, Sharon. 2009. Former e-Bay boss Meg Whitman seeks to run California next. *New York Times*, February 9.

Ozanian, Michael K. 2010. Girls rule. *Forbes*, October 25, 71.

Park, Edward Jang-Woo. 1996. Asians matter: Asian American entrepreneurs in the Silicon Valley high technology industry. In *Reframing the immigration debate:*

A public policy report, edited by Bill Ong Hing and Ronald Lee, 166–67. Los Angeles: LEAP Asian Pacific American Public Policy Institute and UCLA Asian American Studies Center.

Pettigrew, Thomas. 1988. Integration and pluralism. In *Eliminating racism: Profiles in controversy*, edited by Phyliss A. Katz and Dalmas A. Taylor, 19–30. New York: Plenum Press.

———. 2008. Still a long way to go: American black-white relations today. In *Commemorating Brown: The social psychology of racism and discrimination*, edited by G. Adams, M. Biernat, N. Branscombe, C. Crandall, and L. Wrightsman, 45–61. Washington, DC: American Psychological Association.

———. 2010. Commentary: South African contributions to the study of intergroup relations. *Journal of Social Issues* 66: 417–30.

Pitrone, Jeanne Maddern. 2003. *F. W. Woolworth and the American five and dime: A social history*. Jefferson, NC: McFarland.

Pollack, Andrew. 2002. The genome is mapped, now he wants profit. *New York Times*, February 24, section 3, p. 1.

Post, Corinne, and Nancy DiTomaso. 2004. Workforce diversity: Why, when and how. *Research in the Sociology of Work* 14: 1–14.

Preston, Julia. 2010. Immigrants in work force: Study belies image. *New York Times*, April 16, A1, A3.

Raines, Franklin D. (written with Amy Zipkin). 2002. The boss: Quarterback at the lectern. *New York Times*, June 16, section 3, p. 14.

Ransford, H. Edward. 1970. Skin color, life chances, and anti-white attitudes. *Social Problems* 18: 164–79.

Rimer, Sara, and Karen W. Arenson. 2004. Top colleges take more blacks, but which ones? *New York Times*, June 24.

Rivlin, Gary, and John Markoff. 2005. Tossing out a chief executive. *New York Times*, February 14, C1, C4.

Roberts, Sam. 2010. Census figures challenge views of race and ethnicity. *New York Times*, January 22, A13.

Robinson, Eugene. 2010. *Disintegration: The splintering of black America*. New York: Doubleday.

Rodriguez, Clara. 1989. *Puerto Ricans: Born in the USA*. Boston: Unwin Hyman.

Rosen, Gerald H., and Robert Perrin. 2002. Declining returns. *Academe* 78: 8–12.

Rosen, Ruth. 2000. *The world split open: How the modern women's movement changed America*. New York: Viking Penguin.

Rosenberg, Hilary. 1989. The education of TIAA-CREF. *Institutional Investor*, April, 68–77.

Rosin, Hanna. 1998. Texaco takes the diversity tiger by the tail: In a holy crusade against racism, the oil giant is bombarding employees with Orwellian admonishments to "respect the individual." *The Globe and Mail* (Canada), D4.

Rowan, Roy. 1983. How Harvard's women MBAs are managing. *Fortune*, July 11, 58, 60, 64, 68, 72.

Royster, Deirdre A. 2003. Race and the invisible hand: How white networks exclude black men from blue-collar jobs. Berkeley, CA: University of California Press.

Rubenstein, Sarah. 2009. What's next for Schering Plough CEO Fred Hassan? *Wall Street Journal*, March 9.

Rufford, Nicholas, and Zoe Brannon. 1998. The society of rich women. *Sunday Times* (London), December 27.

Ruiz, Hector (written with John Markoff). 2003. The boss: The carrot of education. *New York Times*, section 3, p. 10.

Ryan, William. 1976. *Blaming the victim*. New York: Vintage.

Ryan, Michelle K., S. Alexander Haslam, Mette D. Hersby, Clara Kulich, and M. Dana Wilson-Kovacs. 2009. The stress of working on the edge: Implications of glass cliffs for both women and organizations. In *The glass ceiling in the 21st century: Understanding barriers to gender equality*, edited by Manuela Barreto, Michelle K. Ryan, and Michael T. Schmitt, 153–69. Washington, DC: American Psychological Association.

Saito, John, Jr. 2003. Ko Nishimura. In *Distinguished Asian American business leaders*, edited by Naomi Hirahara, 155–57. New York: Greenwood Press.

Salzman, Harold, and G. William Domhoff. 1980. The corporate community and government: Do they interlock? In *Power structure research*, edited by G. William Domhoff, 227–54. Beverly Hills, CA: Sage.

———. 1983. Nonprofit organizations and the corporate community. *Social Science History* 7: 205–16.

Sandomir, Richard. 2000. Hockey: New owners take over and promise to jump start isles. *New York Times*, June 21, section D, 6.

———. 2003. Chief of U.S. Olympic Committee quits amid a furor over ethics. *New York Times*, March 2, A18.

Sara Lee chief is leaving after a stroke. 2010. *New York Times*, August 10, B6.

Sasseen, Jane. 2008. The changes business wants from Obama. *Business Week*, November 5.

Schoolman, Judith. 2001. Clothed in bankruptcy losses, debt woes force Warnaco to run for cover. *New York Daily News*, June 12.

Schwartz, Jerry. 1997. Roberto C. Goizueta, Coca-Cola chairman noted for company turnaround, dies at 65. *New York Times*, October 19, section 1, p. 45.

Scott, Denise Benoit. 1998. Women at the intersection of business and government: Are they in places of power? *Sociological Spectrum* 18: 333–63.

Sellers, Patricia. 1998. The fifty most powerful women in American business. *Fortune*, October 12.

———. 2000. Seventh Avenue smackdown: Fashion moguls Calvin Klein and Linda Wachner are going toe-to-toe in a bitter suit. *Fortune*, September 4.

Sellers, Robert M., Tabbye M. Chavous, and Tony N. Brown. 2002. Uneven playing field: The impact of structural barriers on the initial eligibility of African American student-athletes. In *Paradoxes of Youth and Sport*, edited by Margaret Gatz, Michael A. Messner, and Sandra J. Ball-Rokeach, 173–86. Albany: State University of New York Press.

Sellers, Robert M., Gabriel P. Kuperminc, and Alphonse Damas, Jr. 1997. The college life experiences of African American women athletes. *American Journal of Community Psychology* 25: 699–720.

Sen, Laura (as told to Amy Zipkin). 2009. The boss: A happy return. *New York Times*, April 25, Business section, 11.

Sennett, Richard, and Jonathan Cobb. 1972. *The hidden injuries of class.* New York: Random House.

Seron, Carroll, and Frank Munger. 1996. Law and inequality: Race, gender . . . and, of course, class. *Annual Review of Sociology* 22: 187–212.

Shapiro, Thomas M. 2004. *The hidden cost of being African American: How wealth perpetuates inequality.* New York: Oxford University Press.

Shapiro, Thomas M., Tatjana Meschede, and Laura Sullivan. 2010. The racial wealth gap increases fourfold. *Research and Policy Brief*, May. Waltham, MA: Brandeis University, Institute on Assets and Social Policy.

Singer, Natasha. 2010. Merck appoints a new chief executive. *New York Times*, November 30.

Skrentny, John D. 2002. *The minority rights revolution.* Cambridge, MA: Harvard University Press.

Smith, Pamela. 2006. You focus on the forest when you're in charge of the trees: Power priming and abstract information processing. *Journal of Personality and Social Psychology* 90: 578–96.

Smith, Pamela, Nils Jostmann, Adam Galinsky, and Wilco Dijk. 2008. Lacking power impairs executive functions. *Psychological Science* 19: 441–47.

Steinhauer, Jennifer. 2010. In California, attack ads take a bizarre turn. *New York Times*, March 21, A1, A19.

Stevenson, Richard W. 1998. A homecoming at Fannie Mae. *New York Times*, May 17, Business section, 1 and 10.

Stodghill, Ron. 2007. Room at the top? *New York Times*, November 1, C1, C11.

Stone, Brad. 2010a. Ex-CEOs show tech can play in politics. *New York Times*, June 10, A20.

———. 2010b. Settlement was paid in Whitman shoving incident. *New York Times*, June 15, A13.

Story, Louise. 2007. Seeking leaders, U.S. companies think globally. *New York Times*, December 12.

Strom, Stephanie. 2007. Ford Foundation selects its new leader from outside the philanthropic world. *New York Times*, August 14, A11.

Sugrue, Thomas J. 2001. Breaking through: The troubled origins of affirmative action in the workplace. In *Color lines: Affirmative action, immigration, and civil rights options for America*, edited by J. Skrentny, 31–52. Chicago: University of Chicago Press.

———. 2008. *Sweet land of liberty: The forgotten struggle for civil rights in the North.* New York: Random House.

Takamine, Kurt. 2000. A profile of current Japanese-American, Chinese-American, and Korean-American lower, middle, and upper level managers in corporate America. PhD diss., Pepperdine University.

———. 2002. Investing in your company's future today: Retaining your Asian Pacific American professionals. Paper presented at the Asian Diversity Conference sponsored by Asian Diversity, Inc., November 14–15, in New York, NY.

Tarquinio, J. Alex. 2008. Selling beauty on a global scale. *New York Times*, November 1.

Tatelli, Caryn Platt. 1999. My job: I stare death in the face. *New York Times*, December 29.

Telles, Edward E., and Edward Murguia. 1990. Phenotypic discrimination and income differences among Mexican Americans. *Social Science Quarterly* 71: 682–96.

Telles, Edward E., and Vilma Ortiz. 2008. *Generations of exclusion: Mexican Americans, assimilation, and race*. New York: Russell Sage Foundation.

Temin, Peter. 1997. The American business elite in historical perspective. Working Paper. Cambridge, MA: National Bureau of Economic Research.

———. 1998. The stability of the American business elite. Working Paper. Cambridge, MA: National Bureau of Economic Research.

Thomas, R. Roosevelt, Jr. 1994. From affirmative action to affirming diversity. In *Differences That Work: Organizational Excellence through Diversity*, edited by Mary C. Gentile, 27–46. Cambridge, MA: Harvard Business Review Book.

———. 1996. *Redefining diversity*. New York: American Management Association.

Thompson, Charis. 2009. Skin tone and the persistence of biological race in egg donation for assisted reproduction. In *Shades of difference: Why skin color matters*, edited by Evelyn Nakano Glenn, 131–47. Stanford, CA: Stanford University Press.

Thompson, Donna, and Nancy DiTomaso. 1988. *Ensuring minority success in corporate management*. New York: Plenum.

Thompson, Maxine S., and Verna M. Keith. 2004. Copper brown and blue black: Colorism and self-evaluation. In *Skin deep: How race and complexion matter in the "color blind" era*, edited by Cedric Herring, Verna M. Keith, and Hayward Derrick Horton, 45–64. Chicago: University of Illinois Press, 45–64.

Timmons, Heather. 2010. Due diligence from afar: Cost conscious companies are outsourcing legal work. *New York Times*, August 5, B1.

Ursula M. Burns. 2009. Times topics. *New York Times*, May 21.

Usborne, David. 2009. From intern to chief executive: Black woman rises to the top. *The Independent*, May 23.

Useem, Michael. 1984. *The inner circle*. New York: Oxford University Press.

Vancil, Richard F. 1987. *Passing the baton: Managing the process of CEO succession*. Boston: Harvard Business School Press.

Vinas, Tonya. 2005. Three quick questions with Alcoa CEO Alain Belda. *Industry Week*, May 1.

Wachner, Linda. 1998. *Current biography yearbook*, 590–593. New York: H. W. Wilson Company.

Warsh, David. 2000. Economic principles/the hidden man. *Boston Globe*, July 2, Business section, H1.

Waters, Mary C. 1999. *Black identities: West Indian immigrant dreams and American realities*. Cambridge, MA: Harvard University Press.

Webber, Michael. 2000. *New Deal fat cats: Business, labor, and campaign finance in the 1936 presidential election*. New York: Fordham University Press.

Weidenbaum, Murray. 1995. The evolving corporate board. *Society* 32: 9–16.

Weintraub, Arlene. 2003. Powering up at eMachines. *Business Week*, November 17.

Wellington, Sheila. 1994. Women on corporate boards: The challenge of change. *Directorship Newsletter*, December. New York: Catalyst.

Wharton, Clifton, Jr. 1987. *Current biography yearbook*, 597–601. New York: H. W. Wilson Company.

Whigham-Desir, Marjorie. 1999. A watershed appointment (Lloyd Ward new CEO at Maytag Corp). *Black Enterprise* 30, p. 15.

Whyte, William H. 1956. *The organization man.* New York: Simon and Schuster.

Wiersema, Margarethe. 2009. Holes at the top: Why CEO firings backfire. *Harvard Business Review on CEO Succession.* Cambridge, MA: Harvard Business School Publishing, 17–37.

Williams, Alex. 2010. The new math on campus. *New York Times*, February 7, Style, 1.

Williams, Lena. 1992. Companies capitalizing on worker diversity. *New York Times*, December 15, A1.

Wilson, Sloan. 1955. *The man in the gray flannel suit.* New York: Pocket Books.

Women in management in the United States: 1950–present. 2010. New York: Catalyst.

Woo, Deborah. 1994. *The glass ceiling and Asian Americans.* Glass Ceiling Commission. Washington, DC: U.S. Department of Labor.

World class: Non-American CEOs are having a big impact at traditional U.S. companies. 2004. *Chief Executive.* Gale Group. April 1.

Wright, S. C., and M. Lubensky. 2009. The struggle for social equality: Collective action vs. prejudice reduction. In *Intergroup misunderstandings: Impact of divergent social realities*, edited by S. Demoulin, J. P. Leyens, and J. F. Dovidio, 291–310. New York: Psychology Press.

Wright, S. C., and D. M. Taylor. 1998. Responding to tokenism: Individual action in the face of collective injustice. *Personality and Social Psychology Bulletin* 28: 647–67.

———. 1999. Success under tokenism: Co-option of the newcomer and the prevention of collective protest. *British Journal of Social Psychology* 38: 369–96.

Yearick, Bob. 2009. She's got game. *Delaware Today*, May 11.

Zate, Maria. 1998. The big jump. *Hispanic Business*, January/February, 32.

Zebrowitz, Leslie A. 1997. *Reading faces: Window to the soul?* Boulder, CO: Westview.

Zeitz, Joshua. 2007. Why did America explode in riots in 1967? www.American Heritage.com, posted July 23.

Zeleny, Jeff. 2010. Reid apologizes for remarks on Obama's color and "dialect." *New York Times*, January 10, A1.

Zweigenhaft, Richard L. 1984. *Who gets to the top? Executive suite discrimination in the eighties.* New York: Institute of Human Relations.

———. 2004. Making rags out of riches: Horatio Alger and the tycoon's obituary. *Extra! The Magazine of FAIR—the Media Watch Group* 17: 27–28.

———. 2007. Diversity in the power elite: What about Atlanta? Paper presented at the annual meeting for the Southern Sociological Association, April 13, in Atlanta, GA.

Zweigenhaft, Richard L., and G. William Domhoff. 1982. *Jews in the Protestant establishment*. New York: Praeger.

———. 1991. *Blacks in the white establishment? A study of race and class in America*. New Haven, CT: Yale University Press.

———. 1998. *Diversity in the power elite: Have women and minorities reached the top?* New Haven, CT: Yale University Press.

———. 2003. *Blacks in the white elite: Will the progress continue?* Lanham, MD: Rowman & Littlefield.

———. 2006. *Diversity in the power elite: How it happened, why it matters*. Lanham, MD: Rowman & Littlefield.

Name Index

Subject Index

AARP, 49, 188n10

A Better Chance (ABC), 123–26, 127, 171, 181

ACLU. *See* American Civil Liberties Union

affirmative action, 36; African Americans with, 109–16; diversity with new CEOs and, 106–16; in education, 111–12; with women, 108–9

African American CEOs, *1*; athletics and, 42–45; babyfaceness of, 45–49, 159–70; breakthrough year for, 32–37; campaign contributions from, 89–90, *91*, 92–95; companies and business sectors hiring, 79, 82–84; compensation for, 33–34, 36, 80, 88–89; conclusions about, 49–50; Democrats supported by, 90, *91*, 92; education of, 41–45, 121–22; *Fortune* 500, 31–50, *38*; heading larger corporations, 82; hirings and gender patterns with, 37–38; in inner circle, 79–80, 84, *85*, 86; insiders, 39–40, 79–80, 84–87; outsiders, 39–40, 79–80, 84–87; progress of, 120–37, 138–39; Republicans supported by, 92; rise in numbers, 2; sit-ins

influencing hiring of, 31, 37, 106, 192n1; skin color ratings of, 45–49, *73*, *74*, 159–70; socioeconomic class of, 40–41. *See also* Raines, Franklin D.; Ward, Lloyd D.; *specific African American CEOs*

African Americans: affirmative action with, 109–16; business and legal education for, 121–22; concubinage and, 159–60; discrimination against, 36, 114–16; home sales among, 33; in Ivy League schools, vii, 32, 39, 41–42; presidential appointees, 141; as threatening to whites, 45–46

agribusiness, 82

Aguirre, Fernando, 60, 63, 146

Alapont, Jose, 146

Allaire, Paul, 39

Allen, Michael Patrick, 190n1

Alvarez, Julia, 189n3

American Can Company, 2

American Civil Liberties Union (ACLU), 18

American Express, 146

The American Class Structure in an Age of Growing Inequality (Gilbert), 186n6

Amerigroup, 194n20

About the Authors

Richard L. Zweigenhaft is the Charles A. Dana Professor of Psychology at Guilford College in Greensboro, North Carolina, where he is also the chair of the Psychology Department and the director of the Communications Minor. He received his BA at Wesleyan University, his MA at Columbia University, and his PhD at the University of California, Santa Cruz. He is the coauthor of *Jews in the Protestant Establishment* (1982), *Blacks in the White Establishment?: A Study of Race and Class in America* (1991), *Diversity in the Power Elite: Have Women and Minorities Reached the Top?* (1998), *Blacks in the White Elite: Will the Progress Continue?* (2003), and *Diversity in the Power Elite: How it Happened, Why it Matters* (2006).

G. William Domhoff is Distinguished Research Professor at the University of California, Santa Cruz. He received his BA at Duke University, his MA at Kent State University, and his PhD at the University of Miami. He is the author of numerous books on power in the United States, including *Who Rules America?: Challenges to Corporate and Class Dominance*. Sixth Edition (2010), and the co-author of *The Leftmost City: Power and Progressive Politics in Santa Cruz* (2009) and *Class and Power in the New Deal: Corporate Moderates, Southern Democrats, and the Liberal-Labor Coalition* (2011).